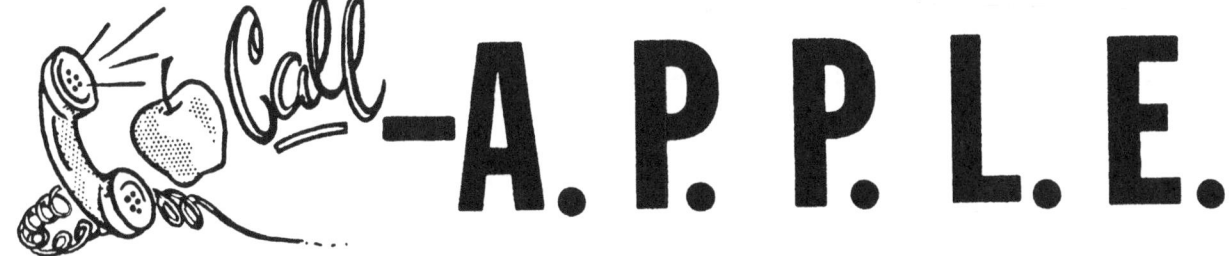

# 1978 Compendium

## The First Year

**Featuring Legend:**
Val J. Golding

**Produced by:**
Brian Wiser & Bill Martens

 Apple PugetSound Program Library Exchange

# Call-A.P.P.L.E. Magazine: 1978 Compendium

Copyright © 1978, 2015 by Apple Pugetsound Program Library Exchange (A.P.P.L.E.)
All Rights Reserved.

Published by Apple Pugetsound Program Library Exchange (A.P.P.L.E.)
www.callapple.org

Paperback ISBN: 978-1-329-66238-4

## ACKNOWLEDGEMENTS

First and foremost, we would like to thank the original contributors: Darrell Aldrich, Ron Aldrich, John Backman, Dan Chapman, Robert Clardy, John Cook, John Covington, Jeffrey Finn, Val J. Golding, Alan Hill, Dick Hubert, Bob Huelsdonk, Gene Jackson, Neil Konzen, S.H. Lam, Steve Paulson, Dana Redington, Michael Scott, Dick Sedgewick, Michael Thyng, Roger Wagner, Michael Weinstock, Randy Wigginton, Don Williams, and Steve Wozniak.

Thanks to everyone who joined the A.P.P.L.E. user group, read *Call-A.P.P.L.E.* magazine, made contributions, and supported our endeavours.

The cover and book was designed by Brian Wiser.

## PRODUCTION

Brian Wiser → Design, Layout, Editing
Bill Martens → Scanning, Introduction, Production

## DISCLAIMER

No part of this book may be reproduced, distributed or transmitted in any form or by any means, including photocopying, scanning, or other electronic or mechanical methods, without prior written permission of the publisher, except in the case of brief quotations contained in articles and reviews, and program listings which may be entered, stored and executed in a computer system, but not reproduced for publication.

*Call-A.P.P.L.E. Magazine: 1978 Compendium* is an independent publication and has not been authorized, sponsored, or otherwise approved by any institution, public or private.

All images are under copyright and the property of Apple Pugetsound Program Library Exchange, or as otherwise indicated. Use is prohibited without prior permission.

Apple and all Apple hardware and software brand names are trademarks of Apple Inc., registered in the United States and other countries. All other brand names and trademarks are the property of their respective owners.

All items containing Apple Computer, Inc. copyright were provided by Apple Computer, Inc. to A.P.P.L.E. for inclusion in *Call-A.P.P.L.E.* magazine. We have gone to great lengths to enhance the visual quality as much as possible, while staying true to the spirit of the original photocopied pages.

While all possible steps have been taken to ensure that the information included within is accurate, the publisher and authors assume no responsibility for any errors or omissions, or for damages resulting from the use of the information and programs contained herein.

# About the Producers

## Brian Wiser

Brian Wiser is a long-time consultant, enthusiast and historian of Apple, the Apple II and Macintosh. Steve Wozniak and Steve Jobs, as well as *Creative Computing, Nibble, InCider,* and *A+* magazines were early influences.

Brian designed, edited, and co-produced many books including: *Call-A.P.P.L.E. Magazine: 1978 Compendium, What's Where in the Apple: Enhanced Edition, Nibble Viewpoints: Business Insights From The Computing Revolution, Cyber Jack: The Adventures of Robert Clardy and Synergistic Software, Synergistic Software: The Early Games, The Colossal Computer Cartoon Book: Enhanced Edition,* and *The WOZPAK: Special Edition* – an important Apple II historical book with Steve Wozniak's restored original, technical handwritten notes.

He passionately preserves and archives all facets of Apple's history, and noteworthy related companies such as Beagle Bros and Applied Engineering, featured on AppleArchives.com. His writing, interviews and books are featured on the technology news site CallApple.org and in *Call-A.P.P.L.E.* magazine that he co-produces. Brian also co-produced the retro iOS game *Structris*.

In 2005, Brian was cast as an extra in Joss Whedon's movie *Serenity*, leading him to being a producer and director for the documentary film *Done The Impossible: The Fans' Tale of Firefly & Serenity*. He brought some of the *Firefly* cast aboard his Browncoat Cruise and recruited several of the *Firefly* cast to appear in a film for charity. Brian speaks about his adventures to large audiences at conventions around the country.

## Bill Martens

Bill Martens is a systems engineer specializing in office infrastructures and has been programming since 1976. The DEC PDP 11/40 with ASR-33 Teletypes and CRT's were his first computing platforms with his first forays in the Apple world coming with the Apple II computer.

Influences in Bill's computing life came from *Creative Computing* magazine, *Byte* magazine and *Call-A.P.P.L.E.* magazine as well as his mentors Samuel Perkins, Don Williams, Joff Morgan, and Mike Christensen.

Bill is a co-producer of many books including: *Call-A.P.P.L.E. Magazine: 1978 Compendium, The WOZPAK: Special Edition, Nibble Viewpoints: Business Insights From The Computing Revolution, What's Where in the Apple: Enhanced Edition,* and co-programmer for the iOS version of the retro game *Structris*. He has written many articles which have appeared in user group newsletters and magazines such as *Call-A.P.P.L.E.*.

Bill worked for Apple Pugetsound Program Library Exchange (A.P.P.L.E.) under Val Golding and Dick Hubert as a data manager and programmer in the 1980s, and is the current president of the A.P.P.L.E. user group. He reorganized A.P.P.L.E. and restarted *Call-A.P.P.L.E.* magazine in 2002. He is the production editor for the A.P.P.L.E. website CallApple.org, writes science fiction novels in his spare time, and is a retired semi-pro football player.

# CONTENTS

Introduction – Bill Martens .................................................................................................. x

Forward – Val J. Golding.................................................................................................... xi

## *Call-A.P.P.L.E.* Magazine

### February 1978

A Call to Arms – Val J. Golding ......................................................................................... 1

Program Exchange – Val J. Golding .................................................................................. 1

Equipment and Material – Val J. Golding .......................................................................... 1

### March 1978

"POKE" This in Your Apple! – Bob Huelsdonk, Val J. Golding ......................................... 1

Call-A.P.P.L.E. ................................................................................................................... 1

IP + E = OP ....................................................................................................................... 1

BASIC For Beginners ........................................................................................................ 1

Tones Dress Up Programs ................................................................................................ 1

Bytes from the A.P.P.L.E. .................................................................................................. 2

Equipment Review: T.I. "Programmer" ............................................................................ 2

Interfacing Printers to Apple II .......................................................................................... 2

Applesauce ........................................................................................................................ 2

### April 1978

Bytes From The Apple – Val J. Golding ........................................................................... 1

Mike's Thing – Michael Thyng ........................................................................................... 1

Apple Source – Dana Redington........................................................................................ 2

Minutes of the Meeting - February .................................................................................... 3

Bugs in the Applesauce..................................................................................................... 3

Don's Translator – Val J. Golding ..................................................................................... 3

Apple BASIC Decoded – Don Williams ............................................................................. 3

A.P.P.L.E. Software Catalogue No. 1 ................................................................................ 4

## May 1978

Bytes From The Apple – Val J. Golding ............................................................................................................. 1

Minutes of the Meeting – March ......................................................................................................................... 2

Minutes of the Meeting – April ............................................................................................................................ 2

Apple Source – Dana Redington ......................................................................................................................... 2

Reviews – Val Golding ......................................................................................................................................... 2

Save Memory on a String – Don Williams .......................................................................................................... 3

An Apple II Memory Test – Bob Huelsdonk ....................................................................................................... 4

Apple II BASIC Structure – Steve Wozniak ........................................................................................................ 4

Apple II Integer BASIC Interpretation of Memory – Val J. Golding, Don Williams ......................................... 6

## June 1978

Appending Applesoft – Val J. Golding ................................................................................................................ 1

Applemash – Mike Thyng .................................................................................................................................... 2

Editorial – Val J. Golding ..................................................................................................................................... 2

Hi-Res Capabilities and Limitations – Darrell Aldrich ....................................................................................... 2

Bytes From The Apple – Val J. Golding ............................................................................................................. 3

Routine to Format Decimal Numbers – Bob Huelsdonk ................................................................................... 3

Routine to Format Remarks Lines and Print Statements In Applesoft II – Val J. Golding .............................. 4

Review: Applesoft II – Val J. Golding ................................................................................................................. 5

Apple Source ........................................................................................................................................................ 6

Minutes of the Meeting – May ............................................................................................................................ 6

Applesoft II Pointers & Tokens – Val J. Golding ............................................................................................... 6

Routine to Display Applesoft Program Tokens – Val J. Golding, Bob Huelsdonk .......................................... 7

Apple Patches ...................................................................................................................................................... 8

Converting Applesoft I to II ................................................................................................................................. 8

Applesoft II Tokens – Val J. Golding .................................................................................................................. 9

Applesoft Conversion Program – Apple Computer, Inc ................................................................................. 10

## July 1978

Bytes From The Apple – Val Golding ............................................................................................. 1

Apple Mash – Mike Thyng .......................................................................................................... 3

Here's an "Oops Fixer" – J.A. Backman ...................................................................................... 3

Call-A.P.P.L.E. "Hot Line" ........................................................................................................... 4

Editorial – Val J. Golding ............................................................................................................ 5

Minutes of the Meeting – June ................................................................................................... 5

Key Kicker Routine – Don Williams ............................................................................................ 5

Routine to Find Page Length ..................................................................................................... 6

Printer Driver Fixes .................................................................................................................... 6

Apple Patch ............................................................................................................................... 6

Discs & Applesoft ROM Delayed ............................................................................................... 6

Apple II Mini-Assembler – Apple Computer Inc ........................................................................ 7

Use of Color Mask Byte in Hi-Res – Darrell Aldrich ................................................................... 9

Memory Map – Apple II with Applesoft BASIC Loaded ............................................................ 9

Our Face is Red (Like an Apple) Dept. – Val J. Golding ........................................................... 10

List of Handy "Call's" ................................................................................................................ 10

System Monitor – Apple Computer Inc ................................................................................... 12

Memory Test – Bob Huelsdonk ................................................................................................ 15

## August 1978

Bytes From The Apple – Val J. Golding ..................................................................................... 1

Disk II and You – John Covington .............................................................................................. 3

Program to Initialize a Diskette ................................................................................................. 4

Editorial – Val J. Golding ............................................................................................................ 4

Write-A.P.P.L.E. .......................................................................................................................... 5

A Disk Utility Program – Val J. Golding ..................................................................................... 6

The Poor Man's Hex-Decimal-Hex Converter – J.A. Backman ................................................... 7

Minutes of the Meeting – July .................................................................................................... 7

Applemash – Mike Thyng .......................................................................................................... 8

System Monitor – Apple Computer Inc ..................................................................................... 8

Applesoft Zero Page Usage ..................................................................................................... 13

Routine to PRINT Free Bytes – Bob Huelsdonk ....................................................................... 13

Loading Machine Language as Part of a BASIC Program – from *Contact* No. 1, May 1978 ......... 14

A Patch for Double Loops – Bob Huelsdonk ........................................................................... 14

## September 1978

The Program That Apple Said "Couldn't be Written" – Rob Aldrich ............................................. 1
Bytes From The Apple – Val J. Golding ............................................................................... 3
Convert – Ron Aldrich ....................................................................................................... 3
Card Shuffling Caution ...................................................................................................... 3
Apple Mash – Mike Thyng .................................................................................................. 4
Video Display Organization Routine – Dan Chapman .............................................................. 4
Routine to Save an Array – from *Apple Stems*, v1 n2, July 1978 .............................................. 5
Program Library ............................................................................................................... 6
Minutes of the Meeting – August ........................................................................................ 6
Editorial – Val J. Golding ................................................................................................... 7
Routine to Allow Execution of Monitor Commands from Integer BASIC Program – S.H. Lam ....... 7
Linkage Routines for the Apple II Integer BASIC Floating Point Package – Don Williams ............ 9
Write-A.P.P.L.E. .............................................................................................................. 10
Integral Data IP 125-225 Driver ......................................................................................... 13
Return to Text from Graphics – Alan G. Hill ........................................................................ 13
Printer Driver Fixes – Bob Huelsdonk .................................................................................. 14
Don't Call Apple, Call-A.P.P.L.E. ! ...................................................................................... 14

## October 1978

Bytes From The Apple – Val J. Golding ............................................................................... 1
Applesoft Tone Subroutines – John D. Cook ........................................................................ 3
6502 Program Exchange .................................................................................................... 3
A Brief History of Apple – Michael M. Scott, President .......................................................... 4
Sample File Handler – Bob Huelsdonk .................................................................................. 6
Write-A.P.P.L.E. .............................................................................................................. 7
Minutes of the Meeting – September .................................................................................. 8
Apple Software Bank ........................................................................................................ 9
Mystery Program Contest .................................................................................................. 9
Wig-Wiz Contest .............................................................................................................. 9
Editing in Integer or Applesoft ........................................................................................... 11
& Now, The Ampersand ..................................................................................................... 11
Modifying Workshop ......................................................................................................... 12
DOS Patches ................................................................................................................... 12
Documentation Package from Apple – *The WOZPAK* ............................................................ 12
Apple II Integer BASIC Interpretation of Memory – Val J. Golding, Don Williams ....................... 13
Applesoft II Tokens – Val J. Golding ................................................................................... 14

# November – December 1978

Bytes From The Apple – Val J. Golding ............................................................................................... 1

Use of Apple II Color Graphics in Assembly Language – Apple Computer Inc ............................... 3

Checkbook Changes for Disk – Gene Jackson .................................................................................. 5

Using Game Paddle Buttons – Steve Paulson .................................................................................... 5

Write-A.P.P.L.E. ................................................................................................................................ 7

& Now, The Further Adventures of the Mysterious Ampersand ...................................................... 8

Minutes of the Meeting – October ..................................................................................................... 8

Transient Voltage Protectors – Steve Paulson ................................................................................... 8

Simple Tones – A Demonstration for Extensions to Applesoft II – Randy Wigginton ..................... 9

Apple-Sharing – Jeffrey K. Finn ...................................................................................................... 10

Lament for the Apple Widows – Cindy Rogers .............................................................................. 12

Applemash – Mike Thyng ................................................................................................................ 12

PEEKs, POKEs, and CALLs ........................................................................................................... 14

Apple Source: Q&A with Mike Scott and Randy Wigginton ......................................................... 15

Identifying Binary Disk Programs – Val J. Golding ....................................................................... 17

Resurrecting a Dead FP Program .................................................................................................... 18

Color Graphics Screen Memory Map .............................................................................................. 18

# INTRODUCTION

## by Bill Martens

In the early 1980's I had the privilege of working with the man who became synonymous with the Apple Pugetsound Program Library Exchange – its founder, Val J. Golding. He was a man who spoke with an easy calm, but seemed to have a lot of details just flowing from his mind.

For every revolution, there is a beginning. That beginning for A.P.P.L.E. was February 16, 1978. It was on that day that a small group of Apple II owners got together because of the actions of Val Golding.

As an original Apple-1 owner, when Val bought the Apple II he expected a bit more information than the original one board machine. However, he found the information available at the local ComputerLand lacking in the realm of what could be done with the machine. Thus, with the encouragement of Max Cook, the store manager, he sent out a newsletter announcing the creation of a user group, calling for like-minded folks to join them in their information sharing endeavors.

Thus was born the Apple Pugetsound Program Library Exchange and, of course, the mainstay over the years – *Call-A.P.P.L.E.* magazine.

Here within the pages of this book is the entire first year of *Call-A.P.P.L.E.*, beginning with that call-to-arms sent out by Val in January 1978 and ending with the first issues of the fully typeset newsletter, with information about all of the changes that were happening at Apple Computer, Inc. as well as programs written by other enthusiasts and club members.

*Call-A.P.P.L.E.* was initially typed on a typewriter and then eventually typed on a teletype. The problem was that if one mistake was made in the typing of the column, the entire document was re-started. Val pushed through these minor issues in production and produced his newsletters.

Towards of the end of 1978, the issues began to take on a more professional look as others began to part in the production process. This style change made the now 16 page newsletter much easier to handle and read and allowed the group to begin growing exponentially with membership nearing 5,000 members by year end.

In 1990, when Don Williams closed down the Renton, Washington office, Val wrote an article in the Winter 1990 issue of *Call-A.P.P.L.E.* of the ride had been taken. But then, like all great rides, there must be a new approach taken once in a while to refresh the ride.

In 2002, when we re-started *Call-A.P.P.L.E.*, Val once again wrote of the ride. I believe the words he wrote that month describe the our direction and goal in re-introducing these materials to the word. Sadly, Val is no longer physically with us, but I believe he would have said something similar to his May 2002 "Editor Bytes Back" column in the forward that follows.

It is our hope that making these magazines available in print once again will give the newer generation of vintage computing enthusiasts that excitement that we felt in 1978 for our favorite computer – the Apple II.

# FORWARD

## by Val J. Golding

May 2002

Twenty-five years and counting, and yes, with a great deal more gray hair, the editor still has a few more bytes left. Many eons ago we thought we had written the last for *Call-A.P.P.L.E.* but one never knows. What goes around, comes around eh?

Early on, we were fascinated with computers, starting in 1977 with a TI-59 programmable calculator. Writing for the 59 came closer to pure machine code programming than one might imagine, what with the need to decrement registers for comparisons, etc. But we soon used up all the TI's available memory slots, so with a cry of "Tally-ho," we went hunting for greener pastures.

A coming together of circumstances – our Christmas bonus money, a gentleman named Max Cook who had just opened a computer store and the advent of a brand new type of personal computer, the Apple II – provided the answer. We soon found ourselves heading a teeny, as yet unnamed, computer user group.

From there on it was all downhill, a visionary leading his disciples. We coined, without objection, the contrived acronym A.P.P.L.E., representing Apple Pugetsound Program Library Exchange. Although the title "From the Very Core of Apple" was to come later, its significance became immediately apparent when, like Nixon's "plumbers," we began snooping about the Apple's software highways and byways, plumbing the depths of this marvelous new device as deftly as a surgeon stitching flesh.

When the IIgs debuted, we were long gone from A.P.P.L.E. We were contracted then to Softdisk Publishing in Shreveport, LA., publishers of the excellent Apple magazine on disk, *Softdisk*. They also published similar disk magazines for the PC and the Commodore C64.

Previously we dibbled and dabbled a bit with the Apple II as editor of *On Three* and in divining its secrets discovered that the III's SOS (Sophisticated Operating System) had become the forerunner of ProDOS for the IIgs, lacking only the III's system of device drivers. "gs" (note the lower case) stood for "graphics and sound," the hallmark of Apple's newest, greatest and final contribution to personal computing.

Of course, we explored and exploited the IIgs as we did its predecessors. We believed then and still believe that it was the finest ever machine of its time. Remember, that was 1985 or so and the PC was still a babe in swaddling clothes compared to the IIgs. It had yet to outclass the Apple, the ill-fated and disastrously overpriced Lisa and the Mac. Alas, Apple corporate typically and misguidedly decided that the Mac, with its totally closed architecture, was the only row to hoe. Much later still, we would see Apple's market share drop like a boulder off a cliff until the Mac finally made its half-hearted comeback in the new century.

And so, full circle. What goes around, comes around eh? Oh. We already said that, didn't we?

**A** pple
**P** uget Sound
**P** rogram
**L** ibrary
**E** xchange

C/O Val J. Golding
6708 39th Avenue SW
Seattle, Wa. 98136
(206) 937-6588 (Home)
(206) 623-7966 (Office)

February 9, 1978

Dear Apple Owner:

The purpose of this letter is to form an Apple Computer users group, as indicated by the tentative name above, and to further the exhange of information and programs of interest to Apple owners and users. A preliminary meeting has been scheduled for 7 PM Tuesday, February 21st at Computerland, 1500 S. 336th St., Federal Way, Wa. 98003 (Phones 927-8585 and 838 9363).

Regretfully, I do not have the time available to continue this project beyond the formative stage; therefore the first order of business will be (hopefully) to find someone that can. I can see this group as a very useful, self-help type of organization, and am most anxious to see it progress. I will, of course, be available for assistance.

The APPLE goals, as conceived, should include establishing a software library for exchanging programs on a cost-only basis, programming and technical assistance, the exchange of information on Apple-compatible equipment and peripherals and the publication of a brief newsletter to serve as a medium for some of the above items. You are urged, therefore, to attend this meeting and help in the formation of your club. If for any reason you can not attend, but are interested in the group, please contact me for further details as they develop.

PROGRAM EXCHANGE

Bring your recorder and tape with you. We have the following at no cost
  ZOT = A snappy one-way conversation with your computer.
  STAR WARS = Galactic target practice with your paddles.
  STOP WATCH = A real time clock and stop watch for your Apple.
  HEX-DEC = A program that converts hexidecimal numbers to decimal and back.
  ANNE APPLE = An interactive rap session with your computer.

EQUIPMENT and MATERIAL

  DAK HEC-60 casettes @ .73 ea. plus shipping. See me to order by Mar. 10.
  I/O board for Apple by Electronics Warehouse, Redondo Beach $74 assembled.
  IP125 dot matrix printer by Integral Data @ 799. They are working with Apple
      to interface it. See their ad in February Byte.
  "HOW TO PROGRAM MICROCOMPUTERS" by Wm. Barden, Jr., SAMS book
      No. 21459, a MUST at 8.95 from Retail Computer Store and Computerland.
  A new RF Modulator from VHF Industries has been ordered by Omega Stereo.
      Reported to offer much better resolution. Priced at 79.95.
  Empire Electronics now carrying Apple line.

*Hope to see you —*    *Val*

# CALL-A.P.P.L.E. V.I, N°2 MAR '78
## APPLE PUGET SOUND PROGRAM LIBRARY EXCHANGE

CALL-APPLE: A monthly publication of the Apple PugetSound Program Library Exchange

Volume I, Number 2   March, 1978

Care of:   Val J. Golding
           6708 39th Avenue Southwest
           Seattle, Washington 98136
           Phone (206) 937-6588 (Home)
                 (206) 623-7966 (Work)

## RESTRICTED PROGRAMS

Certain copyrighted programs carry restrictions in the REMarks lines or elsewhere that they may not be duplicated, reproduced or sold, and for good reason. We would like to discourage from the outset, the practice of duplicating, either on tape or by printouts, of any program that has such a restriction. A recent article indicated that the cost per Basic line of debugged software has risen to an all time high of $8. Selling these programs to the consumer, either directly, or through magazine and book publication, is the only way of recovering those costs. We will not knowingly tolerate, or be a party to such practices.

## "POKE" THIS IN YOUR APPLE!
by Bob Huelsdonk and Val Golding

A subroutine to find the Basic POKE statements for a machine language program or subroutine. Find the starting address of the routine you wish to Poke and convert that to Decimal. Now, in Basic, enter the following program. (n=starting address)

```
1000 A=n B=A+19
1010 FOR I= A TO B: PRINT I, PEEK(I):
     NEXT I
1020 X= PEEK (-16384): POKE -16368, 0:
     IF X>127 THEN 1030: GOTO 1020
1030 A=A+20: B=A+19: GOTO 1010
```

This will give you 20 Poke statements at a time, and Apple will wait for you to "Hit any key" for a new page. Simple? (jsr col2)

## CALL -A.P.P.L.E.

...is the tentative title for this newsletter. The name was chosen with some thought. The Basic (no pun intended) purpose of A.P.P.L.E. is a self help service organization. If you need help, Call Apple. We will attempt to assist you in solving you Apple-related problems and answer questions. If you stump us, we will try to obtain the answer from outside.

## IP+E=OP

Loosely translated, this means there can be no output without input and effort. In order to make this group a success, we need member input in the form of both articles for the newsletter, and programs for the library.

Have you found a sneaky thing your Apple does that is not in the manual? Let us in on the secret with a brief description or story for the newsletter.

We also need to build our program library. If you have written a useable program, send it to us so all can share. We will print submission information in the next issue. All programs submitted will be given freely, and will be considered to be in the public domain.

## BASIC FOR BEGINNERS

A recent letter from Apple Computer announced the publication of a new manual scheduled for late March, designed to teach Apple Basic to those with no prior programming experience. We look forward with anticipation to its publication. (We need it!)

## TONES DRESS UP PROGRAMS

Dress up your Apple program with a simple tone subroutine to direct attention to error messages, etc. From Basic a Call -1050 ($FBE6) will produce a 1000 cycle tone.

To find the starting address for a program in Integer Basic, enter the command:
PRINT PEEK(202) + PEEK(203) * 256.

## BYTES FROM THE A.P.P.L.E.
### Current Software News

Bob Huelsdonk and Val Golding have been hard at work assembling new programs for the software library. See the complete listing below which includes many new programs. Programs from the A.P.P.L.E. library may be ordered as follows: For copies on cassette, send $1.00, along with 35¢ in postage, a self addressed letter size envelope and the names of the programs desired, to Val. For listings only, a self addressed, stamped envelope.

As soon as Val has a printer up and running you will receive your program dumps.

### SOFTWARE CATALOGUE

ALPHABET, 5K. A fancy new color demo from the folks at Apple Computer Company
ALPHA SORT, 1K*. Bob's program will sort your data into alphabetical apple pie order
ANNE APPLE, 5K. You talk to Anne, and she talks back. FUN!
COLOR SKETCH SAVE, 2K. Save your art!
HEXDEC I, 1K*. Converts Hex to Dec & vv
HEXDEC II, 1K. Same but limited to 32767
HURKLE, 2K. A P.C. Co. game. Find the invisible Hurkle on your monitor screen!
MULTIPLY, 1K. Teaches kids the X table.
ROCKET PILOT     Land on the moon!
STAR WARS        Galactic Target practice
STOPWATCH, 1K.   Realtime clock & timer.
ZOT, 3K.         Snappy 1-way conversation with Apple
* = WRITTEN IN APPLESOFT

### EQUIPMENT REVIEW: T.I. "Programmer"

The Texas Instruments Programmer is a unique calculator which provides immediate conversions from, and 4-function calculations in Base 8 (Octal), Base 10 (Decimal) and Base 16 (Hexidecimal). It will also manipulate bits in Hex and Octal modes, with One's and Two's compliments, logical and, or, not and exclusive or, as well as shift left and right functions. Binary conversions are printed on the face, above the appropriate digits, and the machine
JMP / col. 2

performs floating point, negative balance arithmetic in decimal mode. It is simple and fast to operate and, to this writer, more than worth its weight in apples. This little gem is available at Advanced Campus Electronics, Computerland and J.K. Gill at $50 to 60. v.g.

### INTERFACING PRINTERS TO APPLE II

The Apple II paddle I/O Port is immediately available to connect an RS232 type, serial mode printer. Tom Geer, of the Empire Electronics store in Burien is probably first in the area to have a TTY up and running. If you ask, Tom would probably be glad to give you some hints on how to proceed. There is a simple machine language program in the revised Apple II manual to enable a printer. Empire has ordered a number of "Black Box" printers from Expandor, with delivery set for March. The Black Box is an 80 column, 10 CPS, serial mode impact printer which uses 8-1/2" plain paper rolls. It sells for $425.

### APPLESAUCE

The following recipe will save you loading time on your Applesoft programs. 1. Load Applesoft. 2. Do not "run" it. 3. Using the DEL command, delete lines 0, 940, inclusive. 4. Enter this line: 950 POKE 18, 255 This will give you a preset version of Option 1, Applesoft graphics mode. 5. "Save this at the beginning of a blank cassette and follow it with saves of programs written in Option 1. For Option 2, do the same except make line 950 read: 950 POKE 18, 0   Save this on another cassette and follow with programs in Option 2. Note: All Applesoft programs may be written in Option 1 if desired. The LET command is not required, and may be omitted. A REMark line may be handled like this: 530 GOTO 540:REM 540 SETS VARIABLE N. Applesoft will ignore all after the goto.

### CASSETTE SPECIAL OFFER

DAK Enterprises has a special price on cassettes, valid through March 10th. Order from Val Golding. Prices do not include shipping.
HEC60 (Top of the line, cobalt)   .66 each
EC-8  (Four minutes per side)     .68 each

# CALL-A.P.P.L.E.
## V. I, No 3  APR '78
## APPLE PUGET SOUND PROGRAM LIBRARY EXCHANGE

CALL-APPLE Vol. I, No. 3 April, 1978

Apple PugetSound Program Library Exchange
6708 39th Avenue Southwest
Seattle, Washington 98136

Val J. Golding, President  (206) 937-6588
Michael Thyng, Secretary  (206) 524-2744

---

### MARCH MEETING
7:00 PM   Tuesday, March 21, 1978
Empire Electronics
616 SW 152nd St. Burien, Wa. 242-5200

### APRIL MEETING
7:00 PM   Tuesday, April 18, 1978
Omega Stereo
839 106th Ave. NE Bellvue, Wa. 455-1138

---

## BYTES FROM THE APPLE  by Val Golding
Software stuff, etc., etc., etc., etc., etc., etc.,

This month, we have a number of brief programming aids. For starters, here is how you can break your long PRINT statements into pages: For more than two pages, use this as a subroutine, inserting the GOSUB after 20 or less lines: 200 VTAB 22:PRINT "HIT RETURN FOR NEW PAGE": CALL -676: CALL -936: RETURN. This will halt the program with a bell, and wait for a Return to resume.

To divide a program listing into pages, clear the screen, POKE 33,255 and LIST. This will list a single page only. Next, clear the screen again and LIST from the next line you want to see, plus 100 or so. Restore with the TEXT command.

To correct a line in a program listing, POKE 33,33 before listing. This will adjust the right hand window so you can trace your cursor over the line without encountering large gaps in the PRINT statements. Restore screen with text.

Next month, Don Williams will author an article on how to improve Basic performance through indirect addressing in assembly language, and Bob Huelsdonk has also promised a goody.

The January issue of Mini-Micro Systems has a comprehensive survey and equipment listing of printers available to the personal computing field. If you are considering such a purchase, this is well worth your reading.

## MIKE'S THING:  by Michael Thyng
a collection of tidbits worth noting

What is a color monitor worth to you? One of our number has access to same and will consider all serious offers... If you want 16 K chips, tell us. We would have to buy a large quantity, true, but we have to know how many we can handle before we approach a manufacturer. We feel we could do something for under $250. Speak now or forever hold your chips. We have to get moving on this one.

CALL -A.P.P.L.E. has sent word of our existence via news releases to seven major periodicals and Northwest Computer Club.. When you read about us, tell Val or Mike..
Need to see an up and running printer? See Tom Geer at Empire Electronics or Larry Meece at the Bellevue Omega Stereo. Perhaps by the time you read this, Max Cook at Computerland will have one up also. He has several models on order that will interface with Apple... Empire will loan back issues of Kilobaud to members of this group... And, this is a good place to mention that we are grateful to those three gentlemen for the fine support they have offered us, including mailing this newsletter. Remember too, if you are thinking of ordering something by mail, they can order for you for the same price and make a bit on it also. SUPPORT your supporters! ...and they can help you with your problems, as well. All are in weekly contact with Apple Computer, so don't hesitate to ask.
GOTO Page 2, Col. 2.

## APPLE SOURCE
by Dana Redington, Apple Computer, Inc.

A number of exciting software/firmware items will be forthcoming shortly from Apple. Included are a number of revised demo tapes and an extensively modified Star Wars program, which will have many new features, including more areas of action and additional sound effects. All will be available from your local Apple dealer, as well as from the club.

In firmware, a utility ROM has been scheduled for production in the next six weeks and will feature the HIRES color graphics routines and a music synthesis routine. New Basic commands in the ROM include APPEND, which will permit you to load portions of a program from tape separately; VERIFY will allow you to check the tape you have just saved, without reloading and testing it; another will output alphanumeric characters overlaid on a graphics mode screen, and a method of renumbering Basic lines will be provided.

Applesoft Extended Precision Floating Point Basic is currently undergoing revision and will be available shortly to 16K owners through their dealers. Standardization with Integer Basic commands are among the changes, and all of the Integer Basic color commands will now be included in the Applesoft. This version should be available on a ROM board by June.

Also announced for June is a Shugart floppy disc drive, complete with controller and software, retailing for under $700. Two other items that have been designed to interface with Apple II are a music synthesizer which provides a display while it is playing music, this one from PAIA of Oklahoma City, and Mountain Hardware of Ben Lomond, Calif., offers a remote AC controller which handles lights, coffee pot, etc. through your Apple.

Next month, we hope to provide details about the Apple Software Bank, a plan that will give you a chance to submit your programs to Apple and, if accepted, win prizes of cash or similarly submitted programs.

## MIKE'S THING (JMP'd from Page 1)

Don Williams has been kind enough to offer to teach classes in assembly language programming. Is anyone interested in learning? ...if so, let's bring it up at the meeting... Please note that the meeting notice on Page 1 covers both March and April meetings. Call -Apple for May will list the place and date of the May meeting only, and will be issued about the 1st of May...

Val and I need your input to keep this newsletter growing and glowing... Submit comments, questions, programs, anything and everything. Don't worry that your questions may show a lack of knowledge... 75% of the members of this group have NEVER USED a computer before. We are all beginners, and WE ARE HERE TO HELP YOU. Ask, be in the know about your Apple II... That is the function we are providing.

...Mike Thyng

## PROGRAM SUBMISSION GUIDELINES

As we indicated last month, we need your software for our library, in order to make it available to others. You can help cut down on our processing time by observing the following guidelines. All programs should be completely self-prompting. This means all user instructions should be imbedded within the program as "print" statements, so the user can run the program without any additional information at all. Please state the language the program is written in, i.e., Integer Basic, Applesoft or machine. For machine language, the beginning and ending addresses should be shown, along with any special instructions, such as set himem, etc. A brief description of the programs function would also be helpful.

The following information is required in the REMarks lines of the program: Name of program, author, date written and the A.P.P.L.E. logo and address. We anticipate having printed submission forms for your convenience in the near future. Thanks for your help. vg

## MINUTES OF THE FEBRUARY MEETING

We met at Computerland in Federal Way, and Val Golding called us to order at 7:05 PM. A motion was approved to call ourselves A. P. P. L. E., standing for Apple Pugetsound Program Library Exchange. Val was unanimously elected president and Mike Thyng was elected secretary. Other duties will be shared between them. Informality was stressed in the meeting, in order to best follow the purposes of the group: to exchange information and programs. A membership application fee of $2.00 was approved, and an annual rate will be determined at a later date, based on expense experience. Max Cook, owner of Computerland, volunteered to mail out our newsletter at no cost to the group. The meeting was adjourned and the balance of the evening was in fact devoted to answering questions and trading tapes.
A. P. P. L. E. was "Up and Running"!

## BUGS IN THE APPLESAUCE

As stated elsewhere in this issue, Apple Computer plans a new edition of Applesoft on tape, about six weeks hence. They have requested that users advise them as soon as possible of any bugs they have encountered. (This goes for Integer Basic, as well). This is a project in which EVERYONE can contribute. LET'S DO IT NOW, at this coming meeting. Make a list out, as soon as you read this, of any basic bugs you are aware of, and bring it to the meeting. We will compile a master list and forward to Apple. Your cooperation and assistance will result in improved software, to the benefit of us all. Thanks.

## DON'S TRANSLATOR   by Val Golding

I would like to comment briefly on my experience running Don's program the first time. Like most of you, I have had very little to do with low level programming. With Don's program, I was able to see at a glance how a Basic line like "500 PRINT" translated into Hex bytes 08 F4 01 63 01, and in turn, I was able to enter a line of Basic from machine language. Analyzing the result, I was able to determine

JSR COL 2

## DON'S TRANSLATOR   (JSR FROM COL. 1)

that 08 F4 was the line number, 01 was a delimiter and 63 was the print command. This was a real insight for me into the workings of Integer Basic, and I strongly urge everyone to try this short program. Remember, Experimentation is the key to learning! In his notes Don explains an understanding of how Basic statements are compiled and stored will allow you to get the most out of your Basic through storing Hex constants in your programs without fear of conversion errors, building symbol tables and renumbering programs, etc.

## APPLE BASIC DECODED   by D. R. Williams

```
  1 REM  PROGRAM TO DUMP BASIC
  2 REM  STATEMENTS TO HEX
  3 REM  TO USE...ADD A LINE
  4 REM  OF BASIC AFTER #200
  5 REM     AND RUN.
  6 REM  WRITTEN BY
  7 REM  D.R. WILLIAMS 2/78
 10 DIM S$(16):S$="0123456789ABCDEF"
 20 LOCF= PEEK (203)*256+ PEEK (202)
 30 INPUT "STMT #",N
 35 IF N<0 THEN END
 40 LOC=LOCF
 50 K= PEEK (LOC+2): IF K>127 THEN 90
 55 STMT=K*256+ PEEK (LOC+1)
 60 IF STMT=N THEN 100
 70 LOC=LOC+ PEEK (LOC)
 80 IF STMT<N THEN 50
 90 PRINT " ***NOT FOUND"
 92 PRINT " TRY AGAIN"
 94 GOTO 30
 95 K=LOC/256
100 PRINT "STARTS AT ADDR ";K
101 GOSUB 200:K=LOC MOD 256
102 GOSUB 200: PRINT
105 L= PEEK (LOC)-1: FOR I=0 TO L
110 K= PEEK (LOC+I): GOSUB 200
130 NEXT I: PRINT " ": GOTO 30
200 J=K/16:K=K-16*J+1:J=J+1
202 PRINT S$(J,J);S$(K,K);
204 PRINT " ";: RETURN
300 PRINT ABC
```

\*\*\*\*\*\*\*\*\*\*\*\*\*\*\*\*\*\*\*\*\*\*\*\*\*\*\*\*\*\*\*\*\*\*\*\*\*\*\*

CORRECTION to Apple II Reference Manual, Page 39, figure 1. The peeks shown have been transposed and    PP should peek at 202 & 203 while CM peeks at 204 & 205.

APPLE PUGETSOUND PROGRAM LIBRARY EXCHANGE
6708 39TH AVENUE SW
SEATTLE, WA. 98136

SOFTWARECATALOGUE NO. 1
AS OF MARCH 15, 1978
CAT.# TITLE OF PROGRAM    AUTHOR        LNG LEN--- D E S C R I P T I O N ---

### APPLICATIONS, GENERAL

| Cat.# | Title | Author | Lng | Len | Description |
|---|---|---|---|---|---|
| 2001 | ALPHA SORT | HUELSDONK | A | -.-K | THIS PROGRAM SORTS 15 ITEMS INTO ALPHABETICAL ORDER |
| 2002 | BIORHYTHM | APPLE COMP. | B | 1.9K | A FASTER AND CORRECTED VERSION OF BIORHYTHM FROM GAMES I |
| 2003 | MUSIC WRITER | HUELSDONK | B | -.-K | THIS PROGRAM OUTPUTS MUSIC FROM APPLE AND TRANSPOSES |
| 2004 | STOP WATCH | HUELSD/GOLD | B | 1.2K | A REAL TIME CLOCK AND STOP WATCH FOR APPLE II |

### APPLICATIONS, PROGRAMMING

| Cat.# | Title | Author | Lng | Len | Description |
|---|---|---|---|---|---|
| 2501 | CHANGING BASES | ---------- | A | -.-K | THIS PROGRAM CONVERTS FROM DECIMAL TO BASES 2 TO 16 |
| 2502 | HEX-DEC | ---------- | A | -.-K | CONVERTS HEX (BASE 16) TO DEC (BASE 10) AND VICE VERSA |
| 2503 | PICK A BASE FROM.. | D WILLIAMS | B | K | CONVERTS NUMBER FROM ANY BASE TO ANY BASE, RANGE 2-36 |
| 2504 | POKE ROUTINE WRITER | GOLDING | B | 1.5K | TRANSLATES MACH LANGUAGE TO BASIC POKES IN PROGRAM FORMAT |
| 2505 | FORTY VECTORS | STEVE ALEX | B | 1.0K | CALCULATES AND POKES HIRES VECTORS INTO MEMORY |

### DEMOS & AMUSEMENTS

| Cat.# | Title | Author | Lng | Len | Description |
|---|---|---|---|---|---|
| 3001 | ALPHABET | APPLE COMP. | B | 4.0K | A FANCY NEW COLOR DEMO FROM THE FOLKS AT APPLE COMPUTER |
| 3002 | COLOR SKETCH SAVE | APPL/MOD/VG | B | 2.4K | NOW YOU CAN SAVE YOUR VIDEO DISPLAY ON TAPE AND RELOAD IT |
| 3003 | SOFTCORE SOFTWARE | ? | B | 8.2K | SEEING IS BELIEVING... AND IN HIGH RESOLUTION GRAPHICS! |

### GAMES, EDUCATIONAL

| Cat.# | Title | Author | Lng | Len | Description |
|---|---|---|---|---|---|
| 4001 | MULTIPLY | HUELSDONK | | 0.6K | TEACHES KIDS THE TIMES TABLES WITH A TIME LIMIT |

### GAMES, OTHER

| Cat.# | Title | Author | Lng | Len | Description |
|---|---|---|---|---|---|
| 4501 | ANNE APPLE | BROWN/M/VJG | | 5.0K | YOU TALK TO ANNE, AND SHE TALKS BACK TO YOU. FUN! |
| 4502 | HURKLE | P.C.C. | B | 2.4K | FIND THE INVISIBLE HURKLE IN HIS LAIR |
| 4503 | ROCKET PILOT | BISHOP | C | -.-K | SEE HOW YOU FARE LANDING THIS LUNAR LANDER WITH PADDLES |
| 4504 | STAR WARS | BISHOP | C | | GALACTIC TARGET PRACTICE USING YOUR PADDLES. IN HIRES |
| 4505 | ZOT | HUELSD/GOLD | B | 3.0K | SNAPPY ONE-LINERS FROM YOUR APPLE II |
| 4506 | QUBIC | BISHOP | B | -.-K | A FIENDISH GAME OF THREE |

# CALL-A.P.P.L.E.

MAY, 1978                  PAGE 1

BYTES FROM THE APPLE by Val Golding
Software stuff, etc., etc., etc., etc., etc.

Sometimes the problem is not what to write about, but what not to write about. Such is the case this month when we have a large number of items to report. Our software library is first on the agenda. The library, along with the membership, has been growing by leaps and bounds. So much so that by the time a catalogue is issued, it is out of date. We will try to remedy this by listing new programs each month in Call-Apple. In addition, we will try to have an updated catalogue available at each Meeting. We are pleased to see some of our members now writing and submitting good programs, but still more are needed. Copyright/submission forms are also available at meetings, and at participating dealers.

The club is currently negotiating with two different software dealers, the outcome of which will be to greatly increase the amount of available software, and to also give more widespread distribution of member written programs. We hope to establish by the next meeting, a "premium program" exchange, which would permit members to obtain outside programs for a small annual fee, plus a smaller per program charge.

Software in this issue: Bob Huelsdonk has come up with a machine language program to test each specific location in memory which, if you have a bad chip, will pinpoint the exact chip, and Don Williams has written a memory move and store program.

We have at times, been beseiged by phone calls asking for information and assistance, and we welcome them. This is proof we are fulfilling our function. If you need help, "Call-Apple".

CALL-APPLE Vol. I, No. 4    May, 1978

Apple PugetSound Program Library Exchang
8708 39th Avenue Southwest
Seattle, Washington 98136

Val J. Golding, President    (206) 937-6588
Michael Thyng, Secretary    (206) 524-2744

```
***********************************************
*              MAY  MEETING                   *
* 7:00 PM          Tuesday,    May 18, 1978   *
*              Computerland                   *
* 1500 S. 336th St., Federal Way, 838-9363    *
*              JUNE MEETING                   *
* 7:00 PM          Tuesday,   June 20, 1978   *
*           Empire  Electronics               *
* 616 SW 152nd St.  Burien, Wa.   244-5200    *
***********************************************
```

ASSEMBLY LANGUAGE CLASSES

Don Williams will be our instructor for an 18 hour Assembly Language programming course. The cost is $35, which includes the Synertek 6502 Programming manual, and will be taught two nights per week at Empire Electronics, 616 SW 152nd St., Burien, starting in the early part of May, so time is short. Contact Don at 242 6807 or Tom Geer at 244-5200 to sign up.

************************************************

For a limited time only, Computerland Federal Way has sets of Apple 16K chips available to members. This is a rare opportunity to get these chips for just $300.00, which is about 40% off the Apple list price. Call Max Cook at 838-9363 for details.
************************************************
To set HIMEM at locations above 32767, use minus figures, i.e., HIMEM: (-32767-1) would set it at 32768; -32766 sets 32770.

## Minutes of the Meeting = March 21, 1978

The meeting was held at Empire Electronics in Burien. Val Golding called the meeting to order at 7:05 and led the introductions to the 17 members present. The treasurers report indicated a bank balance of $73.50, of which 33.55 is earmarked for preplanned expenditures. Burt Webb reported on the 19" color monitors discussed at the previous meeting. They were made in Canada and designed for use in pubs and arcades. There is a limited number and would cost about $200. Val located a dealer with Mostek 16K chips available for $320 or less. A motion was made and carried to establish an annual dues rate of $5.00; $4.00 for the balance of 1978. Val was voted approval to continue negotiations with software houses whereby the club could obtain outside programs for the library. Questions came up about release forms but nothing was resolved. Don Williams advised his availability for teaching assembly language classes. Details will be worked out. The DAK 8 minute cassettes have not arrived yet; some are still available at 75¢. The meeting broke for discussion at 8:15.

## Minutes of the Meeting = April 18, 1978

The meeting was held at Omega Stereo in Bellevue. Val Golding called the meeting to order at 7:05 and led the introductions to the 22 members present. Mike Thyng read the March minutes, which were then approved. Val reported he had contacted a Softech representative re club use of their software. They appear to be willing to work with the club on royalties, and we voted to have Val further pursue the matter. Don Williams formally announced his assembler classes, with dates to be established later. He also demonstrated his homebrew joystick. Val asked for volunteers to help produce the newsletter. There was no response. We adjourned at 8:15 for program trading and discussion.

## APPLESOURCE
by Dana Redington = Apple Computer, Inc.

More word on the utility Rom. In addition to the routines previously mentioned, this Rom will have new high-res operating routines, including a SHAPGEN command that will eliminate the need to manually write HIRES vectors. You will be able to directly address a dot matrix, and there will also be a HIRES Ascii character set, displayable concurrently with the graphics. The Applesoft Rom board is scheduled for release to dealers July 1st at $99. Also available soon will be a high speed serial I/O board and a Modem I/O board.

## REVIEWS       by Val Golding

At the top of the list is Apple Computer's new Basic programming manual. This falls just short of being a masterpiece. It is well written and easy to understand, even for a novice like this writer and is printed in a small, easy to handle spiral binding. It starts by introducing simple Basic commands in program format and in each simple program, goes on to bring a new command into action. If you have not yet recieved your copy, ask your dealer.

The April-May issue of MICRO, the 6502 journal, reached our desk just in time to be included in this review. Here is a Magazine that is a must for the serious Apple II owner. Every issue to date has had material on Apple II, and this is no exception with an Applesoft Variables chart and an Apple II Programmers guide, an update on a prior article about interfacing a printer to Apple, and comments about the clocking system used by the μp. The guide contains many good hints and routines that are not to be found in the owners manual.

Other articles cover a morse code program for KIM-1, other KIM-1 and PET related stories, words on a standard 6502

GOTO   PAGE   4

## SAVE MEMORY ON A STRING
### by Don Williams

One of the minor deficiencies in Apple Integer Basic is the omission of the Data statement. In search of a remedy for this, I wrote a program to save memory in a Basic string assignment. This is listed as program lines 1020 through 1190.

Upon embarking on the first routine, I quickly found a second ommission in the langauge; a way to store a non-string variable into a string, the remedy for which is shown as program lines 1250 through 1300. Finally, in the interest of completeness, a third routine, given as lines 1200 to 1240, stores the data back into memory.

Running the program that saves memory is fairly straightforward, and is self-prompting. The data to be saved is displayed on the screen, and after the prompt returns, just press the cursor right and repeat keys until you pass the end of the generated statement(s), then hit return. That line is now a part of your Basic program; repeat the procedure for subsequent lines.

Wherever logically in your program you want the same data loaded back into Memory, place a call to the first line generated by the program, and a return after the last line generated. After storing the program, if memory space is at a premium, just delete those lines.

The second routine, (lines 1250-1300), locates any predefined variable in memory, and can readily be interfaced with a tape read/write routine where data needs to move from program to program. (See Apple II Reference Manual, pages 34-43) I have been able to use this program to locate variables for use in an Integer Basic floating point routine, a very fast f.p. which will be published in the June issue. Program listing are in column two.

********************************

For those who have missed the last two meetings, annual dues have now been established at $4.00 and are now payable.

```
1020 REM SAVE MEMORY ON A STRING BY
     DON WILLIAMS, APRIL 1978
1030 DIM S$(255),V$(10)
1040 PRINT "ENTER STARTING ADDRESS,
     ENDING ADDRESS AND LINE NBR"
1050 INPUT IST,IND,STMT
1060 CALL -936 PRINT "ENTER LINES
     BELOW INTO PROGRAM"
1070 PRINT " ";STMT;" L = ";IST
1080 V$="S$*": GOSUB 1260: SL=L
1090 POKE SL,162
1100 K=1: FOR I=IST TO IND:N=PEEK
     (I):M=N/16:N=N-16*M
1110 IF M>9 THEN M=M+7:M=M+176
1120 IF N>9 THEN N=N+7:N=N+176
1130 POKE SL+K,M:POKE SL+K+1,N
1140 K=K+2:IF K<100 THEN 1170
1150 GOSUB 1190
1160 K=1
1170 NEXT I
1180 IF K#1 THEN GOSUB 1190:VTAB 1
     :TAB 1:END
1190 POKE SL+K,162: POKE SL+K+1,0:
     STMT=STMT+10:PRINT " ";STMT;
     " S$= ";S$;" ":GOSUB 1210:RETURN
1200 REM SUBROUTINE TO STORE THE
     HEX DATA IN STRING S$ INTO
     MEMORY AT LOCATION L
1210 FOR I=1 TO LEN(S$) STEP 2
1220 J=ASC(S$(I))-176: IF J>9 THEN
     J=J-7
1230 K=ASC(S$(I+1))-176: IF K>9
     THEN K=K-7
1240 POKE L,J*16+K:L=L+1:NEXT I:
     RETURN
1250 REM SUBROUTINE TO FIND START
     ING ADR FOR VARIABLE WHOSE
     NAME IS IN V$.  L=ADDRESS OR
     -1 IF UNDEFINED
1260 L=PEEK(74)+PEEK(75)*256-1:K=
     LEN(V$)-1:J=PEEK(204)+PEEK
     (205)*256-1
1270 FOR I=1 TO K: IF ASC(V$(I))#
     PEEK(L+I) THEN 1290
1280 IF PEEK(L+K+1)>1 THEN 1290:
     L=L+K+4:RETURN
1290 FOR I=1 TO 100: IF PEEK(I+L)>1
     THEN NEXT I:L=L+I+1:L=PEEK(I)+
     PEEK(I+1)*256-1
1300 IF L<J THEN 1270:L=L-1:RETURN
```
********************************

RETAIL COMPUTER STORE has classes available for both hardware and software. Check with them for details.

## REVIEWS (From Page 2)

Assembly Syntax, Micro's software catalogue and Part III of a 6502 bibliography. It is published bimonthly by "the Computerist" at 8 Fourth Lane, S. Chelmsford, Ma. 01824, $6.00 per year. Run, don't walk!

Last, but certainly not least, is Dr. Dobbs Journal of Computer Calisthenics & Orthodontia, published 10 times per year by Peoples Computer Company, Box E, Menlo Park, Ca. 94025, at $12.00 per annum. Unlike Micro, Dr. Dobbs is not 6502-oriented. However, it appears that the software section each issue has programs for the four popular chips, 6502, 6800, Z-80 and 8080. In addition, it would appear that about every other issue has material pertinent to Apple II., this one being no exception, with a Renum/Append routine being featured. This journal does not accept paid commercial advertising, on the premise of "keeping us honest, while pursuing the role of consumer advocate." We agree.

## AN APPLE II MEMORY TEST
### by Bob Huelsdonk

I wrote this simple program to test new memory chips I bought. Just store the correct end address for your Apple in locat'ns 4 & 5, run 300G and display 800 to the end.

```
*300.32A
0300-  A0 00 A9 55 91 02 D1 02
0308-  D0 1D A9 AA 91 02 D1 02
0310-  D0 15 20 18 03 90 EB 60
0318-  A5 02 C5 04 A5 03 E5 05
0320-  E6 02 D0 02 E6 03 60 20
0328-  3A FF 00

0000-  4C 42 00 08 FF BF 51 17
          SL SH EL EH
*300G
*0800.BFFF

SL=START ADS LO    EL=END ADS LO
SH=START ADS HI    EH=END ADS HI

IF MEMORY PERFECT *0800.BFFF
DISPLAYS ALL AA (FOR 48K)
```

## NEW PROGRAMS

The library is now assembling games and other applications into module form, 2 or three programs on a menu. So far, we have Gamepak 1 with Anne Apple, OneArm Bandit and an updated version of Zot!; No. 2 contains Hurkle, Multiply and Biorhythm, while "Programmers Workshop" is composed of Append, Examine Basic, Renumber, List by Page, Poke Routine Writer, and Pick a Base From ... Blackjack, Checkers and Craps will be in the next Gamepak, while other new programs include Appleodian, Hamurabi and Life. Remember, we need your programs! Programs may be obtained from participating dealers, which include Omega Bellevue, Computerland Federal Way and Empire.

## NEW APPLE DEALERS

We would like to extend a welcome to two new Computerland stores in Bellevue and Tacoma. Tom McConnell manages the new Bellevue store at 14340 NE 20th, phone 746-2070, which opened April 28th and Dennis Griswold is in charge of the Tacoma store at 8700 S. Tacoma Way, scheduled to open May 5th. The phone for Tacoma is 581-0388. Welcome Aboard!

** SUPPORT YOUR APPLE DEALERS **
**** THEY SUPPORT YOU ! ****

## APPLE II BASIC STRUCTURE
### by Steve Wozniak
### Apple Computer, Inc.
(Reprinted from Dr. Dobbs Journal of Computer Calisthenics and Orhtodontia, Box E, Menlo Park, Ca. 94025, Issue No. 23)

An understanding of the internal representation of a BASIC program is necessary in order to develop ... algorithms. Fig. 1 illustrates the significant pointers for a program in memory. Variable and symbol table assignment begins at the location whose address is contained in
JMP PAGE 5

the pointer LOMEM ($4A and $4B where '$' stands for hex). This is $800 (2048) on the APPLE-II unless changed by the user with the LOMEM: command. A second pointer, PV (Variable Pointer, at $CC and $CD) contains the address of the location immediately following the last location allocated to variables. PV is equal to LOMEM if no variables are actively assigned as is the case after a NEW, CLR, or LOMEM: command. As variables are assigned, PV increases.

Figure 1 – MEMORY MAP

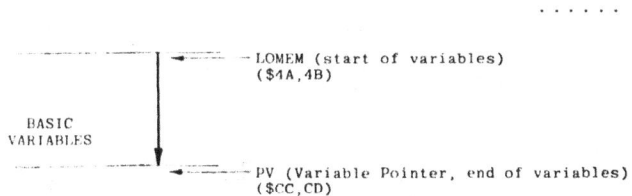

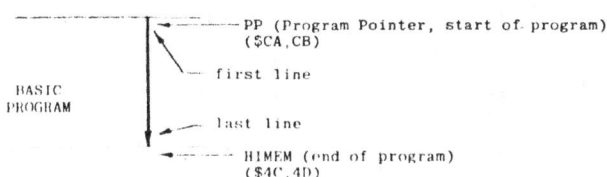

The BASIC program is stored beginning with the lowest numbered line at the location whose address is contained in the pointer PP (Program Pointer, at $CA and $CB). The pointer HIMEM ($4C and $4D) contains the address of the location immediately following the last byte of the last line of the program. This is normally the top of memory unless changed by the user with the HIMEM: command. As the program grows, PP decreases. PP is equal to HIMEM if there is no program in memory. Adequate checks in the BASIC insure that PV never exceeds PP. This in essence says that variables and program are not permitted to overlap.

Lines of a BASIC program are not stored as they were originally entered (in ASCII) on the APPLE-II due to a pre-translation stage. Internally each line begins with a length byte which may serve as a link to the next line. The length byte is immediately followed by a two-byte line number stored in binary, low-order byte first. Line numbers range from 0 to 32767. The line number is followed by 'items' of various types, the final of which is an 'end-of-line' token ($01). Refer to Figure 2.

Figure 2 – LINE REPRESENTATION

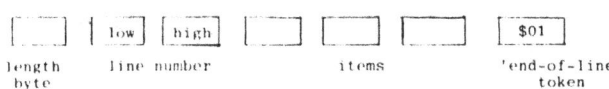

Single bytes of value less than $80 (128) are 'tokens' generated by the translator. Each token stands for a fixed unit of text as required by the syntax of the language BASIC. Some stand for keywords such as PRINT or THEN while others stand for punctuation or operators such as ',' or '+'.

Integer constants are stored as three consecutive bytes. The first contains $B0-$B9 (ASCII '0'-'9') signifying that the next two contain a binary constant stored low-order byte first. The line number itself is not preceeded by $B0-$B9. All constants are in this form including line number references such as 500 in the statement GOTO 500. Constants are always followed by a token. Although one or both bytes of a constant may be positive (less than $80) they are not tokens.

Variable names are stored as consecutive ASCII characters with the high order bit set. The first character is between $C1 and $DA (ASCII 'A' – 'Z'), distinguishing names from constants. All names are terminated by a token which is recognizable by a clear high-order bit. The '$' in string names such as A$ is treated as a token.

String constants are stored as a token of value $28 followed by ASCII text (with high-order bits set) followed by a token of value $29. REM statements begin with the REM token ($5D) followed by ASCII text (with high-order bits set) followed by the 'end-of-line' token.

Figure 3 – ITEMS

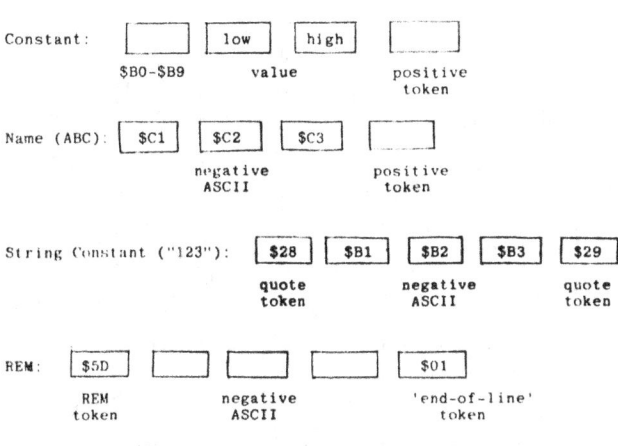

(See token Chart = Page 6)

\*\*\*\*\*\*\*\*\*\*\*\*\*\*\*\*\*\*\*\*\*\*\*\*\*\*\*\*\*\*\*\*\*\*\*\*

OMEGA STEREO Bellevue store has now added Vector Graphics and Axiom to their line of computer products.

\*\*\*\*\*\*\*\*\*\*\*\*\*\*\*\*\*\*\*\*\*\*\*\*\*\*\*\*\*\*\*\*\*\*\*\*

COMPUTER COMPONENTS (Formerly Computer Playground) of Westminster, Ca. offers an Apple II/S-100 bus interface at $100, along with other I/O's and software.

\*\*\*\*\*\*\*\*\*\*\*\*\*\*\*\*\*\*\*\*\*\*\*\*\*\*\*\*\*\*\*\*\*\*\*\*

## COMING UP IN CALL -APPLE

For Applesoft users, a fix decimal point routine by Bob Huelsdonk and a floating point foutine for Integer Basic by Don Williams, along with YOUR programs and YOUR articles. Our pay scale is pretty low (nothing!), but the rewards are gratifying... YOU have helped another member with your contribution!

# APPLE II INTEGER BASIC INTERPRETATION OF MEMORY

Val Golding + Don Williams  3-27-78

|   | 0 | 1 | 2 | 3 | 4 | 5 | 6 | 7 | 8 | 9 | A | B | C | D | E | F |
|---|---|---|---|---|---|---|---|---|---|---|---|---|---|---|---|---|
| 0 | HIMEM: | END OF STMT | — | : | LOAD | SAVE | CON | RUN | RUN | DEL | 9 | NEW | CLR | AUTO | 9 | MAN. |
| 1 | HIMEM: | LOMEM: | + | - | * | / | = | # | >= | > | <= | <> | < | AND | OR | MOD |
| 2 | < | + | ( | 9 | THEN | THEN | = | 9 | " | " | ( | : | . | ( | PEEK | RND |
| 3 | ?/J | ?/J | PDL | RNDX | ( | + | - | NOT | " | = | # | : | ; | SCRN( | 9 | ( |
| 4 | ?/J | ?/J | ( | 9 | ( | 9 | 9 | 9 | ( | = | # | LEN( | ASC( | CALL | DIM | DIM |
| 5 | TAB | END | INPUT | INPUT | INPUT | INPUT | FOR | TO | STEP | NEXT | 9 | TEXT | GR | REM | LET | GOTO |
| 6 | IF | PRINT | PRINT | PRINT | PRINT | POKE | COLOR= | PLOT | HLIN | 9 | 9 | RETURN | GOSUB | 9 | AT | VTAB |
| 7 | = | = | ) | ) | LIST | 9 | LIST | POP | NODSP | NODSP | NO TRACE | AT | VLIN | DSP | TRACE | IN# |
| 8 | NUL | SOH | STX | ETX | EOT | ENQ | ACK | BEL | BS | HT | LF | VT | FF | CR | SO | SI |
| 9 | DLE | DC1 | DC2 | DC3 | DC4 | NAK | SYN | ETB | CAN | EM | SUB | ESC | FS | GS | RS | US |
| A | SP | ! | " | # | $ | % | & | ' | ( | ) | * | + | , | - | . | / |
| B | 0 | 1 | 2 | 3 | 4 | 5 | 6 | 7 | 8 | 9 | : | ; | < | = | > | ? |
| C | @ | A | B | C | D | E | F | G | H | I | J | K | L | M | N | O |
| D | P | Q | R | S | T | U | V | W | X | Y | Z | [ | \ | ] | ^ | _ |
| E | ` | a | b | c | d | e | f | g | h | i | j | k | l | m | n | o |
| F | p | q | r | s | t | u | v | w | x | y | z | { | | | } | ~ | del |

MOST SIGNIFICANT DIGIT (rows): 0–7 TOKENS; 8–F ASCII CHAR. & CONTROLS (ASCII EQUIV 0–7)

LEAST SIGNIFICANT DIGIT (columns)

NOTE: Rows E + F will be output as upper case to Apple II Video Monitor

NOTE: This table is a complement to "Apple II Basic Structure" by Steve Wozniak on Page 4 and 5, and should also be saved as a permanent reference chart.

CALL -APPLE     MAY, 1978     PAGE 6

# CALL -A.P.P.L.E.
## Apple PugetSound Program Library Exchange

## APPENDING APPLESOFT by Val Golding

Here are simple routines that will allow you to append programs in both versions of Applesoft. While appending can be done under program control in Ap. II, it is really simpler to do it without. The routines are the same in both versions; only the pointers have been changed (to protect the innocent!). A word of caution: Applesoft programs store in memory just the opposite of Integer Basic, i.e., from the bottom up. Therefore, the first program appended should be the one with the lowest line numbers. You will get an error message in Ap. I, which should be disregarded. The secret is in changing the values of the pointers (106 & 107 in Ap. I) or (103 & 104) in Ap. II). This "hides" the first program while the second is being loaded. To do this, these pointers must be set to equal the value of the program pointer, less 2. In Ap. I the PP is 112 & 113; in Ap II it is 109 & 110. Here is the routine; just use the proper pointers for version I or II.

```
POKE 103, (PEEK(109)-2)
POKE 104, PEEK(110)
LOAD
POKE 103, 1:POKE 104, 48 (for Ap. II)
POKE 106, 1:POKE 107, 42 (for Ap. I)
```

Do not attempt to list, run, renumber, etc. until all of the routine has been completed or it will blow your Applesoft.

*********************************

### APPLESOFT II WORKSHOP

We will have available sometime within the next month the Applesoft II version of Programmers Workshop, with most of the same routines, Append, Renumber, Examine Basic, Pick a Base, Poke writer.

CALL -APPLE Vol. I, No. 5   June, 1978

Apple PugetSound Program Library Exchan
6708 39th Avenue Southwest
Seattle, Washington 98136

Val J. Golding, President   (206) 937-65
Michael Thyng, Secretary   (206) 524-27

### JUNE MEETING
7:00 PM           Tuesday,   June 20, 1978
Empire Electronics
616 SW 152nd St.   Burien, Wa.   244-5200

### JULY MEETING
7:00 PM           Tuesday,   July 18, 1978
Omega Stereo
5420 196th SW        Lynnwood   775-7585

### SPECIAL APPLESOFT ISSUE

Everything you always wanted to know about Applesoft but. . .

| | |
|---|---|
| Appending Applesoft | Page 1 |
| Applesoft II Review | Page 5 |
| Applesoft II Token Chart | Page 8 |
| Fixing the Decimal | Page 3 |
| Conversion Program | Page 10 |
| REM Formatter | Page 4 |

Plus: our regular features, Bytes from the Apple, AppleMash, new programs, etc.

### ASSEMBLY LANGUAGE CLASSES

Classes scheduled to start June 1st at Empire Electronics. Cost $35 per person including Synertek manual. To sign up, call Tom Geer at 244-5200 or Don Williar at 242-6807. The course includes Number Systems, Boolean Algebra, 6502 Instruction set and Programming.

## APPLEMASH by Michael Thyng

COMPUTER COMPONENTS - formerly known as COMPUTER PLAYGROUND - offers some large storage for APPLE users in the form of PERSCI floppy discs. This is the first in a series of articles about the "large" floppies available for Apple II.

The drive is the PerSci Model 277 dual diskette drive. This means it has two eight inch floppy disc surfaces with approximately 256,000 bytes available per surface. Half a million bytes of disc storage in one drive! Optionally selectable is a double density format which would make the two surfaces capable of storing one million bytes of data in one drive on-line, and available for your program. Each Model 277 weighs 20 pounds and requires + and - 5 volts, and +24 volts.

Computer Components have developed the necessary electronics to connect the system to Apple II and give the programmer an operating system that is not too much more complex than Applesoft. The current price is $2800, but this could change by + or -$200, depending on development costs and demand. It is this writer's opinion that the cost will be dropping, since Computer Components is one of the first on the market with a needed product, and the additional competition will surely let them reduce costs on their proven product, while competitors are still debugging.

Next time: Interface Routines.

## EDITORIAL by Val J. Golding

Is the ugly head of price wars and cut-throat sales about to raise itself? We sincerely hope not. These are bargains in which no one gains. If a dealer can move enough units in a given period of time, he can make money, even with a profit margin as low as 10%. But in order to do this, he must also cut overhead. (JMP Col 2)

## HIRES CAPABILITIES AND LIMITATIONS by Darrell Aldrich

While written for Applesoft II, this article is also applicable to Integer Basic HI-RES graphics mode. The High Resolution Graphics screen is composed of 280 vertical bars (X coordinates), by 160 units high (Y coordinates). The even-numbered bars are violet in color, while the odd-numbered bars are green. The color white is produced by plotting adjacent green and violet bars. (Green/Violet=White.)

By plotting only on even bars, (even X coordinates), violet plots can be made. However, since we are plotting only 50% of the points on the screen, horizontal resolution decreases to 140 points. Plotting green is exactly the same as plotting violet, except plotting is done on the odd-numbered bars (odd X coordinates).

The HIRES routines produce the four available colors, (green, violet, white and black) by allowing us to mask off either the green or violet bars. Remember, when you set the HCOLOR variable (or location $812_{10}$) for green, that a point may not be plotted on a violet bar, and the inverse is true for plotting violet on a green bar.

## OUR THANKS TO:

Randy Wiggington of Apple Computer, inc., for letting us bug him (no pun intended) both by mail and phone, and whose help was invaluable in helping us prepare this special Applesoft II issue.

## EDITORIAL (JMP'd from Col 1)

This is usually accomplished through reductions in sales staff and services to customers. Needless to say, it is the customers who stand to lose the most. Service costs money. And the product is a loser, too. We have seen good audio products go down the drain with uncontrolled price cutting. And this is not too say a dealer can't wheel and deal a bit, but within limits!

BYTES FROM THE APPLE by Val Golding
Software stuff, etc., etc., etc., etc.

We always look forward to writing this column each month, for a number of reasons. One is that since it is usually the last new material written, it is this column that gives us an indication of the length the current issue will run. Secondly, because we look at it as sort of "our own" column we feel free to let our thoughts wander a bit, and we feel this line sometimes will produce some interesting material. In any case, it does give us an opportunity to say our piece.

We have watched with pride our club grow from a handfull of people in mid-february to more than 50 members in a half-dozen states. We have entered into agreements with four outside organizations at this writing, with which we will exchange software. Our program library has grown from a half dozen programs in February, to over three dozen, and more come in every week. And more members are climbing aboard and participating. We would particularly like to welcome Darryl Aldrich who makes an appearance in this issue as the author of an article, and who is now relieving us of some of the load of assembling our programs into module form, as well as writing his own programs.

We enjoy assisting new members with their problems and questions while they are still familiarizing themselves with the power of the Apple II, even though it sometimes becomes a bit hectic. We are glad to know that when we are stumped on a question, there is always another member to whom we can turn for an answer. That is one of the beauties of this organization, and it was from this basic thought that we came up with the title for the newsletter, Call-Apple. CALL-APPLE!

Because of the recent expansion of our membership, next issue (GOTO Pg. 4)

```
10  REM ROUTINE TO FORMAT DECIMAL
    NUMBERS ROUNDED OFF TO TWO
    PLACES AND RIGHT JUSTIFIED
    BY  BOB HUELSDONK

15  REM     4/27/78

20  REM APPLE PUGETSOUND PROGRAM
    LIBRARY EXCHANGE
    6708 39TH AVE SW
    SEATTLE, WA.  98136

70  FOR I = 1 TO 10: READ A:P = A
    : GOSUB 6000
75  PRINT P$: NEXT
80  END
90  DATA  56,2,23456,.95,1,186,34
    5.78,23,678,5123,-98999,820,
    ,2389,789567
100 REM
110 REM   'A' WAS CHANGED TO 'P'
120 REM   TO KEEP THE SUBROUTINE
130 REM   ANONYMOUS.
140 REM   WORKS FOR P<999999
150 REM   BUT CAN BE INCREASED

6000 P$ = STR$ (P)
6010 FOR J = 1 TO  LEN (P$): IF
      MID$ (P$,J,1) < > "." THEN
      NEXT
6015 IF J =  LEN (P$) + 1 THEN P
     $ = P$ + ".0"
6020 IF  LEN (P$) < J + 2 THEN 6
     040
6025 IF  VAL ( MID$ (P$,J + 3,1)
     ) < 5 THEN 6035
6030 P$ =  MID$ (P$,1,J + 1) +  RIGHT$
     ( STR$ ( VAL ( MID$ (P$,J +
      2,1)) + 1),1)
6035 P$ =  MID$ (P$,1,J + 2)
6040 IF  LEN ( LEFT$ (P$,J)) > =
     7 THEN 6050
6045 P$ = " " + P$:J = J + 1: GOTO
     6040
6050 IF  LEN (P$) > = 9 THEN 60
     60
6055 P$ = P$ + "0": GOTO 6050
6060 RETURN
```

Input P may be substituted for 90 DATA above, and other minor modifications made to suit your program. Save routines like the above and append them to your programs.

## BYTES FROM THE APPLE (from Pg. 3)

we will repeat some of the programming hints from past issues in this space, along with many new ones. The alleys of Apple II's monitor remain largely unexplored, and we plan to lead an expedition.

New programs now available include "Doily Doodler" by Ron Nosek, an excellent HIRES demo, "Hires Biorhythm" by Darryl Aldrich, both of which will be in the form of one of our "Apple-Paks", which are modules consisting of three or more individual programs ensconced in a menu. Also available will be a "CasinoPak" which will include an updated version of Karl Gauders' "One Arm Bandit" and Wayne Kraft's "Pin Ball Wizard", all in color graphics. A number of business-oriented programs by Darrel Smith will now be handled by Empire Electronics. These are a property rental program, a universal data base, the Appleditor word processor/text editor and a complete inventory system. Prices range from $50 to $160. We have our own copy of the Appleditor, and it appears to be an excellent program. We hope to be able to announce in the near future a Basic Programming Tutorial for beginners at $40 or less. We are presently working on the "Applesoft II Workshop" a companion program to the popular programmers workshop. It will contain many of the same routines, along with a rem/print formatter, which appears in the form of a program listing in this issue.

Last item for this month is directed to new members. To give your own program library a head start, we have put together a cassette of over 20 programs selected from the club library. This will be available for $5 from selected dealers and direct from the club. Empire Electronics has agreed to handle this item, and we have not yet had the opportunity to contact the other dealers yet. We should be able to announce them by the next meeting.

```
JLIST

10 REM ROUTINE TO FORMAT REMARKS
   LINES AND PRINT STATE-
   MENTS IN APPLESOFT II BY
   VAL GOLDING    5-28-1978

20 REM APPLE PUGETSOUND PROGRAM
   LIBRARY    EXCHANGE
   6708 39TH AVE SW
   SEATTLE, WA.  98136

90  HOME : VTAB 4
100 PRINT "THIS ROUTINE ALLOWS Y
    OU TO FORMAT REM LINES AN
    D PRINT STATEMENTS. DO N
    OT ENTER DATA IN THE SPA
    CES.": PRINT
105 PRINT : PRINT : HTAB 8: PRINT
    "SELECT ONE: ": PRINT : PRINT
    : HTAB 12: PRINT "REM =": PRINT
    : HTAB 12: PRINT "PRINT =": INPUT
    "=";A$
110 IF A$ = "PRINT" THEN 180
120 HOME : VTAB 2
130 REM ENTER GROUPS OF 24 DASH-
    ES AND 4 SPACES
140 PRINT "   000 REM---------
    ------------    --------
    ------------    --------
    ------------    --------
    ------------    --------
    ------------    --------
    ------------"
150 IF PEEK (37) < 18 THEN 140
160 PRINT : PRINT " GOTO 130
    (FOR MORE LINES)"
170 VTAB ( PEEK (37) - 22): END

180 HOME : VTAB 2
190 REM ENTER 39 DASHES 1 SPACE
195 PRINT : PRINT "   000 ?"------
    ----------------------------
    ----------------------------
    ----------------------------
    -- -----------------------
    ---------------- "$
200 IF PEEK (37) < 18 THEN 195
210 PRINT : PRINT " GOTO 190
    (FOR MORE LINES)"
220 VTAB ( PEEK (37) - 19): END
```

REVIEW by Val Golding

APPLESOFT II Extended Precision Floating Point Basic. $20 from Apple dealers or direct from Apple Computer, 10260 Bandley Drive, Cupertino, CA 95014. Supplied free with new 16-48K Apples. A ROM version is expected to be released about July 1st for $99.

One's first impression might be that charging for this updated version of Applesoft is unfair, which was our snap judgement. However, consideration must be given to other facts, the first being that Apple Computer has spent a small fortune in development costs and programming expense, and through the sale of the cassette tapes is attempting to recoup only a small portion of that expense. Secondly, Applesoft II is so much modified from the original that it should properly be considered as a new Basic, rather than a modification. And on this basis, a search through magazine ads reveals that many computer owners, Altair, Imsai, etc., pay hundreds of dollars for a good extended Basic, still not a "rip-off" price, once again taking development costs into account.

Despite it's superior string handling capabilities, we have avoided Applesoft I for a number of reasons, including the many format differences from the faster running Integer Basic, and the lack of immediate error messages, owing to the manner in which the two respective Basics are compiled. Many of these items, minor in themselves, such as the use of a hyphen instead of a comma in the LIST command, have been rectified. In contrast, the listing format has also been revised, with the consequence that, like Integer Basic, one must now utilize the POKE 33,33 routine to avoid tracing over the gaps in long print statements. In addition, it is also necessary to backspace with escape "B" to copy a line number. Apple says this will not be changed. More's the pity.

Applesoft II contains over 35 new or modified commands, in addition to most of the originals. Whenever possible, command names have been changed to match those of Integer Basic, a much needed change. The renamed commands are: GR, PLOT, COLOR=, HLIN, VLIN, TEXT, CALL and HTAB. The new commands include FLASH, INVERSE and NORMAL; TRACE and NOTRACE; STORE and RECALL; ONERRGOTO and RESUME; HOME; POP; SPEED. The latter intrigues us as it provides a means for the first time to control the output speed to either printer or screen, and we have found it most useful in listing programs. We are happy to see the powerful TRACE debug command added, but regret that no room was left to include the handy DSP and AUTO. But then, there is room for only 128 such tokens. (See the Applesoft II token chart elsewhere in this issue.) In addition to the foregoing, there are about a dozen commands committed to the handling of High Resolution graphics, available for the first time in Applesoft.

Apple has indicated that the random number generator has now been repaired, and that math accuracy has been improved. As is the case with earlier Apple documentation, the eight pages that come with the cassette as a supplement to the Applesoft manual leave something to be desired. A case in point. In our first attempt to use the Applesoft II HIRES routines, we struggled through the list of commands, noted one error and one ommission and finally managed to draw some lines on the screen. The colors are still a mystery to us, behaving quite differently in vertical and horizontal modes.

Were this to be used with some of the earlier component-based microcomputer systems we would state that the documentation was adequate, since for the most part users are assumed to have some background in data processing. Such is not the case with Apple II, the forerunner of a new

(Continued from page 5)
generation of "plug-in-and-run" microcomputers. Hopefully, by the time the ROM version is released, Apple will have completely revised the Applesoft manual.

In all fairness, we must also offer our opinion that in the final analysis, Applesoft II will come to be known as one of the most versatile and powerful extended Basics available, and we suspect that we will personally be making a great deal more use of "ASII" than we did of it's predecessor.

## APPLE SOURCE

Apple II the country's top seller? This is what Phil Roybal, Apple Computer's marketing manager believes when we asked him recently. Apple's new Shugart minifloppy has now officially been announced at an unbelievably low $495. Delivery scheduled to commence late June. This drop of $200 was enough to influence our decision to buy. The Applesoft II Rom board will be available at $100 for an introductory period only, running through July 31st, at which time retail becomes $200. Better buy quick! ...Apple has announced price reductions in 16K Apple II's from $1445 to $1195 and in 16K chip sets from $500 to $300. ...We were fortunate to be able to see a pre-release copy of Apple's new editor-assembler, written by Gary Shannon and Randy Wiggington, and tentatively scheduled for fall release. Randy describes it as the most comprehensive editor-assembler ever produced, bar none and says it will even outperform IBM's!

## MINUTES OF May 16, 1978

The meeting got off to a prompt start at 7:25 (after the secretary arrived. ed.) and the minutes were approved as stated in the May Call-Apple. There were 24 members present. (Note the continuing increase). Val started the usual introductions around the room....(JSR Col. 2)

and some names are now becoming familiar. And then on to business.

Val announced that tentative agreement has been reached with Softech, Inc., to sell memberships and software to the club on a greatly reduced basis. (An application form has now been mailed to all members. ed.) Our club shares a major portion of the cost.

Starting with the July Call-Apple, we will be accepting commercial advertising, and classified ads will appear in the June issue. Cutoff date will be the evening of the meeting for both, and non-commercial classified will go at the low rate of .05 per word. Apple has announced the ROM version of Applesoft II for late June at about $99. The card will fit in slot #0 and will be equipped with a switch to select either integer Basic or Applesoft from monitor.

Apple's Software Bank is now open. Val suggests we submit programs through the club so all can share in the programs. Apple will send in exchange. Don Williams' Assembly Language classes will start June 1st. Treasurer's report shows a balance of $152.14. The meeting adjourned at 7:52 and we then exchanged programs.

## APPLESOFT II POINTERS & TOKENS
### by Val Golding

Applesoft & Applesoft II store in memory from the bottom up, unlike Integer Basic, which is just the opposite, storing from the top down. Although pointers and characteristics of Applesoft I and II are similar, they are different. Therefore we will limit ourselves to APII in this discussion.

Programs store starting at decimal location 12289 upwards, and variables are located starting at the high end of program storage. When there is no program present, then the variables will start at 12291. String variables, however, store downwards from the top of memory, 16384 for a 16K Apple. See figure 1 on page 7.

(GOSUB pg. 7 )

## POINTERS & TOKENS (from Page 6)

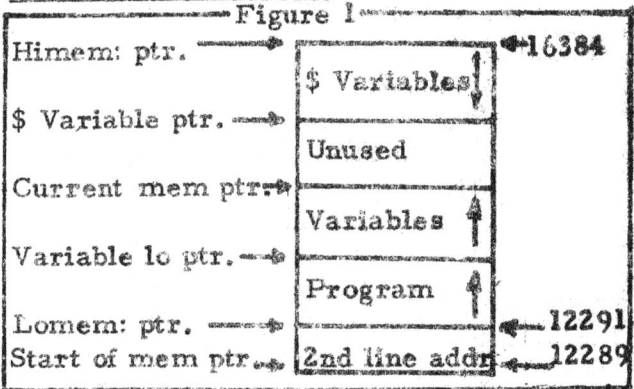

Figure 1

Applesoft has a somewhat complex group of pointers; we're not positive we have covered them all here. All pointers are given in decimal form. 103 & 104 are the start of memory pointer. They always point to 12289 where you can find the address of the second program statement. They are not affected by setting LOMEM:. 105 & 106 are the variable low pointer. They point to the next available location available for either more program or variables. 107 & 108 are the variable pointer. They point to the last location used by variables, plus one. 109 & 110 are the Current Memory pointer. They point to the highest location plus one, used by either program or variables. 111 & 112 are the low string pointers. They point to the next location available for string variable storage. 113 & 114 are the HIMEM: pointer. They always point to HIMEM: which is the first location available for string variable storage. Finally, we have the true program pointer, 175 & 176. These point to the highest location, plus one, used by the program. They are NOT affected by the setting of LOMEM:.

A program to display Applesoft II tokens is listed in column 2. Unlike Integer Basic, which uses the values 0 to 127 for its tokens, ASII uses 128 to 255, while 0 to 127 are the Ascii character set. The Ascii set is as given in the chart in the May Call Apple. ASCII tokens are shown in figure 4 on Page 9. (JSR Page 8)

```
LIST

100  PRINT
110  REM      ROUTINE TO DISPLAY
     APPLESOFT PROGRAM TOKENS
     BY     VAL GOLDING     AND
     BOB HUELSDONK

120  REM APPLE PUGETSOUND PROGRAM
     LIBRARY EXCHANGE
     6708 39TH AVE SW
     SEATTLE, WA. 98136

180  D = 1
200  HOME :A = 19: B = 128:C = 1229
3
210  POKE C,0: LIST 100: VTAB ( PEEK
 (37) - 1)
220  IF D = 1 THEN  GOSUB 700
230  IF D = 2 THEN  GOSUB 520
240  VTAB ( PEEK (37)):B = B + 1:
 A = A + 1
250  IF A = 22 OR A = 65 THEN 400

260  IF A = 40 OR A = 127 THEN 41
0
270  IF A = 64 OR A = 106 THEN 42
0
280  IF A = 128 THEN 500
290  GOTO 210
400  POKE 32,13: VTAB 1: GOTO 210

410  POKE 32,26: VTAB 1: GOTO 210

420  CALL  - 676: POKE 32,0: HOME
 : GOTO 210
500  IF D = 2 THEN  GOTO 800
510  VTAB 6: PRINT " FOR HEX": PRINT
 "TOKENS, HIT": PRINT "RETURN
 ": CALL  - 676:D = 2: POKE
 32,0: GOTO 200
520  X$ = " ":H$ = "0123456789ABCD
EF"
540  XX = ((B / 256) -  INT (B / 2
56)) * 16: GOSUB 600
550  XX = ((B / 16) -  INT (B / 16
)) * 16: GOSUB 600
560  PRINT X$: RETURN
600  X$ = X$ +  MID$ (H$,XX + 1,1)
 : RETURN
700  PRINT B: RETURN
800  VTAB 22: POKE 32,0: POKE C,1
86
810  END

]
```

## POINTERS & TOKENS (RTS Page 7)

A Basic statement in Applesoft II is composed of five bytes, exclusive of any tokens, and is illustrated below in figure 3. Here is a sample program line, along with the hex bytes it is composed of.

Figure 3

```
100 REM
        07 30   64 00   B2   00
         a.       b.     c.   d.
```

- a. = Address of next Basic line.
- b. = Line number.
- c. = Token for "REM".
- d. = End of line delimiter.

## CONTACT!

...is the name of a new monthly newsletter published by Apple Computer, Inc. The first issue (May) was literally packed with good information and program hints.

If you did not get your copy in the mail, contact your dealer.

## APPLE PATCHES

The May contact (see above) has listed the required patches to repair bugs in Applesoft I.

### ARRAY INDEXING PROBLEM FIX

POKE 6331,32: POKE 6332,166: POKE 6333,41: POKE 6334,234: POKE 10646,133: POKE 10647,177: POKE 10648,162: POKE 10649,5: POKE 10650,165: POKE 10651,132: POKE 10652,96

### LONG LINE FIX

POKE 3050,234: POKE 3054,136: POKE 3055,145: POKE 3056,158: POKE 3057,208: POKE 3052,251

### "END" STATEMENT FIX

POKE 2648,210

### FRE(0) FUNCTION FIX

POKE 6143,5

## CONVERTING APPLESOFT I TO II

A complete program listing is given on Page 10 to convert a program written in Applesoft I so it will load in Applesoft II. This program is available from the club library, as is a version of Applesoft I with corrections made.

Load the converter program in Integer Basic and Run. The program will instruct you when to load your Applesoft I program. When conversion is complete and you have resaved your Applesoft I program, load it into Applesoft II and list. You will then need to manually correct commands to the new format, i.e., PLTG becomes GR.

***************************************
*****     CLASSIFIED ADS      *****
***************************************

WANTED Classified advertisers. Members rate .05/word for non-commercial ads. Commercial rate .10/word; $3 min.
FOR SALE One set each Apple II 16K and 4K chips. $225/$40 installed. 232-5637.
BUSINESS SOFTWARE now available at Empire Electronics, 616 SW 152nd, Burien, 244-5200. Complete inventory system $160; Universal Data Base $60; Property Rental and Word Processor/Editor each $50. All for Apple II!
WANTED Commercial advertisers for next issue. Full page $10; half $6.50; quarter $5; eighth $4. Camera ready copy only; same size; no halftones.
SOFTWARE and articles for newsletter wanted from our members. Urgent! Call Val Golding, 937-6588.
***************************************
COMING UP IN CALL-APPLE
Annoted Memory Test by Bob Huelsdonk.
Using Color Mask in HIRES by D. Aldrich.
Mystery Program--a contest by V. Golding.
Programming Hints from Apple to Z.
Integer Basic Floating Point by D. Williams.
Reviews, new product announcements, etc.
***************************************
SUPPORT YOUR APPLE DEALERS...
...THEY SUPPORT YOU!

# POINTERS & TOKENS FIGURE 2

## APPLESOFT II TOKENS — Van Golding 05.28.78

|  | 0 | 1 | 2 | 3 | 4 | 5 | 6 | 7 | 8 | 9 | A | B | C | D | E | F | |
|---|---|---|---|---|---|---|---|---|---|---|---|---|---|---|---|---|---|
| **8** | END | FOR | NEXT | DATA | INPUT | DEL | DIM | READ | GR | TEXT | PR# | IN# | CALL | PLOT | HLIN | VLIN | 128-143 |
| **9** | HGR2 | HGR | HCOLOR= | HPLOT | DRAW | XDRAW | HTAB | HOME | ROT= | SCALE= | SHLOAD | TRACE | NOTRACE | NORMAL | INVERSE | FLASH | 144-159 |
| **A** | COLOR= | POP | VTAB | HIMEM: | LOMEM: | ONERR | RESUME | RECALL | STORE | SPEED= | LET | GOTO | RUN | IF | RESTORE | & | 160-175 |
| **B** | GOSUB | RETURN | REM | STOP | ON | WAIT | LOAD | SAVE | DEF | POKE | PRINT | CONT | LIST | CLEAR | GET | NEW | 176-191 |
| **C** | TAB( | TO | FN | SPC( | THEN | AT | NOT | STEP | + | - | * | / | ; | AND | OR | > | 192-207 |
| **D** | = | < | SGN | INT | ABS | USR | FRE | SCRN( | PDL | POS | SQR | RND | LOG | EXP | COS | SIN | 208-223 |
| **E** | TAN | ATN | PEEK | LEN | STR$ | VAL | ASC | CHR$ | LEFT$ | RIGHT$ | MID$ |  | SYNTAX ERROR | RETURN WITHOUT GOSUB | OUT OF DATA | ILLEGAL QUANTITY | 224-239 |
| **F** | OVERFLOW | OUT OF MEMORY | UNDEF'D STATEMENT | BAD SUBSCRIPT | REDIM'D ARRAY | DIVISION BY ZERO | ILLEGAL DIRECT | TYPE MISMATCH | STRING TOO LONG | FORMULA TOO COMPLEX | CAN'T CONTINUE | UNDEF'D FUNCTION | ERROR | ( | ( | ( | 240-255 |

— LEAST SIGNIFICANT DIGIT —

**Most Significant Digit** (rows labeled 8, 9, A, B, C, D, E, F)

NOTE: Values 00 to 7F (0 to 127 decimal) are used by the standard ASCII character set. As in Integer Basic, Apple II outputs last two rows (60–7F) as upper case.

This table is a complement to "Applesoft II Pointers and Tokens on Pages 6 & 7, and should be saved as a permanent reference chart.

CALL -APPLE    JUNE, 1978    PAGE 9

Note-Illegal line 1, enter manually

```
0 TEXT : CALL -936: VTAB 3: PRINT
  "APPLESOFT CONVERSION PROGRAM:"

1 LOMEM:2048
2 PRINT "
               CONVERTS OLD APPLESOFT PR
  OGRAMS TO": PRINT "APPLESOFT ][
  FORMAT"
3 PRINT "
               COPYRIGHT 1978 APPLE COMP
  UTER, INC.
                                        "
4 PRINT "

                ": POKE 34,10
5 PRINT "WAS PROGRAM WRITTEN IN OP
  TION 1 OR": PRINT "OPTION 2?
                                        "
  : PRINT "OPTION 1: GRAPHICS COMM
  ANDS WITHOUT"
6 PRINT "          LET OR REM STA
  TEMENTS": PRINT "
                         OPTION 2: LET A
  ND REM STATEMENTS BUT NO
     GRAPHICS."
7 INPUT "OPTION #",O: IF O<>1
   AND O<>2 THEN 7
10 CALL -936: PRINT "PUT APPLESOFT
   PROGRAM TAPE IN RECORDER,":
   POKE 60,Z: POKE 61,Z: POKE
   62,2: POKE 63,Z:F=1536:B=4096

20 INPUT "PRESS THE PLAY BUTTON, TH
   EN HIT RETURN",A$: CALL -259

25 IF PEEK (1)<128 THEN 30: PRINT
   "
                      TAPE READ ERROR!": PRINT "TRY R
   E-ADJUSTING VOLUME CONTROLS ON T
   APEPLAYER, THEN RE-RUN THIS PROG
   RAM"
30 POKE 60,Z: POKE 61,16:E= PEEK
   (Z)+ PEEK (1)*256-6657: POKE
   62,E MOD 256: POKE 63,E/256
   : CALL -259
35 CALL -936: PRINT "
                           CONVERTING..."
40 IF B>=E THEN 1000:A= PEEK (
   B)+F MOD 256: POKE B,A MOD
   256: POKE B+1, PEEK (B+1)+F/
   256+(A>255)

50 FOR B=B+4 TO B+999:T= PEEK
   (B): IF T<133 THEN 250: IF
   T<>135 AND T<>142 OR O=2 THEN
   200:C=B
55 IF T<>142 THEN 60:T=137: GOTO
   250
60 C=C+1:U= PEEK (C): IF U=32 THEN
   60: IF U=67 OR U=71 OR U=72
    OR U=80 OR U=86 THEN GOTO
   U: PRINT "BAD STATEMENT IN PROGR
   AM": GOTO 250
67 T=168: GOTO 90
71 T=135: GOTO 90
72 T=142: GOTO 67
80 T=141: GOTO 90
86 T=143
87 CC=Z:D=B
88 D=D+1: IF PEEK (D)<>44 AND
    PEEK (D)<>58 AND PEEK (D) THEN
    68: IF PEEK (D)=44 THEN 89:
    PRINT "BAD STATEMENT IN PROGRAM
   !": GOTO 250
89 CC=CC+1: IF CC=1 THEN 88: POKE
   D,187
90 POKE C,32: GOTO 250
100 REM :MAP OLD TOKENS TO NEW
200 IF T>185 THEN 250:T=T+1+(T>
    134)*34+(T>139)+(T>168)+(T>
    177)*2
250 POKE B,T: IF B/500=500=B THEN
    PRINT "STILL CONVERTING!"
251 IF T<>0 THEN NEXT B:B=B+1: GOTO
    40
870 C=Z:D=C
1000 CALL -936: POKE 60,Z: POKE
     61,Z: POKE 62,2: POKE 63,Z:
     PRINT "DONE!
                    ": INPUT "START REC
     ORDING, THEN HIT 'RETURN'",
     A$
1001 POKE E-2,Z: POKE E-1,Z: POKE
     E,Z
1005 D=E-4096: POKE Z,D MOD 256:
      POKE 1,D/256: POKE 2,Z: CALL
     -307
1010 POKE 60,Z: POKE 61,16: POKE
     62,E MOD 256: POKE 63,E/256
     : CALL -307
1020 PRINT "O.K.
                    ": PRINT "THE TAPE JU
     ST RECORDED CAN NOW BE LOADED IN
     TO APPLESOFT ][.": END
```

BULLETIN: Our library now has a LCOS (Limited Cassette Operating System)

# CALL -A.P.P.L.E.
## Apple Pugetsound Program Library Exchange

BYTES FROM THE APPLE by Val Golding
Software stuff, etc., etc., etc., etc., etc.

As usual, we are down to the wire again as it comes time to write this column. We are still receiving applications from all over the country as we pass the 110 mark in membership, and we would also at this time like to extend a special welcome to our first overseas member, Paul Moortgat who lives in Nieuwkerken, Belgium! There are many special features for new members in this issue, and we would like to refer you to the "In This Issue" column on this same page.

Many new programs have been received in the last two weeks, and more are on the way. They will all be made available through our library at the earliest possible moment.

This is a good time and place to mention that we need YOUR original programs. Not only do we need them for the library, but we also have obligations now to other groups and individuals who have furnished us with programs.

Should we introduce a "Letters" column? Because we have members now scattered in just about every part of the country, phone calls are a bit on the expensive side. We certainly welcome your questions, either on the Call -Apple "hot line" (206) 932-6588 or by mail. Marvin Eidinger in Pullman Wa. has written to ask, among other things, how the "save" routine (page 40, red manual) works, and how is the append routine to be used. We would like to answer both questions here. The data save routine will write to tape all of the variable data stored between the LOMEM: pointers 74&75 and the variable pointers, 204&205. APPEND, which is a routine within our PROGRAMMERS WORKSHOP program is designed to
(JMP Page 11)

CALL -APPLE Vol. I, No. 6 July, 1978

Apple Puget Sound Program Library Exchange
6708 39th Avenue Southwest
Seattle, Washington 98136

Val J. Golding, President (206) 932-6588
Michael Thyng, Secretary (206) 524-2744
Darrell Aldrich, Prog. Ed. (206) 782-7802

```
**********************************************
            JULY MEETING
7:00 PM           Tuesday,    July 18, 1978
            Omega Stereo
5420 196th SW     Lynnwood    775-7585

            AUGUST MEETING
7:00 PM           Tuesday    August 15, 1978
            Computerland of Bellevue
14340 NE 20th     Bellevue    746-2070
**********************************************
```

MEETINGS are held the third Tuesday of each month at 7:00 PM, rotating between Computerland, Omega Stereo and Empire.

### IN THIS ISSUE....                Page No.

| | |
|---|---|
| Bytes from the Apple............... | 1 |
| Applemash.......................... | 3 |
| Oops..(How not to hit reset)........ | 3 |
| New Member Info................... | 4 |
| Apple "Hot Line".................... | 4 |
| The Key Klicker.................... | 5 |
| Editorial........................... | 5 |
| Minutes of the Meeting.............. | 5 |
| Page Length Routine................. | 6 |
| Printer Drive Fix................... | 6 |
| Apple II Mini-Assembler............. | 7 |
| Color Mask Byte in Hires............ | 9 |
| Apple II Memory Map................ | 9 |
| How the Program Library Works..... | 10 |
| Handy Calls........................ | 10 |
| Classifieds........................ | 11 |
| Apple II Monitor System............ | 12 |
| Annotated Memory Test............. | 15 |

## AUTOMATED TRAINING SYSTEMS

Automated Training Systems has been a Washington State Licensed Proprietory School since 1968. These classes are taught by Cliff Gazaway who has had 20 years of electronics hardware experience and ten years of teaching. He is now assistant manager at Max Cook's Computerland store in Federal Way.

```
$$$$$$$$$$$$$$$$$$$$$$$$$$$$$$$$
$$          SAVE $20.00       $$
$$$$$$$$$$$$$$$$$$$$$$$$$$$$$$$$
$$                            $$
$$ Register at COMPUTERLAND in $$
$$ Federal Way and pay your   $$
$$ tuition before July 22 and $$
$$ COMPUTERLAND will pay $20  $$
$$ of your fee.               $$
$$                            $$
$$$$$$$$$$$$$$$$$$$$$$$$$$$$$$$$
```

.BEGINNING APPLE BASIC.

.Mon. July 24-Aug14, 7-9pm.
.1500 S.336th.,Federal Way

.This class, held at Computer-
.land in Federal Way, is for
.beginners who have never pro-
.grammed in BASIC or for those
.who already know BASIC but
.have never had their hands on
.an APPLE computer. The grad-
.uates of this class will be
.able to use ALL of the Integer
.BASIC & Applesoft I &II com-
.mands. $55.00 plus materials.

.POKING & PEEKING AT YOUR APPLE.

.Mon.Sept.11-25,7-9pm. plus
.additional hands-on time ar-
.ranged.1500 S.336th.,Fed.Way.

.This class shows you how to
.use the powerful POKE,PEEK,&
.CALL commands to do exciting
.things with you APPLE.
.$55.00.

APPLE CIRCUIT THEORY.

Wed.Aug.9-30,7-9pm.
7906 34th.S.W.,Seattle,98126

You will know the purpose of every IC chip in your APPLE upon completion of this course. You will get more out of your APPLE if you know how it works.
$55.00 plus materials

CONNECTING TO THE REAL WORLD.

Wed.,Sept. 13-27, 7-9pm.
7906 34th.S.W.,Seattle 98126

We will study a collection of magazine articles on interfacing and adapt the articles to the APPLE. We will help you custom build the hardware. Subjects of special intrest include clock and calendar, burglar alarms, AC appliance controls, temperature and photo input.
$55.00 plus materials.

CHRISTMAS PRESENTS FOR APPLELOVERS.

Wed., Nov.8-29, 7-9pm.
7906 34th. S.W., Seattle 98126

Every APPLE owner wants something for his APPLE for Christmas. 1978 will be the first"home computer Christmas". This class helps you build or buy something for your APPLE computer owner.
$55.00 plus materials.

For more information call CLIFF at COMPUTERLAND - Phone 838-9363 or 927-8585

## AUTOMATED TRAINING SYSTEMS

## APPLE MASH   by Mike Thyng

Last issue I talked about the general specs of the PERSCI 277 eight inch floppy disk drive. This issue I want to discuss some of the uses for a floppy disc and why anyone would even want one.

But first, let me digress. Since Apple has announced its own Disc II, why should I be telling you about the Persci floppy? Two reasons. 1) Computer Components announced its own floppy as available before Apple did, and 2) I'm using one in another system.

WHY would you want a floppy disc?

The two tasks that a floppy performs most often are program storage and data file storage. I feel that data file storage is the most important use you can put your floppy to. Files--data files--can be written in three basic ways. A file is a list of data grouped together for subsequent retrieval. There are three common ways of reading or writing data files. (You might think of this in terms of INPUT or PRINT).

1) SEQUENTIAL - This writes out your data in the same order it was read into the file.
2) RANDOM - This allows you to get your data any way (i.e., in any order) that you choose. Your records are accessed by their relative number on the file.
3) INDEXED SEQUENTIAL - This is by far the most flexible for a programmer, but is the most complex of the three accessing methods and costs (read wastes) a lot of side overhead. For your early needs, skip this one.

All files are composed of records. Records are made up of fields or variables. A typical kind of file is a Name & Address file. In this, the file would be the names and addresses of, say, all the Call-Apple club members. (Mike, you may have hit upon something! ...ed.) The record would be all the information about one club member. It might contain seven fields (or variables). For example:

(GOTO Pg. 11)

## HERE'S AN "OOPS FIXER" ©

J.A. BACKMAN   6-27-78

If you have dumped a program by hitting "RESET" when you meant to hit "RETURN" and $C^C$ wouldn't bring the program back - - I'll bet the air was as blue around your APPLE II as it was around mine! - ! - !

A sweet little fix is a simple gadget that stops accidental keying "RESET" but does not stop its operation when it is needed. It does not hide the key, and doesn't require lifting a lid to get to it.

The gadget is made in a few minutes from an old - tired - empty cassette storage box lid. Just cut off 1-1/2" from the left end of the cover, shorten the remaining length to 2-1/4", soften the plastic over gentle heat and bend the long flat side up about 15° 1-1/8" from the single edge.

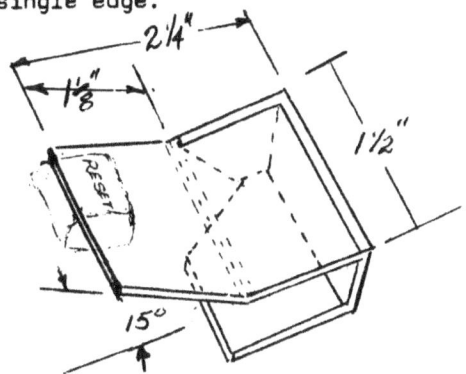

Now, to use this gadget, press down slightly on the lower right hand corner of the top cover of your APPLE II, just above the "RESET" key. This will make a thin gap - just wide enough to slip the narrowest side under the keyboard housing and the top cover. If the bend angle is right, the plastic shield will cover, and just clear the "RESET" key. There is enough tension from the top cover to hold it in place.

Wonder-of-wonders!!! the "RESET" key still works by pressing the cover, but, when you reach for the "RETURN" key - - your finger stubs. Voila!! no more unintentional program dumps.

## A.P.P.L.E. PORTLAND

We are pleased to report the formation of an Apple user group south of the border, Apple Portland Program Library Exchange. We attended their organizational meeting in May and spent an enjoyable evening in Portland as the guest of Terry Ashton of Computerland of Portland, who also hosted the initial meeting. We are happy to see that their membership now numbers in the 30's. Their dues and program rate structure approximates ours, and we anticipate a good deal of interaction between the two groups. Those interested may contact Ken Hoggatt, President, at 9195 SW Elmrose Ct. Portland, OR 97223 or (503) 639-5505.

## CALL-APPLE "HOT LINE"

We would like to announce the installation of the Apple "Hot Line", (206) 932-6588. This number is now available so your club can assist you with questions, problems, etc. If we don't have an answer immediately available, which is quite likely, we will either attempt to find an answer or refer you to another member who can answer.

If might be well to mention at the same time (especially for distant members who may tend to overlook time zones), call at reasonable hours unless you know odd-hour calls are O.K.

## WELCOME NEW MEMBERS

This issue is devoted to you, and particularly those that live without the Seattle metropolitan area. We have recently received tremendous amounts of mail, largely a result of being mentioned in the club columns of some of the major computer periodicals. Letters have been coming in at the rate of 6-12 per day, and it has certainly solved any problem as to what to do in our spare time!

Those members who live out of state are at a distinct disadvantage in that, since they cannot attend meetings, they will fre-

## Welcome New Members (Cont'd.)

quently miss announcements of interest that are made at the meetings and not reprinted in Call-Apple. This, then, is for you.

If you have requested back issues of Call-Apple, you should previously have received the April and May issues. You should receive the June issue in the same envelope as this (July) issue. If not, let us know (with a S.A.S.E.). The February and March issues were relatively inconsequential and are out of print. A couple of items will be reprinted in this issue.

We have been asked a number of times why our Premium Program plan is unavailable outside Washington; it is really very simple. This is an agreement we negiotiated with an outside software vendor (at a great savings to our members), and participation is very strictly limited in terms of members they will accept at this low rate. And the roster is nearly full.

Why S.A.S.E.'s? Also very simple. Both our dues and our software are structured on a very minimum cost we feel we can get by with, and the time we have available is also very limited, so by enclosing a self addressed, stamped envelope with your requests for information or software, you can substantially reduce the time it takes to get a response back to you, and help keep our treasury intact.

Program submission/copyright forms can be had at meetings or for an S.A.S.E. We need your good, debugged programs, and want to make them available to others through the library.

We do not currently have a software catalogue in print. We will be doing a revised catalogue once our printer is up and running. (Still waiting for I/O card from Southern California). In the meantime, see the item elsewhere in this issue which describes Library Pak 1A and Basic Tutorial.

## EDITORIAL  by Val J. Golding

A problem that arises in any such organization as A.P.P.L.E. is that of "Bootlegging programs." We have a number of programs in our personal library which we have purchased from a software vendor, and when a friend says: "Gosh, that's a neat program..will you run me a copy off?", we have to decline. Not because we don't want to pass the program on, but because we happen to believe that the author/owner of software is entitled to remuneration for his efforts, which is not possible when a program is freely duplicated and passed from person to person. This is why the author has placed a copyright line somewhere in the program.

Our club policy is oriented towards providing the membership with a maximum amount of software at the lowest possible cost, but this does not include adding saleable programs to our library unless we can make an agreement with a vendor to distribute his program, which we have done in some cases.

We would like to discourage from the outset the practice of duplicating, either on tape or printout, programs that carry copyright restrictions. We will not knowingly tolerate, or be a party to such practices.

## MINUTES OF THE MEETING 6/20/78

The meeting got off to a flying start at 7:07 PM as we introduced ourselves. Our official membership now stands at about 64, with 31 present at this meeting. (And in the two weeks since the meeting, has increased to over 100! ..ed) Val reported that the new Call-A.P.P.L.E. "Hot Line" has been installed and that the number is 932-6588. (Where have we heard that number before?) This number can be called for current Apple information, answers to problems, gossip, etc. It is also equipped with our minimodem to handle programs. (Don't tell Ma.)

(JSR Pg. 6)

## KEY KLICKER ROUTINE

If you have a newer Apple with the silent keyboard, Don Williams has written a short and sweet machine language routine to solve your problem.

```
0300:   48          PHA
0301:   A9 20       LDA  #$20
0303:   8D 30 C0    STA  $C030
0306:   20 A8 FC    JSR  $FCA8
0309:   8D 30 C0    STA  $C030
030C:   68          PLA
030D:   4C 1B FD    JMP  $FD1B
0038:   00 03
```

Once you store the address ($0300) in location $38 and hit return, your keys will click merrily away until you hit reset. To restart the routine, reenter the address.

A minor modification of this routine will give you a slow list (with tones) feature. Change the JMP and 030D to F0FD and store the address in $36. The value stored at $0302 may be increased for a slower list.

## BASIC CLASSES

Don Williams will be our instructor again for two levels of Integer Basic Programming, beginning and intermediate, beginning sometime in August. Details will be available in the next Call-Apple.

## PREMIUM PROGRAM PLAN

For those members that have paid their $10 annual membership but have not returned the Softech membership form..... These forms must be turned in before your application can be processed. If you have not received your application, please let us know right away at 932-6588.

## ADVERTISING

Call-Apple is now accepting both commercial and classified advertising. Inquire

## ROUTINE TO FIND PAGE LENGTH

This handy little subroutine can be used in two manners; to fill a screen page with repetitive material or to determine the length of a screen page of print statements. Assume line 100 is a print statement with which you wish to fill the page.

```
100   PRINT " ":GOSUB 400
400   IF PEEK(37) < 18 THEN RETURN
410   POP:PRINT "FOR NEW PAGE HIT
      ANY KEY":CALL 756:GOTO 000
```

Line 400 reads the cursor and finds where it is on the page. If less than 18 lines, print more lines. Line 410 "Pops" the return address from the stack. Instead of Call 756 you could use INPUT A$ or Call -676, all of which are a means of halting the program to await further instructions.

## PRINTER DRIVER FIXES

Some protocol is a must if you use a printer with greater than 40 columns with your Apple. This comes about because it tries to write beyond the screen area and into the variables area in Integer Basic or into the operating system in Applesoft. The following will prevent problems.

Start your printer driver routine with a JSR FC58. This will home the cursor and clear the screen. Do not return to the screen via FDF0. You will not get any output to the CRT but this is usually o.k. There is also a problem with leaving Applesoft with a PR#0. To solve this, use the routine below to re-enter the CRT output. This is done by a Call 1866 if you load it at the location shown. This also resets the window width to 40 characters.

```
*3F0L

03F0-   A9 F0       LDA   #$F0
03F2-   85 36       STA   $36
03F4-   A9 FD       LDA   #$FD
03F6-   85 37       STA   $37
03F8-   A9 28       LDA   #$28
03FA-   85 21       STA   $21
03FC-   60          RTS
```

## MINUTES of 6/20 (RTS Page   )

We are waiting for (and have now received ..ed) a program tape from Apple Corps of Long Beach containing 106 programs, mostly games, to be delivered to Val.

Through the efforts of Val, Darrell and Ron Aldrich, we have produced "Library Paks" from the club's library, which are offered to members at $5.00. About 50% of the new members have opted to purchase the Library Pak, and this in turn has paved the way toward commercial printing of Call-Apple. Printing costs are estimated at about .02 per copy. We are also working toward being recognized as a non-profit educational group in order to take advantage of the tremendous price break in postage.

The cost of the Apple II floppy discs is $495 now, but will go up by $200 as of July 31st. Best order now from your favorite Apple dealer. It was unanimously agreed that the club would purchase a floppy disc for Don Williams in appreciation for the fine assembly language class he presented.

## APPLE PATCH

Here is a patch to correct one of the few bugs found in Applesoft II. The HTAB function will space 2 places further to the right than intended unless corrected with this patch: POKE (HM-28), 202 where HM = the value of HIMEM: for your Apple. This should be done after loading & prior to running.

## DISCS & APPLESOFT ROM DELAYED

Documentation has been cited by Apple Computer as a cause of delay in shipping both the new ROM board and Disc II. Discs have been rescheduled for shipping during the first week of July, while the Applesoft ROMs should follow within two or three weeks. Well worth waiting for!

WELCOME TO: Steve Paulson who will be assisting with membership files and John Backman, who has contributed an article.

## Apple II Mini-Assembler

The following section covers use of the Apple II mini-assembler only. It is not a course in assembly language programming. The following section assumes the user has a working knowledge of 6502 programming and mnemonics. The Apple II mini-assembler is a programming aid aimed at reducing the amount of time required to convert a handwritten program to object code. The mini-assembler is basically a look-up table for opcodes. With it, you can type mnemonics with their absolute addresses, and the assembler will convert it to the correct object code and store it in memory.

Typing "F666G" will put the user in mini-assembler mode. While in this mode, any line typed in will be interpreted as an assembly language instruction, assembled, and stored in binary form unless the first character on the command line is a "$".

If it is, the remainder of the line will be interpreted as a normal monitor command, executed, and control returned to assembler mode. To get out of the assembler mode, reset must be pushed.

If the first character on the line is blank, the assembled instruction will be stored starting at the address immediately following the previously assembled instruction. If the first character is nonblank (and not "$"), the line is assumed to contain an assembly language instruction preceded by the instruction address (a hex number followed by a ":"). In either case, the instruction will be retyped over the line just entered in disassembler format to provide a visual check of what has been assembled. The counter that keeps track of where the next instruction will be stored is the pseudo PC (Program Counter) and it can be changed by many monitor commands (eg., 'L', 'T',...). Therefore, it is advisable to use the explicit instruction address mode after every monitor command and, of course, when the mini-assembler is first entered.

Errors (unrecognized mnemonic, illegal format, etc.) are signalled by a "beep" and a carrot ("^") will be printed beneath the last character read from the input line by the mini-assembler.

The mnemonics and formats accepted by the mini-assembler are the same as those listed by the 6502 Programmers Manual, with the following exceptions and differences:

1. All imbedded blanks are ignored, except inside addresses.

2. All addresses typed in are assumed to be in hex (rather than decimal or symbolic). A preceding "$" (indicating hex rather than decimal or symbolic) is therefore optional, except that it should not precede the instruction address.

3. Instructions that operate on the accumulator have a blank operand field instead of "A".

4. When entering a branch instruction, following the branch mnemonic should be the target of the branch. If the destination address is not known at the time the instruction is entered, simply enter an address that is in the neighborhood, and later re-enter the branch instruction with the correct target address. NOTE: If a branch target is specified that is out of range, the mini-assembler will flag the address as being in error.

5. The operand field of an instruction can only be followed by a comment field, which starts with a semi-colon (";"). Obviously, the mini-assembler ignores the field and in fact will type over it when the line is typed over in disassembler format. This "feature" is included only to be compatible with future upgrades including input sources other than the keyboard.

6. Any page zero references will generate page zero instruction formats if such a mode exists. There is no way to force a page zero address to be two bytes, even if the address has leading zeros.

In general, to specify an addressing type, simply enter it as it would be listed in the disassembly. For information on the disassembler, see Apple II System Monitor in the previous section. A complete listing of the mini-assembler appears at the end of this section. An example of the mini-assembler appears below. Note that the second "BRK" has no space before it hence Apple refused the input, sounded the bell and typed a "↑" underneath the "R". In "LDA3R45", Apple also refused the instruction because "R" is not a legal hex digit. Remember to hit the "RESET" key to get out of the mini-assembler.

```
*F666G

!0: INX

0000-    E8           INX
! TXA

0001-    8A           TXA
! JSR $FDED

0002-    20 ED FD     JSR   $FDED
! JMP $0

0005-    4C 00 00     JMP   $0000
! BRK

0008-    00           BRK
!BRK
 ↑
! BRK

0009-    00           BRK
! LDA 3R45
       ↑
!
```

# ComputerLand™

In Federal Way.

**HOBBY/PROTOTYPING BOARD.**
A two sided printed circuit board that will accept all IC's, transisters, capacitors, etc. For building experimental circuitry or a unique interface for peripheral or hobby accessory. Comes with a good eight page "manual", that tells how to use the board and peripheral slots. $24.00. IN STOCK.

**EXPERIMENTER KITS:** Temperature Input, $9.95. Light Detector Input, $9.95. RS232 Teletype Interface Kit (as shown in red manual) under $15.00.

**PARALLEL PRINTER INTERFACE CARD.**
This card allows the APPLE to produce hard copy on a wide variety of printers, but is also useful in non-printer applications, as a general purpose 8-bit parallel output port to drive Music Synthesizers, Digital-to-Analog Converters, etc. The price is $180.00 and is IN STOCK.

**COMMUNICATIONS INTERFACE CARD (RS232 Serial).**
We are using this to run our IP125 printer. This weekend we will try talking to the Nordata timeshare computer with this card, a Novation modem, and our APPLEs. Incidently, Did you know that your APPLE can use that Nordata computer for only 50 cents an hour on weekends and after 6:00 pm on weekdays. All you need to do is buy our used Novation modem and the APPLE communications interface card, both in stock.

---

**BOOKS AND MAGAZINES FOR APPLES.**

<u>An Introduction To Microcomputers, Vol.II, Some Real Products</u> by Osborne. Out of a total of 20 chapters, one chapter of 75 pages is devoted to the 6500 family of chips. Worth the $15.00 to any APPLE owner who wants to know how his computer works. IN STOCK.

<u>MICROPROCESSOR ENCYCLOPEDIA, VOL.I, 8-BITS</u> by Sybex. Chapter 8 is <u>29 pages on the 6500 series.</u> $9.95. IN STOCK.

<u>HOW TO PROGRAM MICROCOMPUTERS</u> by William Barden. A third of this book <u>is devoted to the 6502. Cliff</u> highly reccomends this book if you are just started machine language or assembly programming your APPLE. $8.95. IN STOCK.

<u>SY6500/MCS6500 MICROCOMPUTER FAMILY HARDWARE MANUAL</u> by MOS TECH or by SYNERTEK. Written mostly for the <u>designer</u> but should be added to your library. $15.00. IN STOCK.

<u>6502 PROGRAMMING MANUAL</u> by MOS or SYNERTEK. $15.00.

<u>TV TYPEWRITER COOKBOOK</u> by Don Lancaster. It helps if you have had some electronics circuit background, but this book is nice in that it tells you how to direct-wire a computer to a TV set without using an RF module. Also tells you how the character generator works in your APPLE. See Cliff in Federal Way to show what parts apply to the APPLE. $9.95. IN STOCK.

## ComputerLand™

1500 South 336th St. • Parkway Center, Suite 12 • Federal Way, Washington 98003
Tacoma (206) 927-8585 • Seattle (206) 838-9363

## USE OF COLOR MASK BYTE IN HIRES
### by Darrell Aldrich

This is a brief description of the use of the color mask byte (Location $812_{10}$) for high resolution graphics in Apple Integer Basic.

This mask specifies an 8 bit pattern of plottable X coordinates, with the pattern repeating itself every eight coordinates, going from left to right. The bits in this byte represent the colors violet and green, alternately. (See Figure 1).

Suppose we want to mask off every other green bar on the screen as in Figure 2a, where "X" indicates a point we want masked off. Set up an 8 bit byte as in Figure 2b, with all masking bits=0 and all non-masking bits=1. Convert this value to decimal & Poke in decimal location 812.

Figure 1.

| | LSB | | | | | | | MSB |
|---|---|---|---|---|---|---|---|---|
| | V | G | V | G | V | G | V | G |
| | 1 | 2 | 4 | 8 | 16 | 32 | 64 | 128 |

Figure 2a.

| V | X | V | G | V | X | V | G |
|---|---|---|---|---|---|---|---|

Figure 2b.

| 1 | 0 | 1 | 1 | 1 | 0 | 1 | 1 |
|---|---|---|---|---|---|---|---|

## Memory Map — Apple II with APPLESOFT BASIC LOADED

| MEMORY RANGE* | DESCRIPTION |
|---|---|
| 0.1FF | Program work space; not available to user. |
| 200.2FF | Keyboard character buffer. |
| 300.3FF | Available to user for short machine language programs. |
| 400.7FF | Screen display area for text or color graphics. |
| 800.2FFF | APPLESOFT BASIC compiler. (Cassette Tape Version) |
| 800.XXX | User Program (ROM version - A2B0009X installed) where XXX is maximum available RAM memory |
| 2000.3FFF | High Resolution Graphics Display page 1. May be used by ROM (A2B0009X) version of Applesoft II only. |
| 3000.XXX | User program (Cassette Tape Version) and variables where XXX is maximum available RAM memory to be used by APPLESOFT. This is either total system RAM memory or less if the user is reserving part of high memory for machine language routines. |
| 4000.5FFF | High resolution graphics display page 2. |
| C000.CFFF | Hardware I/O Addresses. |
| D000.DFFF | Future ROM expansion |
| D000.F7FF | Applesoft II ROM version with select switch "ON". |
| E000.F7FF | Apple Integer BASIC |
| F800.FFFF | Apple System Monitor |

## OUR FACE IS RED (Like an Apple) Dept.
### by Val J. Golding

In Applesoft II Pointers and Tokens, Call-Apple, June, 1978, we made a couple of boo-boos, the most serious of which was stating the HIMEM: pointer as 113 and 114, rather than 115 and 116 which are the correct HIMEM: pointer. We also neglected to mention another peculiarity of Applesoft II String handling: The string variable itself (A$=) is stored in the Variable storage area, while the string data (the information between quote marks) is stored in the string variable area. Another of life's minor mysteries that we have been unable to solve is where in Applesoft II variables, variable matrices and string variables are dimensioned. If anyone has the answer to that one Call-Apple!

### LIST OF HANDY "CALL'S"

| DECIMAL | HEX | FUNCTION |
|---|---|---|
| -1321 | FAD7 | DISPLAYS REGISTERS |
| -676 | FD5C | BELL,HALT,WAIT FOR CR |
| -673 | FD5F | HALT,WAIT FOR CR |
| -668 | FC9E | CLR CURS TO LINE END |
| -922 | FC66 | LINE FEED W/O CR |
| -912 | FC70 | SCROLL UP ONE LINE |
| -936 | FC58 | HOME,CLR SCREEN |
| -958 | FC42 | CLR CURS TO END PAGE |
| -1392 | FA92 | BRK,DSP ADDR,REG,MON |
| -336 | FE84 | SCRATCH BASIC PROG |
| -317 | FECD | WRITE TO TAPE |
| -259 | FEFD | READ FROM TAPE |
| -155 | FF65 | ENTER MON W/O RESET |
| -1052 | FBE4 | IMMEDIATE BELL |
| -211 | FF2D | BELL, PRINT 'ERR' |
| -468 | FE2C | MOVE MEM, MUST POKE |
|  |  | 60,61 LO ADDR |
|  |  | 62,63 HI ADDR |
|  |  | 66,67 STRT LO NEW ADDR |

LOAD ANY MACH LGE SUBROUTINE ADDRESS INTO $3F8 (DEC 1016),,$3F9 (DEC 1017) AND A CONT "Y" WILL JUMP TO IT.

## HOW OUR PROGRAM LIBRARY WORKS

In the last few weeks, we have been expanding very rapidly. So much so that the library has not really been able to fill requests on a completely current basis. We felt that it would be worthwhile to take some space, both to let all members know of recent additions to the library, and to acquaint new members with what is available. With the rapid changes, we have more or less been making policy on the go. A number of changes have been made in the manner in which we produce and distribute programs, with an eye to keeping both handling and reproduction costs to a minimum.

Currently, when we receive a request for an application blank, we also send out available software lists and prices. We have designed "Library Paks" to help new members establish their personal libraries. Each Library Pak has 20 or more programs in modular form, and cost $5.00 plus .41 postage (if from the club). The library Paks are available by mail from the club, or from participating dealers. Individual programs and/or modules may be copied at club meetings at no charge, or from dealers. This is also the way in which you will acquire new programs before they are assembled into Library Paks. Index lists of Paks may be obtained at meetings, dealers or with a S.A.S.E. Here's our current list:

| | |
|---|---|
| Library Pak 1B | 5.00 |
| Library Pak 2 (ready about 8/1) | 5.00 |
| Programmer's Workshop II | 5.00 |
| Integer Basic Tutorial | 15.00 |
| Text Editor/Word Processor | 45.00 |

We plan to distribute these to all area dealers. Some are in stock now. If you have ordered a Pak by mail and not received it, it will be along soon!

*******************************************

Any Ascii control character can be used within a print statement and will function under program control.

*******************************************

## BYTES FROM THE APPLE (JMP'd fm pg.1)

join together two or more individual programs to form a whole. This is what we use when we take a number of programs & put them together on a menu in the form of one of our Game Paks. Its most useful function, however, is appending a program on to the workshop so that the program may be examined and modified, using many of the different Workshop routines. It is also a good learning tool, to aid you in learning hex and in general, more about how your Apple II functions.

A final note for this month, also with regard to learning. USE YOUR RED MANUAL! There is an entire world of information contained therein. You don't need to know assembly language, although it is, of course, helpful. READ and STUDY the monitor listings. Find out what they do. USE them. They can all be called from Basic. Convert the hex addresses to decimal. If > than 32-767, subtract from 65536 to get the negative value and CALL them. Remember, you can only blow a program, not your monitor.

## APPLE MASH (from pg. 3)

1) Name
2) Street Address
3) City
4) State
5) Zip Code
6) Telephone number
7) Special interests

The Persci 277 would be able to read 2000 records in five minutes. If you wanted to read and print all the names of the people in your name and address file, your printer is liable to be slowing you down, not your floppy disc system.

I'll be happy to answer any "file" questions at our next club meeting. As soon as I get my APPLE disc up and running, I will write about that. Next issue: File Commands.

## ****** CLASSIFIED ADS ******

Members rate .05/word for non-commercial ads. Commercial rate .10/word.

FOR SALE The "Apple Box" a mini-modem for your cassette I/O port. With this modem you can get your programs on the Call-Apple Hot Line. $15 with documentation. from Apple, 6708 39th Ave. SW., Seattle, WA 98136. Phone 932-6588.

APPLE CLASSES See our display ad on pg. 2. Automated Training Systems 838-9363.

FOR SALE One set each Apple II 16K and 4K chips. $225/$40 installed. 232-5637.

SOFTWARE for Apple II. Library Pak 1B, Programmers Workshop, Basic Tutorial, others. Computerland Fed. Wy. 838-9363.

WANTED Commercial advertisers. Rates through Sept. issue only: Full page $10.00; half, $6.50; quarter $5; eighth, $4. Same size, camera-ready copy only; no halftones.

BUSINESS SOFTWARE Complete line. Inventory, Data Base, Word Processor, Property Rental $50.00 up. Empire Electronics, 616 SW 152nd, Burien. 244-5200.

INFLATION FIGHTER. According to a recent issue of Newsweek, inflation scarism is the most dangerous enemy our families are facing in today's financial waters!! Using our computer (Apple II, of course), let us show you how, by replacing your expensive, low-yield cash-value life insurance with inexpensive, guaranteed renewable to age 100, plus high-yield tax-favored savings, you can sink the inflation shark!!! Give us a call.    JIM WILSON
ARROW ASSOCIATES Life Insurance and Financial Planners.   542-3695

WANTED Urgent! Articles from our members for Call-Apple. Val, 932-6588.

LIBRARY PAK 1A owners: There is a partial dropout in program No. 8 (Color Game Pak) in early copies. Try loading at a higher volume setting. If this does not work, let us know and we will replace. Also early copies of Basic Tutorial.

# System Monitor

by (and courtesy of) APPLE COMPUTER, INC., Cupertino, Ca.

## Introduction

The APPLE II System Monitor is an aid to using your Apple to its fullest capabilities. With this monitor, one may store, examine and execute assembly language programs with a minimum of time and effort.

Previous personal computers required a front panel to enter binary data into memory. This loading process, consisting of setting 8 switches for the data, 16 switches for the address, and another switch for storing, was very time-consuming and extremely monotonous. To set a memory location requires up to 26 toggles on a front panel, in contrast with 8 or fewer keystrokes on the Apple keyboard. This represents a time and effort savings of over one-third.

When your APPLE II is turned on, press the reset key (top row — far right) on the keyboard to use the computer. After you depress the reset key, the speaker will beep, and an "*" (asterisk) prompt character and a flashing cursor will appear on the bottom left of the screen indicating that the computer is ready. The screen will now be in all-text mode with the entire screen of 24 lines of 40 characters each available for display. If this does not happen, the computer is not working properly. The APPLE II system monitor is now ready for use.

## Examining Memory

The first use of the monitor is for examining memory. To examine a location in memory, simply type the address followed by a carriage return. The address is one to four hexadecimal digits (0-9 and A-F). For example, type a 0 followed by pressing the carriage return button. The computer will respond by typing the contents of location zero.

Suppose, however, that you wished to examine locations zero to seven. This could be a very time consuming task if you had to type each address on a new line. Instead, you may examine a block of memory by typing the beginning address of the block, followed by a period ("."), followed by the ending address. For example, to examine the memory from location 0 to location 7, type:

    0.7 (CR)[1], and

the computer will respond with the data, in order from 0 to 7. Note that when a single location is examined, the computer types the location the data is coming from followed by a dash, followed by the actual data itself and when a range or block of memory is displayed, the computer will display the beginning location, followed by a dash, followed by up to 8 bytes of data, then on the next line it will continue displaying data in this fashion until the end of the range. For example, type:

    0.1E (CR)

    0000 — 8 bytes of data from 0 to 7
    0008 — 8 bytes of data from 8 to F
    0010 — 8 bytes of data from 10 to 17
    0018 — 7 bytes of data from 18 to 1E

For another example type:

    3.7 (CR)

    0003 — 5 bytes of data from 3 to 7

Further on we will use the term "address range" to specify a range of memory referred to by "beginning address.ending address". Examples address ranges are:

    0.7
    3.1E
    800.AFFF

In addition, one may use the format ".ending address" to specify an address range beginning at the current address to the specified ending address. For example type:

    F000.F006 (CR)

and the computer will respond with:

    F000 — A0 00 84 A0 84 4A 84

now type:

    .F00E (CR)

and the computer will respond with:

    F007 — 4C
    F008 — A9 08 85 4B 85 4D E6

## Changing Memory

Another important function of the monitor is to alter the contents of memory. To change memory, type the starting address for the data, followed by a colon, followed by the data. <u>Each byte of data must be separated by a space</u> and a carriage return must be entered at the end of the data. For example, type:

  0:00 11 22 33 44 55 66 77 (CR)

Then type:

  0.7 (CR)

to examine the memory locations you just changed. The computer should respond with:

  0000 — 00 11 22 33 44 55 66 77

Note 1.: "(CR)" stands for "depress the carriage return button" and not to type a left parenthesis, the letter C, etc. The carriage return is used to tell Apple that you have finished a line of data.

Note 2.: A control character is typed by holding down the control key (sometimes marked "CTRL") at the same time the specified character is typed. We will use a superscript "C" to indicate a control character thus $H^C$ is a "control H". If you have an Apple supplied keyboard, it will have two additional keys on the second row to the far right. The "←" key performs the same function (backspace) as $H^C$ without depressing the control key; the "→" key is the same as $U^C$ (forward space with copy).

Note 3.: Note that Apple does not display control characters on screen but it will act on them.

Note that the APPLE II keeps track of where the next byte of data is supposed to go, allowing you to type several lines of data at a time. It is recommended that when you enter a program through the monitor, you occasionally check to be sure that you are putting the correct data in the correct locations. To do this, simply enter a small amount of the data, then check the last location deposited into. If the data is misaligned, you must re-enter the last data group. For example, type:

  0:11 2233 44 (CR)

Note that a space was not typed between 22 and 33.

Now type:

  0.3 (CR)

to display contents of 0 to 3.

Location 3 will not be the correct data since it was incorrectly entered and data must be re-entered.

A useful feature of the APPLE II monitor is the "last opened address pointer". When you examine a location, the Apple monitor remembers the location, so that if you type a ":" on the next input line, the data will be entered starting from that location that was just examined. If an address range is examined, the last-opened location is the first address in the range. For example, type:

  0.3 (CR)

The computer will display the contents of locations 0 to 3. Now type:

  :0 11 22 33 (CR)

This deposits data from location 0. Now type again:

  0.3 (CR)

and the computer will respond with:

  0000 — 00 11 22 33

Since the following sections build upon the premise of understanding the above completely, the reader is encouraged to review the above sections if anything presented so far is not clearly understood.

## Executing Machine Language Programs

Another important use of the APPLE II monitor is to execute machine language programs as opposed to "BASIC" programs. To execute a program, type the starting address of the program followed by a "G" and a carriage return. The computer will "GO" to the specified location and execute the program there.

You are now ready to run your first assembly-language program through the monitor. This program outputs all of APPLE II's text characters to the screen. Type:

  0:E8 8A 20 ED FD 4C 0 0 (CR)

Now type:

  0.7 (CR)

to check and make sure all data is correct. The computer should type back:

  0000 — E8 8A 20 ED FD 4C 00 00.

Now type:

  0G (CR)

to execute the program. Depress "RESET" button to stop program. The screen now displays APPLE II character set in three modes: normal, inverse and flashing.

## Editing Line Entries

When typing an input line on the APPLE II, you are limited to typing 255 characters at a time. Once you have typed 247 characters on a line, the computer will beep each time another character is typed, warning you that you are about to overflow the line. If you do overflow type more than 255 characters, Apple will print a backslash, ignoring everything on that line and you must then re-enter your data.

The Apple II has special editing features that allow you to edit a line as it is being typed in. There are three special functions that allow you to backspace, forward space with pickup, and cancel line. Each is described below:

## Backspace

A "control H" (H$^C$) or the "←" key will move the cursor back one position. (See Note 2). If a character is present in the position it just backed into it will flash that character to indicate the position of the cursor. If another H$^C$ is typed, the cursor will again move back, the character it was on previously will return to normal video (white on black) and the computer will now believe it was never typed. After backspacing the cursor to the character to be changed, type the character it should be.

## Forward Space With Copy [2]

A "control U" or the "→" key will copy the current character that the cursor is on from the screen into memory and then advance the cursor one position.

After backspacing to a character and changing it, you may wish to read back in all the characters you just backspaced over. Hold down the "repeat" key as well as U$^C$ or "→" to ease copying. Remember that when a character is backspaced over, it is erased as far as the input line is concerned. When a U$^C$ is typed, the computer reads the character off the screen that the cursor is on. The cursor will then move forward one position. Try it with the example, type:

    0:0 15 22 33 44 (no CR)

Now after the second 4, type a control-H or "←" 10 times. The 5 should be flashing. Type a 1, then 9 control-U's or "→". The computer now believes that you typed the line as it now appears.

Note that a control U always uses display for input instead of the keyboard.

## Cancel Line

When a control-X is typed during an input, the computer acts as if nothing on the current line had been typed, types a backslash and goes to the next line, waiting for input.

## Screen Functions

The backspace and forward space functions move the cursor and modify the input line. With the cursor controls about to be presented, the user may move the cursor anywhere on the screen without modifying the input line. All the cursor move functions consist of typing the escape key, releasing it and then typing the appropriate character. These cursor moves are referred to as "escape-functions" because of the fact that all are preceded by the escape key.

- escape A  (escape key followed by the A key) moves the cursor forward one space without reading the character as part of the input line.
- escape B  moves the cursor back one position without erasing any characters from the input line.
- escape C  moves the cursor down one line without altering the input line the computer sees.
- escape D  moves the cursor up one line without altering the input line the computer sees.
- escape @  returns the cursor to the upper-left-hand corner of the screen and erases the screen.
- escape E  erases all the characters on the current line from the current cursor position to the end of the line on the screen.
- escape F  erases all the characters from the current cursor position to the end of the screen.

## Error after Carriage Return

In the monitor, if an illegal character is typed, after carriage return is hit, the monitor will do everything up to where the illegal character is typed, then it will beep and stop scanning the line. For example, if you type an illegal Hex number while depositing data into memory, the monitor will store all data typed before the illegal digit, then it will stop depositing data and beep the speaker

## Multiple Operations

An exclusive feature of the APPLE II monitor is the ability to do several things on one input line before pressing carriage return, except during a store operation. For example, to examine the blocks of memory from 0 to 7 and from 300 to 31F, type:

    0.7 300.31F (CR)

Note that the two address ranges are separated by a blank. To perform multiple commands per line, each command must be separated from the previous command by at least one blank. Single character commands need not be separated by a space; thus LLL (CR) is legal.

When the Apple monitor is expecting an address, it will examine only the last four digits typed for the address if more than four digits were typed. For example, 2300 is the same as 12300, since in the second case the Apple will only "see" the 2300. Similarly, when the monitor is expecting a data byte, it will only examine the last two digits if more than two digits were typed. This is a useful way to correct errors quickly without backspacing.

<u>NEXT MONTH</u> "System Monitor" concludes with descriptions and instructions on Cassette I/O's; Memory Move & Verify; Miscellaneous Commands; Debugging Aids; Single Stepping; Multiple Stepping and Tracing.

Work in your Apple II's Monitor "Lab" and discover the secrets of its power!

```
0010  ;       THIS PROGRAM TESTS MEMORY BY LOADING EACH LOCATION
0020  ;       WITH 55, TESTING, LOADING WITH AA, AND TESTING.
0030  ;       IF ANY LOCATION IS BAD, THE PROGRAM RINGS THE BELL
0040  ;       AND STOPS.  THE OFFENDING ADDRESS WILL BE SHOWN
0050  ;       IN LOCATIONS 02 AND 03.
0060  ;            START BY LOADING LOCATIONS AS FOLLOWS
0070  ;  02 - LO BYTE OF START ADDRESS
0080  ;  03 - HI BYTE OF START ADDRESS
0090  ;  04 - LO BYTE OF END ADDRESS
0100  ;  05 - HI BYTE OF END ADDRESS
0110  ;  TYPICAL ENTRY *02:00 08 FF 3F  FOR 16K MACHINE
0120  STLO .DL 0002
0130  STHI .DL 0003
0140  ENLO .DL 0004
0150  ENHI .DL 0005
0160  BELL .DL FF3A,     BELL IN MONITOR
0170       .OR 0300      START ADDR
0180  TEST LDY 00        ZERO Y         ;0300  A000
0190  LOAD LDA 55        BI 01010101    ;0302  A955
0200       STA (STLO),Y  55 TO MEM      ;0304  9102
0210       CMP (STLO),Y  IS IT THERE?   ;0306  D102
0220       BNE ERR       ERR IF NOT     ;0308  D01D
0230       LDA 0AA       TO 10101010    ;030A  A9AA
0240       STA (STLO),Y  TO MEM         ;030C  9102
0250       CMP (STLO),Y  IS IT THERE?   ;030E  D102
0260       BNE ERR       ERR IF NOT     ;0310  D015
0270       JSR INCR      TO INCR ROUT   ;0312  201803
0280       BCC LOAD      BACK TO LOAD   ;0315  90EB
0290       RTS           TO APPLE MON   ;0317  60
0300  INCR LDA *STLO     THIS ROUTINE   ;0318  A502
0310       CMP *ENLO     INCREMENTS     ;031A  C504
0320       LDA *STHI     THE MEMORY     ;031C  A503
0330       SBC *ENHI     LOCATION       ;031E  E505
0340       INC *STLO                    ;0320  E602
0350       BNE RTN                      ;0322  D002
0360       INC *STHI                    ;0324  E603
0370  RTN  RTS           GO DO AGAIN    ;0326  60
0380  ERR  JSR BELL                     ;0327  203AFF
0390       BRK           HALT-SEE 02,03 ;032A  00
0400  ;    ENDING ADDRESSES FOR LOCATIONS 04 AND 05
0410  ;  4K-0FFF 16K-3FFF 32K-7FFF 48K-BFFF
0420  ;       TO RUN,  *300G
0430  ;  YOU MAY SEE THE AA LOADED MEMORY BY - *800.3FFF 'RETURN'
0440  ;  FOR 16K. THIS PROGRAM DOES NOT TEST THE 1ST 2K.
0450       .EN
```

SYMBOL TABLE
```
STLO  0002
STHI  0003
ENLO  0004
ENHI  0005
BELL  FF3A
TEST  0300
LOAD  0302
INCR  0318
RTN   0326
ERR   0327
```

```
*********************************
*                               *
*         MEMORY TEST           *
*       by Bob Huelsdonk        *
*********************************
```

Dear Apple Lover,

Max Cook at Computerland of Federal Way has put me in charge of making his store the APPLE Center of the Northwest. I intend to make the store exactly that. The store will have all the books, magazines, hardware, software, classes, advice, and every service that an APPLE LOVER wants.

You can help me get this APPLE center ready by coming into the store and telling me what you want to see in the store. Right now, in stock, in the store, we have proto boards, communication interface, used MODEMS (so you can talk to other APPLES, or to NORDATA), 6502 programming and hardware manuals, and more. We have a printer up and running and will print your program lists for you. See me in Federal Way.

Cliff Gazaway

| ACCESSORIES | Retail Price |
|---|---|
| Disk II — Drive and Controller | 495.00 |
| Monitor-II (Black and White) | 205.00 |
| Monitor-IIA (Color) | |
| Vinyl Carrying Case | 30.00 |
| Printer II-Centronics µP1 w/Interface | 695.00 |
| Printer IIA-Centronics 779 w/Tractor & Interface | 1445.00 |
| Mt. Hdwe. Introl — AC Controller Assembled | 189.00 |
| Mt. Hdwe. Introl — Dual Chan AC Remote Assembled | 149.00 |
| Memory Expansion Module 4K | 75.00 |
| Speechlab™ — Heuristics, Model 20A | 189.00 |
| Memory Expansion Module — 16K | 300.00 |
| Modem IIA w/Interface | |
| Programmers Aid #1 Firmware | 50.00 |

| TAPES, DISKETTES, PAPER | |
|---|---|
| Blank Diskettes (Box of 10) | 50.00 |
| Blank Cassettes (Box of 25) | |
| Centronics µP Paper (Box of 5) | 4.00 |
| Checkbook Cassette | 20.00 |
| Startrek/Starwars Cassette | 15.00 |
| Color Demo/Breakout Cassette | 7.50 |
| Applesoft II/F.P. Demo (w/Manual) Cassette | 20.00 |
| Hi Res Graphics/Hi Res Shapes Cassette | 7.50 |
| RAM Test Cassette | 7.50 |
| Color Math Demo/Hangman | 7.50 |
| Blackjack/Slot Machine Cassette | 7.50 |
| Biorhythm/Mastermind Cassette | 7.50 |
| Apple II Capabilities Demo Cassette | 20.00 |
| Finance I — 2 Cassette Package | 25.00 |
| Datamover/Telepong Cassette | 7.50 |

| | |
|---|---|
| Prototyping/Hobby Card | 24.00 |
| Parallel Printer Interface Card | 180.00 |
| Communications Interface Card | 180.00 |
| High-Speed G.P. Serial Interface Card | 195.00 |
| Applesoft II Firmware Card | 100.00 |

| LITERATURE, MANUALS, LISTINGS | |
|---|---|
| Apple II Reference Manual | 10.00 |
| 6502 Hardware Manual | 15.00 |
| 6502 Programming Manual | 15.00 |
| Parallel Printer Interface Manual | 2.00 |
| Apple II BASIC Programming Manual (Box of 30) | 5.95 |
| Applesoft II Reference Manual | 7.50 |
| Communications Interface Manual | 2.00 |
| High-Speed G.P. Serial Interface Manual | 2.00 |

1500 South 336th St. • Parkway Center, Suite 12 • Federal Way, Washington 98003
Tacoma (206) 927-8585 • Seattle (206) 838-9363

# CALL -A.P.P.L.E.
## Apple Pugetsound Program Library Exchange

BYTES FROM THE APPLE by Val Golding
Software stuff, etc., etc., etc., etc., etc.

And now a word from our sponsor..., you! Look elsewhere in this issue for an as yet untitled letters to the editor feature. We are now actively soliciting your letters and will reproduce in part some of the interesting ones. If you have a question or a problem, and we can't find the answer in time to print it, we'll throw it open to our readers for solution.

Money talks. Unfortunately, we have a number of words on that subject. As you will see in other stories, the prices on the Apple Box, software and dues are all to be increased. We don't like to see this, particularly since one of our prime objectives is low cost software, but it is a necessary evil, if we want to adequately support Call -Apple, the cost of which has grown to over $100 per month, not counting postage. Your understanding will be appreciated.

New software. Library Pak 2 should be ready for release as you read this. It contains many new color games and demos, music programs, a Greeting Pak which has a variety of Xmas and other greetings, a nifty game called "Nightmare No. 6", which in its opeing title states "The object of this game is to figure out the object of this game!". You take it from there. Also available now is "Disk Workshop", a new version of Workshop II, designed to work with Disk II and adds two new commands: DSAV saves an appended program to disk and CONNECT appends a Disk program to the Workshop. This is available at $6, postpaid, and if you have previously ordered Workshop as a separate program, we will send you this one for just $2.

CALL -APPLE Vol.I, No.7 Aug., 1978

Val J. Golding, President  (206) 932-6588
Michael Thyng, Secretary   (206) 524-2744
Darrell Aldrich, Prgm Ed   (206) 782-7082

```
************************************************
*                                              *
*           AUGUST    MEETING                  *
*   7:00 PM      Tuesday, August 15, 1978      *
*           Empire Electronics                 *
*   616 SW 152nd Street  Seattle  244-5200     *
*                                              *
*         SEPTEMBER MEETING                    *
*   7:00 PM      Tuesday, September 19, 1978   *
*           Computerland of Bellvue            *
*   14340 NE 20th    Bellvue, Wa.  746-2070    *
************************************************
```

## DISK II IS HERE!

### Special Disk Issue !

See the Index below for Disk Features

Save six disk programs to tape in one operation with the disk Utility-Save Program listed on Page Six.

How to use your disk and more!

```
         IN THIS ISSUE...           Page
Bytes from the Apple................   1
Disk II and You.....................   3
Program to Initialize a Diskette....   4
Editorial...........................   4
Write -Apple (Letters)..............   5
Disk Utility Program................   6
Poor Man's Hex-Dec Converter........   7
Minutes of July 18th................   7
Apple Mash (Persci Disks Part 3)....   8
System Monitor (Part II)............   8
Is There a Doctor in the House?.....   8
Back Issue Availability.............  12
Library Orders; Current  Programs...  12
Dues Structure......................  12
Applesoft Zero Page Useage..........  13
Routine to Print Free Bytes.........  13
Machine Language as Part of Basic Prgm  14
A Patch for Double Loops............  14
```

# ComputerLand™

In Federal Way.

## HELP WANTED

Apple enthusiast or Apple owner needed, part time, to demonstrate the Apple. A good way to have fun while earning extra money.

••••••••••

Come in to Computerland of Federal way, to sign up for one of the Apple computer classes advertised by AUTOMATED TRAINING SYSTEMS elsewhere in this newsletter.

••••••••••

IBM SELECTRIC with Apple interface card (almost ready). Includes software for Selectric, modem, or RS232 printers to 30,000 baud. Selectric, card, &software $999.00. Board only, $18; card kit, $45; assembled card, $65.

••••••••••

NON APPLE-OWNERS who want free time on our machines are welcome to work with our Apples for a few hours to decide if it is the right machine for them. Additional free time may be earned by writing tiny programs for us. No experience is needed. Please spend as much time with our Apples as you need.

••••••••••

We can ship Apple products anywhere. We welcome your long distance calls (no collects of course). Phone orders by bank cards.

••••••••••

- Ask for Cliff Gazaway.
- Phone 927-8585 or 838-9363.

## THE MINI-MEDIA LIBRARY OF PERSONAL COMPUTER PROGRAMS

IN STOCK

Audio explanations with every program, PLUS standardized instructions to take out the guesswork.

**DRAWING (4K)**
Great at a party, yet practical for the classroom, this program has countless applications. Use the drawing program for choosing a name at random from the list of names you give the computer. Fascinating to watch, impartial in its decision, this program will be an exciting addition to any scene.

**MATCHING QUIZ**
Match an item on the left with one on the right and they both disappear! There are three different quizes in every program. You can replace the original list with your own categories. (Why not develop a whole library of interesting facts?) What a way to learn!

**DON'T FALL ™ (8K)**
Don't Fall is a multi-color arcade-type game to use for pure entertainment or for learning a list of words (spelling, Bible Characters etc.). It works like "Hangman". You guess the letters (hopefully before you fall off the cliff). The you give the computer a word and watch him try to guess it.

**TRUE/FALSE QUIZ (4K)**
This True/False Quiz is a teaching tool (why just "test" when you can "teach"?). It is easy to enter your own questions. Then quiz your friends (or students). Use it as a game, a review, or a test. When the fun is over the computer gives you your score.

**MEMORY AIDE (4K)**
Memorizing used to be pain, but now there's Memory Aide! Tell the computer what you need to memorize. It uses several different ways to make the words stick in your mind. Repetition, prompting, missing words -- they all help you (or your child or student) enjoy memorizing.

**STUDY AIDE (8K)**
This interesting program lets students enter their own questions and answers (Or the parent or teacher can program questions for the student). The computer gives them back in random order. If he misses, it gives the answer and saves the question for a later try. When all the questions have been answered correctly, it gives the score.

**KEYBOARD ORGAN (4K)**
You have to try it to believe it! This program turns your Apple II into a practical musical instrument. Play the keys just like you would on the piano or organ. Meanwhile, on the screen, the computer shows you what note you are playing. This is just another way the computer combines learning and recreation.

**GRADING ROUTINE (16K)**
Every teacher will love this one! The Grading Routine takes the drudgery out of finding class curves. It saves hours of tedious work when figuring your final grades. You use your own categories, grading scales and methods. With it, you can analyze your class in every category. It lets you save the information for later review.

## ComputerLand™

1500 South 336th St. • Parkway Center, Suite 12 • Federal Way, Washington 98003
Tacoma (206) 927-8585 • Seattle (206) 838-9363

## DISK II AND YOU
### by John Covington

Finally!!! Disk II is out. If you're lucky, you will be able to play with one in your local computer store until yours arrives from Cupertino. That is what I have been doing this last week, and this article comes from using the disk and my varied background in Data Processing. Hopefully, I'll be able to explain some of the HOWS and WHYS of the disk system and clear up some of the blind spots in Disk II's documentation. So let's get on with it and explore the mysteries of DOS.

DOS is simply short for DISK OPERATING SYSTEM, the heart of Disk II. With it, Apple is able to talk to the disk and treat it like any other I/O device. The DOS is just a program (which resides in the top of RAM) so like Applesoft, if you write over it, you can kill it. However, with normal use, you don't have to worry about that. If you are like me and have only 16K of RAM, the DOS will lock you out of using HIRES, because HIRES Page 1 uses your upper 8K of RAM. Now, let's bring the DOS up and find out how to use it.

### HOW DO YOU DO THAT???
First, follow the instructions that came with the Disk System and plug the controller card into slot 6 in your Apple (with the power off). Then connect the ribbon cable from the drive into the controller card connector marked "Drive 1" (on the top of the card) and power your Apple up and hit reset twice. Insert the master diskette in the drive and type a 6 (for slot number), followed by Control P. This will bootstrap in the DOS and bring the disk system up. If all goes well you will see some titles and an Integer Basic prompt. This means DOS is up and you can begin running programs.

One of the first to run is the COPY program, but there is a hitch; it requires two drives. I'm sure the owner of your local computer store will let you run this program in his store, using your drive as the second drive. The purpose of running the copy program is to duplicate your master. It may save both of you a lot of headaches later. (We found out the hard way. ...ed) The reason is your master can be lost in a number of ways, ranging from oxide breakdown to operator error. Therefore it is prudent to have a backup disk to recover from.

To copy your master, you must first initialize a blank disk. To do this, boot the DOS up and then enter a short Integer Basic program (as per example) and use the INIT routine as follows:
  INIT (program name), V(vol. no.), S(slot no.), D(drive no.). Then run the COPY routine and Disk II will make you a second master.

### WHAT's THIS INIT THING???
The INIT command INITializes new disks. Because the Apple system uses soft sector drives, the floppies must be formatted to fit the DOS software. Any mini-floppy has 35 tracks (similar to a track on a phonograph record, except it does not spiral in; it meets itself after one revolution.) each of which must be divided into a certain number of sectors (a sector is where the data actually goes, and is composed of 256 bytes). To perform the INIT, you must have an Integer Basic program in RAM, which serves as a model for the formatter. It can be any runable Basic program, but keep it short, as this program will automatically run each time the disk is booted. The short program listed on Page 4 will serve as well as any, and will also call the catalog up for you each time you boot the disk up. Well, I guess I've given you enough to make you dangerous!

HAPPY DISKING!

## PROGRAM TO INITIALIZE A DISKETTE

```
100 CALL -936:PRINT " (insert your name,
    address and phone)"
200 PRINT "THIS DISK CONTAINS INTE-
    GER BASIC PROGRAMS" (or game
    programs, etc.)
300 FOR I=1 TO 1000: NEXT I: CALL
    -936
400 PRINT "D^C CATALOG":END
```

Note: In line 400 after the first quote, hit the Control key and the "D" key at the same time. This is how the disk system responds to commands within a Basic program, with Control D in a print statement.

## EDITORIAL by Val J. Golding

The big news story of this issue is obviously the arrival in town of Disk II and Applesoft II ROM. Rather than do a review, we have hidden behind the pretext of an editorial to state our feelings on the failings of Disk II and A/S ROM (I've got a feeling I'm failing? (Oh dear!))

Applesoft II ROM for $100 is like buying 10K of memory for less than half price, since it frees that amount of RAM for program use. Unfortunately, according to the documentation, the Applesoft ROM and disk versions are incompatable, although it is relatively easy to convert one to the other. However, in our estimation, the nusance factor is of prime importance, since one of the reasons for purchasing either version of Applesoft was to have it instantly accessable. One of the plans for our library was an Applesoft Pak. Now it appears we will have to make a Pak in three different versions, cassette, ROM and disk. (The documentation does not indicate whether the cassette version is compatable with either of the others.

The new Applesoft manual comes coverless, and commences with eight pages of corrections and additions to the manual.

This indicates a lack of planning by Apple Computer in rushing to get the ROM board into production without fully completing and checking the documentation. It is inexcusable for a computer system which is designed to plug in and run, and used by a pure beginner. Additionally, the HIRES color commands we found so helpful in the cassette version, DRAW, XDRAW, ROT=, SHLOAD and SCALE=, are not available in the ROM version. This means that even though one has the ROM card, one must also have the cassette version in order to use those commands.

The above shortcomings pale, however when one looks at the documentation accompanying the Disk II. While the information is all there, it is arranged in more or less haphazard manner, and concrete examples are missing. Jeff Raskin (who wrote the excellent manual on Integer Basic) where are you? No doubt the instructions can be easily understood by anyone with computer background, but how about all us newcomers, Apple?

Finally, because DOS uses the COUT and KEYIN routines at $36 and $38, it is not possible while the DOS is up, to use the printer driver routine from the red manual. We have an Integral Data IP-225 printer, which works just fine at 1200 baud from the red book routine (modified), but it is not possible to run the printer without first killing the DOS. Of course, we could always get an Apple parallel printer card for $180, and that might solve the problem...

But before you change your mind about buying, let us remind you that all of the above is relatively minor and we believe both the disk and ROM are a wise investment. We would not be without either, having once had the opportunity to use them.

\*\*\*\*\*\*\*\*\*\*\*\*\*\*\*\*\*\*\*\*\*\*\*\*\*\*\*\*\*\*\*\*\*\*\*\*\*\*

See additional comments on Disk II documentation on Page 5

## WRITE -APPLE

To: Call -Apple

I purchased a set of 16K dynamic ram from "Advanced Computer Products". they passed the memory test in a previous issue of this newsletter. The price was 8 for $200, with a 6 week delay waiting for their "same day shipment". remember to have a set of three 14 pin sockets on hand for your memory select jumpers. Thanks for telling how the Hi Res system handles the colors. I wondered why my blue and green spaceships were disappearing at certain points on the screen.

Mark Cross
1906 Goodwin Road
Ruston, La. 71270

Dear Mr. Golding:-

Received my July issue of Call -Apple after joining the group. I think you are doing a great job on Call -Apple! In STOPWATCH (Library Pak 1a), the display flickers, this can be fixed by changing Line 190; change POKE 34,22 to POKE 34,24 And I have a question that others might be interested in too: How do you use HIRES with Integer Basic )LOAD without asking the operator to manually enter )HIMEM: 8192? By listing your program, I see a Basic line "5 HIMEM: 16384"; what does this do?

S. H. Lam
256 Hartley Avenue
Princeton, N. J. 08540

THANKS for your kind comments.
This is not easy to answer in a short space. In fact, if space permits, we will reprint, elsewhere in this issue, an article from Apple's newsletter CONTACT, issue 1, which explains in detail just how to manipulate the program pointers to load a HIRES program in Basic, which is just about what we did in our HIRES demo. What you did not notice was line 0, which disappears, once the program has been run. Again, due to playing games with the program pointer. Line 0 reads: HIMEM: 8192, and if you try to enter it normally, you will get a ***SYNTAX ERR. It was accomplished by first entering the line as "0 PRINT 8192" and then locating the line in memory and changing the PRINT byte ($63) to HIMEM: ($10). Our Programmer's Workshop II is helpful for this, in that it has a routine to locate and display a Basic line as viewed by memory. The HIMEM: 16384 you referred to would have been in the Softcore Software program, which in truth is not a program, but merely a screen display that has been saved on tape. ...ed.

## WRITE -APPLE (Continued)

Dear Call -Apple

I am writing to say I am very impressed with the Call -Apple newsletter. It is not only informative, it is also very useful, particularly the section dealing with the System Monitor and Mini-Assembler, since I am especially interested in Assembly Language. How about making available an Assembly Language Tutorial tape? Also, how would I go about getting a copy of the listing for Integer Basic?

Linda Egan
6471 E. Nixon Street
Lakewood, Ca. 90713

LINDA, if you had made a killing in the stock market, we might be able to get that listing for you. Seriously, that is one very closely guarded secret. And we are looking into the possibility of an Assembly Language Tutorial. ...ed.

## DISC DOCUMENTATION FLASH

As we were going to press, we were handed a copy of NEW documentation on Disk II. We are pleased to report that this documentation, running nearly twice the length of the original, It is far more concise and detailed and has a very good introductory section. So all you gentle folk at Apple Computer, we retract (sort of) some of the nasty things we said on page 4. However, we still feel that the Disk II should not have been released until this obviously superior documentation was also ready.
...Val Golding

## AND NOW, the ROM...

here is a quickie about setting up the APPLESOFT rom card. First, as the instructions indicated, this card will function only in Slot #0 in your Apple. This card allows you to make a choice of whether you want Integer Basic or Applesoft to be called with control B after you power up. If the switch is in the down position, Integer Basic will be selected. If it is in the up position, Applesoft will be selected. In addition, it is not necessary to change the switch position to call the non-default basic. if the switch is up, hit "reset" and type C081 followed by Control B to get Integer Basic. If the switch is down, hit "reset" and type C080 followed by Control B and return to get Applesoft.

## A DISK UTILITY PROGRAM
### by Val J. Golding

Perhaps this may be the first disk program published for Apple's new Disk II. If so, a feather for our cap! The "SAVE" program, listed in column two will ask the user to input the file names of six disk programs, start recording on tape and hit return. SAVE will then consecutively load from disk and save to tape, in one operation, the six named programs. A neat way to make a tape for a friend from your disk collection.

Since this program uses the Basic SAVE command under program control, it is necessary to enter the SAVE commands as something else and then go into memory and change them to SAVEs. If you don't know how to do this, here is another routine that will do it for you. Just substitute the command TEXT where you see SAVE in the program and then add lines 1100 to 1250 as given below and RUN 1100. This will convert the TEXT commands to SAVE. After this has run, you can DELete 1100 to 1250, as they are no longer required. This routine can be modified to change any token or Ascii character in memory to another one, and of course, the program SAVE can be modified to save however many programs you would like in one operation by adding or taking away input statements and SAVE and LOAD statements. Remember in line 1000, Z$="D^C". A Control D must be within the quotes for the DOS to recognize a Disk command.

```
1100 REM PRGM TO CHANGE TOKENS IN MEMORY
1150 REM EN=MEMORY RANGE TO BE SEARCHED
1200 LOCN= PEEK (202)+ PEEK (203)*256
     :EN=LOCN+735
1210 REM  PEEK AT VALUE OF ORIG TOKEN
1220 IF PEEK (LOCN)=75 THEN 1250:LOCN=
     LOCN+1: IF LOCN=EN THEN END : GOTO
     1220
1240 REM POKE VALUE OF NEW TOKEN
1250 PRINT "CONVERTING ";LOCN: POKE LOCN,
     5: GOTO 1220
```

```
>LIST
 10 REM   "SAVE" BY VAL GOLDING 7/23/78
 20 REM   THIS PROGRAM SAVES 6 NAMED DISK
         FILES TO TAPE IN ONE OPERATION
 50 GOTO 1000
 60 POKE 0, PEEK (76): POKE 1, PEEK
    (77)
 70 POKE 76, PEEK (202): POKE 77, PEEK
    (203)
 90 PRINT Z$;"LOAD ";A$
100 SAVE
180 PRINT Z$
190 PRINT Z$;"LOAD ";B$
200 SAVE
280 PRINT Z$
290 PRINT Z$;"LOAD ";C$
300 SAVE
380 PRINT Z$
390 PRINT Z$;"LOAD ";D$
400 SAVE
480 PRINT Z$
490 PRINT Z$;"LOAD ";E$
500 SAVE
580 PRINT Z$
590 PRINT Z$;"LOAD ";F$
600 SAVE
649 REM   INSERT 6 CONTROL G WITHIN QUOTES
650 CALL -936: VTAB 10: TAB 10: PRINT
    "FILES SAVED TO TAPE"
700 POKE 202, PEEK (76): POKE 203, PEEK
    (77): POKE 76, PEEK (0): POKE 77
    , PEEK (1): END
999 REM   INSERT CONTROL D WITHIN QUOTES
1000 DIM A$(36),B$(36),C$(36),D$(36),
     E$(36),F$(36):Z$=""
1010 TEXT : CALL -936: VTAB 4
1020 INPUT "   FILE NAME ? ",A$
1030 INPUT "   FILE NAME ? ",B$
1040 INPUT "   FILE NAME ? ",C$
1050 INPUT "   FILE NAME ? ",D$
1060 INPUT "   FILE NAME ? ",E$
1070 INPUT "   FILE NAME ? ",F$
1080 VTAB 20: PRINT "START RECORDING AND H
     IT RETURN TO SAVE  THE ABOVE LISTED F
     ILES TO TAPE": CALL -676
1090 GOTO 60
```

Are there any corrections or additions to the minutes? Yes, Mr. President. It was moved, seconded and carried unanimously that for 1979, the application fee would be increased to $2.50 and that dues would be raised to $7.50. Primarily, this would be in support of our magazine, Call -Apple, including card stock covers. Thank you, Thyns!

## THE POOR MAN'S HEX -- DECIMAL -- HEX -- CONVERTER

| HEX | "DECIMAL VALUE" | | | | HEX |
|---|---|---|---|---|---|
| | MSB | 3rd | 2nd | LSB | |
| 1 | 4096 | 256 | 16 | 1 | 1 |
| 2 | 8192 | 512 | 32 | 2 | 2 |
| 3 | 16288 | 768 | 48 | 3 | 3 |
| 4 | 16384 | 1024 | 64 | 4 | 4 |
| 5 | 20480 | 1280 | 80 | 5 | 5 |
| 6 | 24576 | 1536 | 96 | 6 | 6 |
| 7 | 28672 | 1792 | 112 | 7 | 7 |
| 8 | 32768 | 2048 | 128 | 8 | 8 |
| 9 | 36864 | 2304 | 144 | 9 | 9 |
| A | 40960 | 2560 | 160 | 10 | A |
| B | 45056 | 2816 | 176 | 11 | B |
| C | 49152 | 3072 | 192 | 12 | C |
| D | 53248 | 3328 | 208 | 13 | D |
| E | 57344 | 3584 | 224 | 14 | E |
| F | 61440 | 3840 | 240 | 15 | F |

A pencil, scratchpad and you - that's all you need to convert HEX TO DECIMAL, or DECIMAL TO HEX. Based on the fact that unit, ten, hundred, and thousand columns have a unique set of values for hexadecimal, the above table will assist you convert either way.

EXAMPLE: HEX TO DECIMAL
013C =?

```
MSB  3rd  2nd  LSB      DECIMAL VALUE
 0 - - - - - - - - - - - -  00000
      1 - - - - - - - - -    256
           3 - - - - - -      48
                C - - - -     12
           total - - - - -   316
```

EXAMPLE: DECIMAL TO HEX

14632 = ?
In the table, in the MSB column, the number is less than HEX(4) and more than HEX(3), so the MSB =3. To get the third, put down 14632
(value for MSB(3))        -12288
                           2344

In the 3rd column, this is more than HEX(9) and less than HEX(A), so the 3rd = 9. Again enter 2344
value for 3rd(9)          -2304
                             40

in the 2nd column this remainder is more than HEX(2) and less than HEX(3), so the 2nd=2. Again enter          40
value for 2nd(2)          -32
                            8

This remainder = 8 in the LSB column, and = HEX(8). So, the HEX number for 14632 is 3928.

This might seem cumbersome, but it is surprising how rapid this conversion can become with a little practice.

J.A. Backman

## MINUTES OF JULY 18th MEETING

Meeting began promptly at 7:16. We again introduced ourselves in Lynnwood OMEGA's meeting room and found 41 members attending.

Tom Geer, who is recovering from a broken leg, sent word that he orders his APPLE hardware directly from APPLE in California and dispelled any contrary rumors that had been circulating.

We've got about 800 dollars in the treasury and most of it is commited to prior obligations.

Ron and Darrell Aldrich have been busy working on a mini "kind-of" modem connector. It's currently available (one of the few things you can get shortly after ordering) for

Mike Thyng answered some questions about disks and what to look for. Val told us about our members in Belgium and Singapore. Are we expanding?

The club is getting so big that now it becomes very hard to get the neat little programs that everyone brings in each meeting. So, we're asking for members who are fairly up to date in their tape libraries to make programs available at their homes (this will give us broader coverage ) and also to bring their apple's APPLE's to the meetings. Whoa. Not everybody. Just 5 are needed.
Please call Val and confirm.

Meeting adjourned at 8:11

## APPLE MASH by Mike Thyng

### BASIC FILE HANDLING

In the previous articles, we've discussed types of files - sequential and random - and general facts and figures about the PERSCI floppy disk drive.
This issue I'd like to explore some of the actual commands necessary to get data to and from the diskettes.
Before you can write a file, you have to do something called "opening" it. This defines to your program that some related data - let's say names and addresses - is going to be available for your use and can be referenced by the name you give your file. If you want to access (either read or write) to your file you need to specify OPEN AFILE. (AFILE is the name I gave a file for example).
What if you want to write a whole new file that hasn't existed in your system before. Fine, use the FILE statement. FILE BFILE opens a file called BFILE and makes it available to you to write sequential data.
FILE BFILE(130) opens a file called BFILE that hasn't previously existed also. But the difference is that each record you write will be allowed to be a maximum size of 130 bytes. You would use the FILE BFILE(130) format whenever you wanted to deal with random files. Personally I use the random file format exclusively. It gives me greater flexibility for file handling. You can always read a random file sequentially but the reverse isn't true.
So now we've gotten into 2 files; AFILE we'll use for gaining previously stored information, and BFILE we'll use to write new information.
To get the information from AFILE, you need to READ # 1; field 1, field 2, field 3 ....
The READ is comparable to
The READ command is to a disk (or tape) file what the INPUT command is to the keyboard. The #1 is a direct reference to AFILE - the first file opened. Fields 1, 2, and so on are the variables you output to AFILE when you wrote it.      (GOTO Page 12)

## IS THERE A DOCTOR IN THE HOUSE?

Apparently, quite a few. You can look forward in the near future to receiving a questionaire in connection with your medical and other applications for Apple II. It would seem that about 10% of our current membership is in the profession, and our objective is to put this large minority in contact with one another. You will also be receiving names and addresses. This also will apply to any other special interest group; we will attempt to put you in contact with others of similar interests.

## APPLE BOX PRICE INCREASED TO 18.50

Sorry to do this, but we underestimated both cost and demand on this mini-modem. For those that are unaware, Apple Box acts as an interface between your cassette and your telephone. After connecting it to an FCC type-approved telephone coupler, it allows you to transmit or receive programs over telephone lines. This requires the ability to monitor your line, and if your recorder is not so already equipped, Apple Box II at $23.50 will do it for you.

## OUR THANKS TO . . .

Apple Computer, Inc., ...for allowing us to steal "System Monitor", which is concluded below.

## SYSTEM MONITOR (Continued from July)

**Cassette Input/Output**

To read an address range of data or a machine language program from a cassette tape, type the address range followed by an R, start the tape recorder playing, and press carriage return. Example:

   300.3FFR (start cassette in play mode) (press carriage return)

will read the address range from 300 to 3FF inclusive from the tape.

If there is a bad tape read, (determined by a checksum byte at the end of each record) the monitor will type the letters "ERR". At the completion of reading a record or address range off of the tape, the speaker will beep and a "*" and a flashing cursor will appear indicating that the read is finished.

To write an address range onto the cassette, type the address range followed by the letter W. Press record on the cassette recorder, then press return. The speaker will beep upon completion of the write. Example 2:

    300.3FFW (start cassette in record mode) (press carriage return)

will write the address range from 300 to 3FF on to the tape.

Example 3:

    300.3FFW 800.8A0W (start cassette in record mode) (press carriage return)

will write the range from 300 to 3FF, then will write the range from 800 to 8A0 onto tape.

Definition of a record on the cassette is an address range written on the cassette, preceded by a 6 second header. A record may be of any length from 1 byte to 48K-bytes (maximum size of the system).

## Memory Move ("M")

Occasionally it becomes necessary to move a block of memory to another address range. For example, after writing a record onto cassette, you may desire to check if the write was good by reading the data back out. You would simply write the tape, copy the current memory range to another block of memory, and try reading your program back in. If the read is good, everything is fine. If not, move the correct data back into the original range, and start over.

To move memory, type the beginning destination address followed by a less-than sign, "<", followed by the address range to move and the letter "M" for "MOVE". For example:

    800 <300.3FFM (CR)

will copy location 300 to location 800, location 301 to location 801, etc. through 3FF to 8FF.

The above line should be read as eight hundred from three hundred to three F F move.

Another use of the memory move is to set a range of memory to a specific value, such as zero. To do this, set the first location of the range to the value, then type the second location of the range, followed by a "<", the first location of the range, a ".", and the next to last address in the range. For example, to zero locations 800 to 8FF type:

    800:0 (CR)
    801 <800.8FEM (CR)

What the above does is copy location 800 to 801, 801 to 802, 802 to 803, etc. up to 8FD to 8FE, then 8FE to 8FF.

## Memory Verify ("V")

Sometimes it is useful to check two ranges of memory to see if they are identical. The format for doing this is similar to moving memory, but instead of a M, a V should be typed. For example, to check if the range from 300 to 3FF contains the same data as 800 to 8FF, type:

    300 <800.8FFV (CR)

This will compare location 300 to 800, then 301 to 801, etc. If two corresponding locations match, the verify continues on to the next two corresponding locations; if on the otherhand, location 305 contained an F7 while location 805 contained an FF, the following would be printed:

    305 — F7 (FF)

indicating that a non-match was discovered.

## Miscellaneous Commands

The APPLE II display system has three modes of displaying characters: normal video (white on black), inverse video (black on white), and flashing (alternates between normal and inverse). Through the monitor, you can specify either normal or inverse mode for monitor output. Monitor input is always printed in normal video. By typing an N on an input line, the monitor will output in normal video. By typing an I on an input line, the monitor will output in inverse video. For example, type:

    0.1F I .3F N (CR)

The monitor will display locations 0 to 1F, switch to inverse video mode, display locations 20 to 3F, then switch back to normal video mode.

The APPLE II computer comes supplied with BASIC in ROM. To enter BASIC type a control-B in the monitor and a carriage return, and you will be in BASIC. To return to the monitor, hit the reset key. If you hit the reset key while in BASIC and wish to re-enter BASIC without destroying your program, type a control-C and depress return key and you will be back in BASIC.

By typing a control-Y on a line, the APPLE II monitor does a jump to location 3F8. This is supplied mainly to save typing time. For example, by putting a jump instruction at location 3F8, you can do a "GO" to any location in memory with one keystroke. $Y^C$ may also be used for user programs requiring up to three arguments.

To specify a port for keyboard input, type a single digit (0-7) followed by a control-K to specify I/O slot number. The default port is port number 0, or the keyboard not slot 0.

To specify a port for output, type a single digit (0-7) representing the I/O port number, followed by a control-P. Default output port is 0, or the screen and not slot 0.

### Debugging Aids

The process between writing a program and making it actually work is called debugging. Assembly language programs over 20 bytes long will most probably require debugging. The following monitor section describes several features of the monitor for quick and easy debugging.

After entering a program, you may desire to examine a certain portion of the program in 6502 mnemonics instead of the machine code. To list out memory in Mnemonic, type the starting address of the part you wish to list out, followed by the letter "L" and a carriage return. The monitor will list the next 20 mnemonic instructions starting at the address specified.

Four output fields are generated for each disassembled instruction: (1) Address of first byte of instruction in Hex; (2) Hex object code listing of instruction, from 1 to 3 bytes long; (3) 3-character mnemonic, or ??? for undefined opcodes (which assume a length of one byte); (4) address field, in one of the following formats:

| Format | Address Mode |
|---|---|
| -empty- | Invalid, Implied, or Accumulator |
| $12 | Page zero |
| $1234 | Absolute or branch target |
| #$12 | Immediate |
| $12,X | Zero page, indexed by X |
| $12,Y | Zero page, indexed by Y |
| $1234,X | Absolute, indexed by X |
| $1234,Y | Absolute, indexed by Y |
| ($1234) | Absolute indirect |
| ($12),X | Indexed indirect |
| ($12),Y | Indirect indexed |

Note that unlike MOS Technology assemblers, which use "A" for accumulator addressing, the Apple disassembler outputs an empty field to avoid confusion and facilitate byte counting. Upon displaying twenty instructions, if another "L" and carriage return are typed, the next twenty instructions will be disassembled.

For an example of the "L" (list) command type:

    F000L (CR)

and Apple will respond with:

```
F000-   A0 00       LDY     #$00
F002-   84 A0       STY     $A0
F004-   84 4A       STY     $4A
F006-   84 4C       STY     $4C
F008-   A9 08       LDA     #$08
F00A-   85 4B       STA     $4B
F00C-   85 4D       STA     $4D
F00E-   E6 4D       INC     $4D
F010-   B1 4C       LDA     ($4C),Y
F012-   49 FF       EOR     #$FF
F004-   91 4C       STA     ($4C),Y
F016-   D1 4C       CMP     ($4C),Y
F018-   D0 0X       BNE     $F022
F01A-   49 FF       EOR     #$FF
F01C-   91 4C       STA     ($4C),Y
F01E-   D1 4C       CMP     ($4C),Y
F020-   F0 EC       BEQ     $F00E
F022-   4C AD E5    JMP     $E5AD
F025-   4C 79 F1    JMP     $F179
F028-   20 32 F0    JSR     $F032
*
```

### Single Stepping

Another useful debugging aid is single-stepping. Single-stepping allows the user to execute the program, one step at a time, while watching the registers as the program is executed. To single step, type the address to begin single-stepping, followed by an "S" and carriage return. The monitor will execute the instruction at that location, then display the instruction in disassembled format, (see above), followed by a display of the registers in the format:

    A=BB X=BB Y=BB P=BB S=BB

where BB represents a Hexadecimal byte. P stands for processor status, and S stands for stack pointer. To use the processor status byte, see processor status register section of the MOS Technology Software Manual. To execute the next program instruction, simply type another "S" and (return).

During single-stepping, you may desire to change the contents of the registers. To do so, after the registers are displayed, type a ":" (colon) followed by the data to go into the A register, followed by data for the X Register (if desired), followed in order the registers were displayed. To display the contents of the registers, type a control-E followed by a carriage return.[2] For example, suppose the registers were displayed as:

    A=01 X=2E Y=53 P=78 S=AC

to change A to 00 and X to 30, type:

    :0 30

Then, if you typed a control-E to examine the registers, the following would be displayed:

    A=00 X=30 Y=53 P=78 S=AC

For an example of single step ("S") command, retype in our previous program example:

    0: E8 8A 20 ED FD 4C 0 0 (CR)

Now type:

    0S (CR)

and the computer will respond:

```
0000-    E8              INX
 A=06  X=07  Y=0B  P=30  S=6D
```

The 6502 registers are now open; change the A and X registers by typing:

:A FF (CR)

Now type a control-E and a carriage return to re-examine the registers. Apple will respond with:

```
*
 A=0A  X=FF  Y=0B  P=30  S=6D
```

Type "S" and carriage return a few more times to explore "single-stepping".

```
*S

0001-    8A              TXA
 A=FF  X=FF  Y=0B  P=B0  S=6D
*S

0002-    20 ED FD        JSR     $FDED
 A=FF  X=FF  Y=0B  P=B0  S=6D
*S

FDED-    6C 36 00        JMP     ($0036)
 A=FF  X=FF  Y=0B  P=B0  S=6D
```

## Multiple Stepping

Another tool for debugging is the BRK instruction. In the APPLE II, any time a BRK instruction is encountered, it acts as if the BRK instruction were just single-stepped, and goes into the monitor, where you may continue single-stepping or whatever you want to do. Note that although BRK is only one byte ($00), the 6502 microprocessor treats it as a two-byte instruction. Therefore, to properly use the BRK instruction, you should put the BRK instruction at the point you wish to start single-stepping from, execute your program, and when the program encounters the BRK instruction, it will return to the monitor as described above. Then you should replace the BRK instruction with the original instruction, and initialize single-stepping from that point.

## Tracing

Another debugging tool is the trace ("T") command. This command executes a program, instruction by instruction, and as it executes each instruction, it displays the instruction in single-step format. Trace will continue tracing until either a BRK instruction is encountered or the reset key is hit. Example:

0T (CR)

will "trace" a program starting at location 0.

```
0000-    E8              INX
 A=00  X=07  Y=00  P=30  S=12
0001-    8A              TXA
 A=07  X=07  Y=00  P=30  S=12
0002-    20 ED FD        JSR     $FDED
 A=07  X=07  Y=00  P=30  S=12
FDED-    6C 36 00        JMP     ($0036)
 A=07  X=07  Y=00  P=30  S=12
0389-    84 35           STY     $35
 A=07  X=07  Y=00  P=30  S=10
038B-    48              PHA
 A=07  X=07  Y=00  P=30  S=0F
038C-    20 A5 03        JSR     $03A5
 A=07  X=07  Y=00  P=30  S=0F
03A5-    A0 0B           LDY     #$0B
 A=07  X=07  Y=0B  P=30  S=0D
03A7-    18              CLC
 A=07  X=07  Y=0B  P=30  S=0D
03A8-    48              PHA
 A=
*
```

The above trace would have continued until a "BRK" command was encountered, but we stopped it by hitting the "RESET" key.

The above described the usage of the monitor directly from the keyboard. In addition to the above, the monitor contains many useful subroutines that can be utilized in your programs.

## WHAT... LIBRARY PAKS AGAIN ?

Yes, again! We have been asked by members who have purchased Library Pak 1A, whether they should order Pak 1B. The answer to this one is no. The letter designates only minor modifications have been made. In this case, one program was removed and another updated. Should you want an updated copy of any program or Pak, we will do that for just a $2.00 handling charge. Assuming we let you in on it!!!

## INTEGER BASIC FLOATING POINT

We admit at last to having Don Williams' Integer Basic routines actually in our hands, and guarantee herewith that they will be published in the September Call-Apple. We will have complete program listings and supporting documentation.

...And speaking of what's coming up in Call-Apple, we'd certainly like to be able to print your software and articles. How about it, out there?

## BACK ISSUES of CALL -APPLE

Currently, only the July issue is available. We plan to reprint April, May and June as time and money permit. If you have not received the back issue you want, please send a self-addressed envelope and 41¢ postage, along with the issues you desire. We will fill the orders, but it may take quite some time.

## LIBRARY ORDERS

We are fairly current on filling orders at this time. All orders received prior to July 15th should have been filled. If you do not receive your tape within 30 days, please check with us. However, we have every hope of being able to handle a 10 day turnaround time.

## CURRENT PROGRAMS

| | |
|---|---|
| Library Pak 1B | $ 5.00 |
| Library Pak 2 | $ 5.00 |
| Programmers Workshop II | $ 6.00 |
| Disk Workshop | $ 6.00 |
| Integer Basic Tutorial | $ 15.00 |
| Danny's Text Editor | $ 45.00 |
| Apple Box (mini-modem) | $ 18.50 |
| Apple Box II (with speaker) | $ 23.50 |
| Applesoft Workshop (watch for notice) | |

Programs submitted to our library and accepted will receive a free library Pak.

## DUES STRUCTURE

Fees for 1979 will be $2.50 Apple-cation fee (new members only) plus $7.50 dues. Those members who have already renewed at the prior rate will not be charged the new rate. New members paying for the first time after September 1st will not be required to pay 1978 dues. Membership cards are being mailed with this issue. If you are current and have not received a card, please let us know.

## (From Page 8)

To output data to BFILE we will do something a bit more familiar. PRINT #2, 14; field 1, field 2, field 3 .... The PRINT portion of this command works the same as for output to your CRT. The #2 means you are referencing BFILE - which was the second file you opened. 14 refers to the fourteenth record on the random file BFILE. Fields 1, 2, and 3 are the same as for AFILE.
Later in your program close to the end you must CLOSE files AFILE and BFILE. Why? To keep the data. Writing to and reading from disk files means you must get used to a discipline known as file handling. Errors in file handling can cost you a bundle in effort to recover lost files. If you've written data to a file but not closed the file when you're through with it, you might lose all the data that you stored. I can't say always because sometimes the operating system gives you a break. CLOSE 1, 2 will close AFILE and BFILE.
Not closing a file is like putting marbles in a box without a bottom. When you try to use it, your data isn't where you can easily get to it.
Next time, some preliminary comments about the APPLE II disk.

## INTEGRAL DATA TO THE RESCUE!

Much of this issue of Call -Apple was done on our own Apple II computer, nobly assisted by an Integral Data IP-225 printer, along with our own modification of Phil Roybal's Lower Case Character Generating Program (see Contact 1, May, 1978) The IP-225 has performed beautifully, and because you can software-select eight different type fonts, it is ideal for this task. We believe the smallest available type face, which we are using here, is easily readable, and it contributes further by making it possible to include more editorial matter in a given space. reader input on this subject would be welcomed.
Write -Apple!

## LIBRARY PAK 1A PROBLEMS

Sorry to say, many of the "corrected" versions of LPak 1A still have a bad copy of Program 8. If you are ordering LPak 2 and ask us with your order, we will add program 8 from LPak 1a to your tape. The main reason for this was simply our lack of time to check the tapes. Forgive?

## APPLESOFT Zero Page Useage

| HEX LOCATION | USE |
|---|---|
| 0-5 | Jump instructions to continue in Applesoft. (0G for Applesoft is equivalent to Control C in Integer Basic.) |
| $A-$C | Location for USR( ) function jump instruction. |
| $D-$17 | General purpose counters-flags for Applesoft. |
| $20-$4F | Apple II system monitor reserved locations. |
| $50-$61 | General purpose pointers for Applesoft. |
| $67-68 | Pointer to beginning of program. Normally set to $0801 for ROM version, or $3001 for RAM (cassette tape) version. |
| $69-$6A | Pointer to start of simple variable space. Also points to the end of the program plus 5, unless manually changed with the LOMEM: statement. |
| $6B-$6C | Pointer to the beginning of Array space. |
| $6D-$6E | Pointer to end of numeric storage in use. |
| $6F-$70 | Pointer to start of string storage. Strings are stored from here to the end of memory. |
| $71-$72 | General pointer. |
| $73-$74 | Highest location in memory available to Applesoft plus one. Upon initial entry to Applesoft, is set to the end of memory available. |
| $75-$76 | Current line number of line being executed. |
| $77-$78 | "Old line number". Set up by a control-C, STOP or END statement. Gives line number that execution was interrupted at. |
| $79-$7A | "Old text pointer". Points to location in memory for statement to be executed next. |
| $7B-$7C | Current line number where DATA is being read from. |
| $7D-$7E | Points to absolute location in memory where DATA is being read from. |
| $7F-$80 | Pointer to where input is coming from currently. Is set to $201 during an INPUT statement, or during a READ statement is set to the DATA in the program it is READing from. |
| $81-$82 | Holds the last used variable name. |
| $83-$84 | Pointer to the last used variable's value. |
| $85-9C | General useage. |
| $9D-$A3 | Main floating point accumulator. |
| $A4 | General use in floating point math routines. |
| $A5-$AB | Secondary floating point accumulator. |
| $AC-$B0 | General useage flags-pointers. |
| $B1-$C8 | CHRGET routine. Applesoft calls here every time it wants another character. |
| $B8-$B9 | Pointer to last character obtained through the CHRGET routine. |
| $C9-$CD | Random number. |
| $D0-$DF | High resolution graphics scratch pointers. |
| $D8-$DF | ONERR pointers-scratch. |
| $E0-$E2 | High-resolution graphics X and Y coordinates. |
| $E4 | High-resolution graphics color byte. |
| $E5-$E7 | General use for high resolution graphics. |
| $E8-$E9 | Pointer to beginning of shape table. |
| $EA | Collision counter for high resolution graphics. |
| $F0-$F3 | General use flags. |
| $F4-$F8 | ONERR pointers. |

## ROUTINE to PRINT FREE BYTES
### by Bob Huelsdonk

Only line 30001 is required for less than 32K of memory. The first GOTO 30000 shows result with >32K of memory. The second GOTO 30000 shows the result with <32K of memory.

```
30000 IF PEEK (203)>128 THEN 30002

30001 PRINT PEEK (202)+ PEEK (203
      )*256- PEEK (204)- PEEK (205
      )*256;" BYTES FREE": END
30002 PRINT 32767-( PEEK (204)+ PEEK
      (205)*256);" BYTES + "; PEEK
      (202)+( PEEK (203)-128)*256
      +1;" BYTES FREE": END

>GOTO30000
30719 BYTES + 16226 BYTES FREE

>GOTO30000
27793 BYTES FREE
```

## LOADING MACHINE LANGUAGE AS PART OF A BASIC PROGRAM

### from Contact No. 1, May, 1978

Often we want to include machine language data inside a Basic program. Apple Basic loads programs into memory with the highest program line at the highest RAM location (HIMEM). Preceeding lines are located lower and lower in RAM. The beginning of the program is at PP, an address which is held in memory locations CA and CB (hexadecimal) or 202 and 203, decimal. When you type SAVE, the computer transfers to tape everything between PP and HIMEM. Thus, to tuck machine language into your program so it can be loaded like Basic, it is merely necessary to move the PP down below the beginning of the extra code, put in two POKES to reset the pointer before running the program, and type SAVE. Later, you will be able to LOAD the whole thing just as if it were all Basic. Just follow these steps:

1. Get the Basic program into memory, exactly the way you want it. If you make any changes, you must redo steps 2 and 6.
2. In the command mode, type PRINT PEEK(202),PEEK(203) and write down the results. Call them m and n, respectively.
3. Load your machine language code into memory using the monitor load capabilities. This will put the machine language program into memory below the beginning of the Basic program, starting at hexadecimal address xxxx.
4. Take the starting address of the machine language program and divide it into two parts: xx:xx. Convert each pair of digits from hex to decimal values: a & b, corresponding to the left and right xx pairs, respectively. Write them down.
5. Now enter the Basic command mode and type: POKE 202, b-1 (value b from step 4, above). POKE 203, a (value a from step 4, above).
6. You have now moved the pointers down below your machine language program, and must insert code to move them back again when the program is run. To do that, type: POKE 202,m: POKE 203,n: GOTO a.. where m and n are the values from step 2 and a is the first line number in your Basic program. That line number can be 0.. it will not be erased by the above entry.
7. Now you're done! Don't try to list your program because before it runs, all you will see is a meaningless set of numbers and symbols. Just type SAVE (before running the program) and it will all go on to tape. Later a LOAD command will bring it all back in.

### CAUTION !

Once you have RUN such a program, you cannot SAVE it, for the pointers will have been moved. You can only copy a program like this before it has been RUN.

## A PATCH FOR DOUBLE LOOPS
### BY BOB HUELSDONK

WHEN INPUTTING TO A DOUBLE LOOP BY ROW, THEN JUMPING OUT TO A DOUBLE LOOP TO TOTAL BY COLUMN, IT IS NECESSARY TO REVERSE THE SUBSCRIPT ORDER.

THIS WILL NOT WORK IN APPLESOFT BECAUSE THE RIGHT COUNTERS DO NOT RESET. THE FOLLOWING SIMPLE EXAMPLE WILL DEMONSTRATE:

```
80   PRINT " INPUT '-1' TO TERMINATE
     INPUTS"
100  FOR R = 1 TO 3
120  FOR C = 1 TO 3
140  INPUT A(R,C)
160  IF A(R,C) = - 1 THEN 300
180  NEXT C
200  NEXT R
300  FOR C = 1 TO 3
320  FOR R = 1 TO 3
340  PRINT A(R,C)
360  NEXT R
380  NEXT C
```

IF THE FOLLOWING CHANGES ARE MADE, THIS PROBLEM IS OVERCOME:

```
160  IF A(R,C)=-1 THEN 250
250  FOR R=0 TO 0:NEXT R
```

THE EMPTY 'R' LOOP RESETS THE COUNTER.

---

### BASIC CLASSES !

don Williams will again be our instructor for the A.P.P.L.E. Classroom, starting late August at Empire Electronics. Tuition for members will be

**only $25.00**

Two different classes will be taught:
**Beginning Basic** and
**Intermediate Basic**.
We suggest you sign up now while space is still available. Call Tom Geer at 244-5200.

# AUTOMATED TRAINING SYSTEMS

Automated Training Systems has been a Washington State Licensed Proprietory School since 1968. These classes are taught by Cliff Gazaway who has had 20 years of electronics hardware experience and ten years of teaching. He is now assistant manager at Max Cook's Computerland store in Federal Way.

```
$$$$$$$$$$$$$$$$$$$$$$$$$$$$$$$$
$$            SAVE $20.00     $$
$$$$$$$$$$$$$$$$$$$$$$$$$$$$$$$$
$$                            $$
$$                            $$
$$  REGISTER FOR ANY CLASS 15 $$
$$  DAYS IN ADVANCE AND RECEIVE $$
$$  $20.00 COMPUTERLAND GIFT  $$
$$  CERTIFICATE.              $$
$$                            $$
$$                            $$
$$$$$$$$$$$$$$$$$$$$$$$$$$$$$$$$
```

IN ADDITION TO THE TIME SHOWN IN THE SCHEDULES EACH STUDENT IS ENCOURAGED TO SPEND ADDITIONAL "LAB" TIME AT A MUTUALLY AGREEABLE TIME.

$10 off if you bring your own Apple to each class.

POKING & PEEKING AT YOUR APPLE.

Mon.Sept.11-25,7-9pm. plus additional hands-on time arranged. 1500 S.336th.,Fed.Way.

This class shows you how to use the powerful POKE, PEEK, & CALL commands to do exciting things with you APPLE.
$55.00.

APPLE CIRCUIT THEORY.

Wed.Aug.9-30,7-9pm.
7906 34th.S.W.,Seattle,98126

You will know the purpose of every IC chip in your APPLE upon completion of this course. You will get more out of your APPLE if you know how it works.
$55.00 plus materials

CONNECTING TO THE REAL WORLD.

Wed.,Sept. 13-27, 7-9pm.
7906 34th.S.W.,Seattle 98126

We will study a collection of magazine articles on interfacing and adapt the articles to the APPLE. We will help you custom build the hardware. Subjects of special intrest include clock and calendar, burglar alarms, AC appliance controls, temperature and photo input.
$55.00 plus materials.

CHRISTMAS PRESENTS FOR APPLELOVERS.

Wed., Nov.8-29, 7-9pm.
7906 34th. S.W., Seattle 98126

Every APPLE owner wants something for his APPLE for Christmas. 1978 will be the first "home computer Christmas". This class helps you build or buy something for your APPLE computer owner.
$55.00 plus materials.

For more information call CLIFF at COMPUTERLAND - Phone 838-9363 or 927-8585

# AUTOMATED TRAINING SYSTEMS

# Empire ELECTRONICS, INC.

**TV SALES • HIGH FIDELITY SALES • WHOLESALE PARTS • SERVICE**
**• COMPUTERS**

616 S.W. 152nd Street
Seattle, Washington 98166
206-244-5200

894 Southcenter Shopping Center
Tukwila, Washington 98188
206-246-6120

---

### *** Thank You ***

I would like to thank all the club members for the beautiful Fuschia plant you sent me during my stay at the hospital. **Tom Geer**

---

### ** PRINTERS **

* Integral Data
* Expandor Black Box

All copy for this ad was set with an Integral Data IP-225 Printer.

---

### ** SOFTWARE **

* A.P.P.L.E. Library Paks
* Savings
* Loans
* Leases
* Finance
* Appleditor
* Data Base
* Programmer's Workshop

* Basic Tutorial
* Vendor
* Inventory
* Calendar
* Home Improvement
* Home Inventory
* Applesoft II
* Disk Workshop

---

### ** BOOKS **

* Howard Sams
* Osborne & Associates
* Kilobaud
* Kilobaud
* Interface Age
* Micro

* Tab Books
* Apple Manuals
* Byte
* N.W. Computers News
* Call -Apple

---

### ** PARTS **

* Jim Packs
* Vector
* Sprague
* Joy Sticks

* Injectrol
* ECG Sylvania
* G C Electronics
* Ascii Keyboards

<<< ALL APPLE PERIPHERALS >>>

---

Memorex Diskettes for Apple Disk II
Member Price  $ 3.60  each

***** FREE Punching to use Both Sides *****

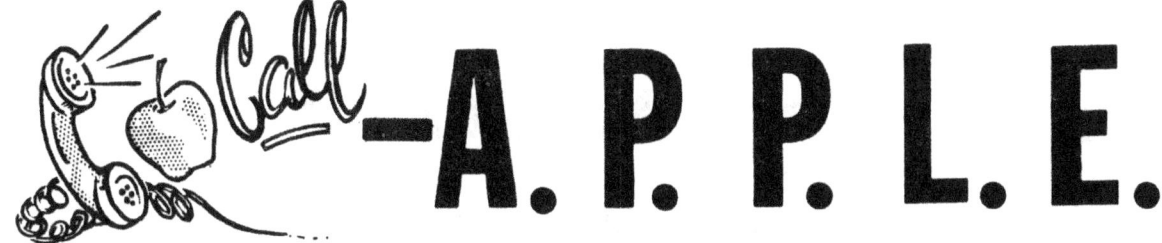

# A.P.P.L.E.

## APPLE PUGETSOUND PROGRAM LIBRARY EXCHANGE

SEPTEMBER, 1978     $1.00     Vol. 1, No. 8

6708 39th Avenue SW    Seattle, Washington 98136    (206) 932-6588

### The Program that Apple Said "Couldn't be Written" !!!
#### by Ron Aldrich

The Aldrich brothers strike again!. Remember, folks, you read it first in Call -Apple. "Convert", by Ron Aldrich, using the disk, will create a text file from an Integer Basic program listing, call Applesoft, then read the file into Applesoft and presto, your program has been converted! After conversion, list it out and note all lines that need to be changed to conform to the Applesoft format. This means that the Integer commands that are not compatible with Applesoft must be changed. For example: TAB must be changed to HTAB and commas in input statements must be changed to semi-colons, etc. The program listing may be found on Page 3.

    WELL, RANDY?

### SPECIAL NOTICE

The September meeting will be held on the second Tuesday of September instead of the usual third Tuesday. The occasion for this being an appearance "on the scene" by Mr. **Randy Wiggington** of Apple Computer, Inc. We would like to take this opportunity to thank Randy for his interest in the group, and also to Bob Huelsdonk, who was instrumental in arranging for Randy to appear. We are not certain just what will go on at the meeting, other than many questions. But there can be no doubt that it will be a most interesting one. Plan to attend. 7:00 PM September 12th at Computerland of Bellevue, 14340 NE 20th Street.

| | |
|---|---|
| Val J. Golding, President | (206) 932-6588 |
| Michael Thyng, Secretary | (206) 524-2744 |
| Darrell Aldrich, Program Editor | (206) 782-7082 |
| Ron Aldrich, Asst. Prgm. Editor | (206) 782-7082 |
| Bob Huelsdonk, Technical Consultant, Basic | (206) 362-4910 |
| Don Williams, Technical Consultant, Assembly | (206) 242-6807 |
| Steve Paulson, Circulation | (206) 242-2700 |

### SEPTEMBER MEETING
7:00 PM TUESDAY, SEPTEMBER 12, 1978
Computerland of Bellevue
14340 NE 20th St., Bellevue, wa.   746-2070

### OCTOBER MEETING
7:00 PM Tuesday, October 17, 1978
Omega Stereo   5420 196th SW   Lynwood

### IN THIS ISSUE...   Page

| | |
|---|---|
| Integer-Applesoft Conversion Program | 3 |
| Bytes from the Apple | 3 |
| Card Shuffling | 3 |
| Apple Mash | 4 |
| Video Display Routine | 4 |
| Saga of Old No. 8 | 5 |
| Nightmare Gamepak | 5 |
| CQ all Hams de Call -Apple | 5 |
| New User Group Formation | 5 |
| Routine to Save an Array in Applesoft | 5 |
| Program Library | 6 |
| Minutes of August 16th | 6 |
| Editorial | 7 |
| Linkage Routines for Integer Floating Point | 9 |
| Write Apple (letters) | 10 |
| Integral Data Printer Driver | 13 |
| Return to Text from Graphics | 13 |
| Printer Driver Fixes | 14 |
| Classifieds | 14 |

CALL -APPLE        SEPTEMBER, 1978             PAGE 2

# Bellevue ComputerLand
14340 N.E. 20th Street
746-2070

Prices go up September 30.

## MODEM TYPE 103 — ORIGINATE OR ANSWER

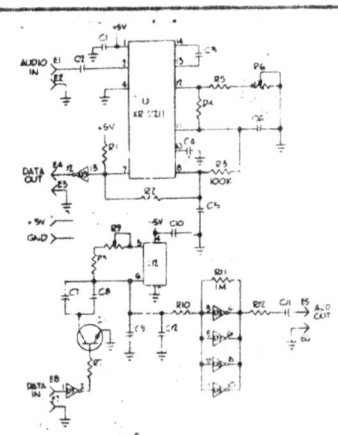

This circuit uses the XR-2211 FSK demodulator. The XR-2211 is a monolithic phase-locked loop system designed for data communications. This circuit connects to a crystal mike for an input and an eight ohm speaker for an output. Only a single supply of +5 volts is required. The data inputs and outputs are TTL. The receive frequencies are 2225 Hz (logic 1), and 2025 Hz (logic 0). The transmit frequencies are 1270 Hz (logic 1), and 1070 Hz (logic 0). The circuit works up to 300 baud.

Board only $7.60 Part No. 109; with parts $27.50 Part No. 109A

Cliff plans to plug this MODEM directly into the game paddle connector. The Apple should, then, function as a terminal on the Nordata computer (for 50¢ per hour) and other time share systems.

## RS-232/TTL INTERFACE

The RS-232 board has two separate circuits. One circuit converts RS-232 to TTL. The other converts TTL to RS-232. The board has a ten-pin edge connector. Power required is +12V and -12V.

Board only $4.50 Part No. 232; with parts $7.00 Part No. 232A

## RS-232/TTY INTERFACE

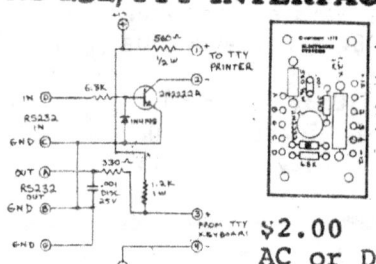

This board has two separate circuits. One converts RS-232 to 20 mA current loop, the other converts 20 mA current loop to RS-232.

Board only $4.50 Part No. 600, with parts $7.00 Part No. 600A

AC power control is a bonus you receive from this printer and teletype interface. It connects to the game paddle connector. If a $2.00 relay is connected in place of the teletype, any AC or DC devices can be turned on and off by addressing the annunciator outputs. Can also start and stop the cassette recorder. One or both of these cards may be needed, depending on the type of printer or control.

## APPLE II SERIAL I/O INTERFACE

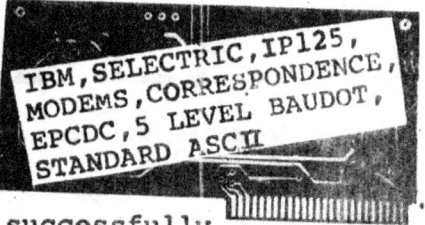

This serial I/O port works up to 30,000 baud. Software included are, an input and output routine from the Apple monitor or basic to a teletype or other serial printer. Also a program for using the Apple II for a video terminal or an intelligent terminal. It plugs into one of the Apple II peripheral connectors. It uses very low current. The input and output are RS-232.

Board only $15.00 Part No. 2; with parts $42.00 Part No. 2A. Assembled and tested $62.00 Part No. 2C.

This is the interface card that Cliff has used very successfully with the TRENDATA IBM's and Integral Data Systems IP125's.

# Bellevue ComputerLand

14340 N.E. 20th. St.
B E L L E V U E, WA. 98007

Phone Cliff at (206) 746-2070.

Mail, telephone, and bank card orders accepted. Shipping: add $3.

## BYTES from the APPLE
Software stuff, etc., etc., etc., etc., etc., etc., et

by Val J. Goldins

This month, many of the topics we often cover in this column, such as the software library, etc., are discussed fully elsewhere. So, we would like to take this page this month to deliver what most journals would egotistically call "the President's Message"!!! As much as possible we prefer to remain relaxed and informal, making occasional bad puns, etc. But this is one time we would like to pat ourselves on the back a bit. We have recently received a number of complimentary letters and phone calls, related to all aspects of the club. And we believe for the most part, it is deserved. We have worked long and hard, as have many of the members, to make the club a success. And, of course, we've made many a goof along the way. But the point we want to strongly make is that a national organization with a 200 plus membership, can not be a one man operation. And essentially, it has. The time has come when we must have some additional assistance. And this is difficult to ask, because what needs to be done most are the menial chores like stamping and stuffing envelopes, processing applications, etc. But these are all things necessary to the operation and continued success of the club. Most of all, we would like to have some input from others on how to best go about this.

We have received some comments from out of state members who feel they should be entitled to lower annual dues, since they are unable to participate in local meetings, etc. Now on the face of it, this would seem to be a legitimate idea, but notwithstanding the complexities of a two level dues structure, what many do not realize is that all of the income from dues and the majority of the income from software all go toward the expense of publishing Call -Apple, which runs in the neighborhood (or should we say slum) of about $250.00 per month. And Call -Apple is of course, the major membership benefit to out of state members.

One final note! Thanks to all who have recently been contributing software, articles and letters. Each of you, as individuals have a right to be proud of your club, and it is through your own efforts that you have earned than right.

THANKS.

## OUR SPECIAL THANKS TO:

MICHAEL WEINSTOCK of Ft. Walton Beach, Fla. for the masthead (GOSUB TOPOFFRONTPAGE) that graces our cover this issue.

```
0 REM "CONVERT" BY RON ALDRICH
1 REM PROGRAM LOADS INTEGER BASIC PROGRA
  M FROM DISK, SAVES TO A TEXT FILE ON D
  ISK
2 REM THEN EXECUTES THAT FILE IN APPLESO
  FT II
3 REM SOME COMMANDS WHICH ARE LEGAL IN I
  NTEGER BASIC WILL NOT WORK IN APPLESOF
  T II (TAB,INPUT...)
10 POKE 76, PEEK (202): POKE 77, PEEK
   (203)
20 DIM A$(35):D$="": REM   D$="(CTRL) D"
30 PRINT D$;"NOMON C,I,O"
40 TEXT : CALL -936: VTAB 3: PRINT "A.P.P
   .L.E.  PRESENTS:": PRINT : PRINT
   "APPLE INTEGER BASIC - APPLESOFT II"
   : PRINT "CONVERSION PROGRAM"
50 PRINT : PRINT : INPUT "PROGRAM TO BE C
   ONVERTED ?";A$
60 PRINT D$;"LOAD ";A$
65 PRINT D$
70 POKE 33,33
80 PRINT D$;"OPEN ";A$;"FILE": PRINT
   D$;"WRITE ";A$;"FILE"
90 LIST
100 PRINT D$;"CLOSE ";A$;"FILE"
105 PRINT D$
110 PRINT D$;"OPEN I-A FILE": PRINT D$
    ;"WRITE I-A FILE": PRINT "FP": PRINT
    "EXEC ";A$;"FILE"
120 PRINT D$;"CLOSE I-A FILE": PRINT
    D$;"EXEC I-A FILE"
130 END
```

## Card Shuffling Caution

The last 90 days or so have seen a tremendous influx of peripheral equipment available for the Apple II, much in the form of plug in cards. Cliff Gazaway of Computerland has told us numerous sad tales of mishaps that have occured while changing cards. Here are two prime rules to follow:
1. NEVER plug a card in or out while the power is on.
2. Wait a minimum of 10 seconds after the power is off, before pulling a card.

## APPLE MASH   by  Mike Thyng

### ARRAYS

This issue we'll discuss numerical arrays and dimensioning of single variables. We'll find out what an array is, how to use one and why it is so useful. Next issue, we'll discuss alpha variables and touch on matrices - arrays of multiple dimension.

First, what is an array? An array is a collection of related variables. You can tell one variable from another by using a subscript. A subscript is an independent variable that you use to access (there's that word from our disk file series) data from the array. As the subscript changes, so does the variable you will be getting data from. Note well- the data does not change when you change the value of the subscript; only the variable changes.

An example of a numerical array would be A(1),A(2),...,A(n), where the variable is A and the subscript is n. You might want a collection of numerical variables - an array - to store the passing distance of Seahawk quarterback Jim Zorn. So in our example, A(1) would be the value in yards that he threw in pass one; A(2) the distance in pass two and so on for as many passes as we want to record. Which brings me to an important point in our collective understanding.

Before we start our array, we must decide how many elements - in our example, passes - we plan to record. Let's choose 95. Now we need to tell the computer that we want to set aside space to record the distance for 95 passes. We do this with a DIM (or dimension) statement. DIM A(94) sets aside space for exactly 95 variables, A(0) through A(94). This is the most efficient use of the array space. In actual practice though, most programmers would just DIM A(95), then they could just refer to the last array element as A(95). The element known as A(0) would then become an extra variable that could be used for another purpose. You could also use DIM A(s) to set aside array space. However, you must then set s equal to 94 or 95, prior to the dimension statement, else your only element will be A(0).

O.K. Now we've decided what our array A represents. We have set aside space for it. Now we need to set some data into it. We could set each of the 95 variables equal to the values we want to record.
```
    A(1) = 23
    A(2) = 50
       :
       :
    A(95) = 46
```
But that's not really putting the computer to its best use. A better way would be:

```
100 INPUT "NEXT PASS ";A(N)
110 N=N+1
120 IF N < 96 THEN 100
200 REM  OTHER LOGIC FOLLOWS
```

An array is really useful (in 25 words or less) because you can access a bunch (technical word) of variables without writing separate logic statements for each one. As an example, if we assigned names to each of the 95 variables we used to record Jim Zorn's yardage, we'd have to write statements naming each of them individually. With the array, all we'd have to do to say, average them all, would be the following:
```
    FOR N= 1 to 95
    TOT = TOT + A(N)
    NEXT N
    AVER= TOT /95
```
Ask your boss for arrays!

The readers attention is also directed to the program listing on Page 5 on how to use arrays in Applesoft II.

---

```
100 REM THIS ROUTINE DEMONSTRATES HOW THE
    VIDEO DISPLAY IS ORGANIZED

110 REM IT DISPLAYS HOW THE HIGH ORDER BIT
    S CONTROL "INVERSE", "NORMAL" AND "FLA
    SH" DISPLAYS

120 REM NOTE THAT THE VIDEO DISPLAY MEMORY
     LOCATIONS ARE NOT ARRANGED IN SIMPLE
     SERIAL FORM

130 REM THIS ROUTINE WILL POKE CHARACTERS
    INTO THE VIDEO DISPLAY AREA WITHOUT US
    ING TAB OR VTAB

140 REM THIS FUNCTION MUST BE USED IN ORDE
    R TO PEEK AT A LOCATION ON THE VIDEO S
    CREEN

150 REM "X" IS THE HORIZONTAL POSITION; "Y
    " IS THE VERTICAL POSITION WITH "0" AT
    THE TOP

160 REM  BY DAN CHAPMAN

170 CALL -936
180 FOR Y=0 TO 7: FOR X=0 TO 31:LTR=32
    *Y+X: GOSUB 220
190 POKE POS,LTR
200 NEXT X: NEXT Y
210 VTAB 12: END
220 POS=1024+X+128*Y-984*(Y/8): RETURN
```

## THE SAGA of OLD No. 8

(Or what else could possibly go wrong ???)

"Program 8 won't load" was the complaint we heard in droves, when Library Pak 1B was first released. Unfortunately, by that time, we had released over 30 copies of that infamous pak. So, we decided, we would make that program the first program on the soon-to-be-released pak 2. This would be a way to make amends without re-recording a large batch of tapes. But we had not taken into account the whims of the computer gods. For lo and behold, on Library Pak 2, there came to be a duplication of Color Gamepak 2, and no Color Gamepak 1. So we are once again on our knees, begging for mercy!

This error occured on all copies of pak 2 numbered <48. If you still need old no. 8, then send a note and a self-addressed envelope and we'll make amends. Shameful, shameful!

## NIGHTMARE GAMEPAK

In another maddening example of shoddy craftsmanship, here are some patches to be made in Nightmare Gamepak for copies number <48. Load the program, make changes as shown below, and resave it.

Renumber line 2392 to 2389 and delete 2392
Renumber line 2394 to 2391 and delete 2394
Correct line 2106 to read GOTO 2496
Line 2216 change END to GOTO 2496
Add line 2496 FOR I=1 TO 2500:GOTO 20160: NEXT I:

## CQ ALL HAMS DE CALL -APPLE

We have had inquiries from a few hams as to any ham software we might have available. We will have a morse code training program shortly, so if this is of interest, please let us know. We would also request that each ham member so advise us of that fact, and we in turn will attempt to put you in contact with one another.

## NEW USER GROUPS

Many new Apple user groups are currently forming around the country. Our membership is now some 200 strong, with members in most states and a few foreign countries. If you are interested in forming your own local user group, we will help by supplying you with a membership list of members in your state or area, so let us know your needs.

## ROUTINE to SAVE an ARRAY

Reprinted from Apple Stems, Vol I, No. 2, July, 1978, the newsletter of Apple Portland Program Library Exchange.

Here is a routine to save both integer or floating point real numbers in an Applesoft II array. This will not work in alpha strings until they are converted, using the CHR$ function. Any variable may be used.

```
90   TEXT : HOME : VTAB 5
100  PRINT "THIS PROGRAM DEMONSTRATES T
     HE USE OF ": PRINT : PRINT "STORE
     AND RECALL FUNCTIONS OF APPLESOFT
     II"
110  PRINT : PRINT : PRINT "FIRST WE WI
     LL GENERATE AN ARRAY 'A(10,3)'."
120  FOR X = 1 TO 10: FOR Y = 1 TO 3
140  A(X,Y) = X * Y: NEXT Y,X
160  PRINT : PRINT "HERE IS THE ARRAY":
     PRINT
170  FOR X = 1 TO 10: FOR Y = 1 TO 3: PRINT
     A(X,Y);: NEXT Y,X
210  PRINT : PRINT
220  PRINT "HIT ANY KEY TO CONTINUE": CALL
     - 756: HOME : VTAB 5
300  PRINT : PRINT "NEXT WE STORE THE A
     RRAY": PRINT : PRINT "START THE TA
     PE RECORDER IN RECORD MODE": PRINT
     : PRINT "AND HIT ANY KEY"
320  : PRINT : CALL - 756
330  STORE A
340  HOME : VTAB 5: PRINT "NOW WE WILL
     ZERO THE ARRAY": PRINT : PRINT
370  FOR X = 1 TO 10: FOR Y = 1 TO 3:A(
     X,Y) = 0: NEXT Y,X
410  FOR X = 1 TO 10: FOR Y = 1 TO 3: PRINT
     A(X,Y);: NEXT Y,X
450  PRINT : PRINT "NOW WE WILL RECALL
     THE ARRAY": PRINT : PRINT "REWIND
     AND START RECORDER ON PLAY": PRINT
     : PRINT "AND HIT ANY KEY"
470  CALL - 756: HOME : VTAB 5: PRINT
     "NOW WE WILL RECALL THE ARRAY": PRINT
490  RECALL A
500  FOR X = 1 TO 10: FOR Y = 1 TO 3: PRINT
     A(X,Y);: NEXT Y,X
540  PRINT : PRINT "AND NOW WE HAVE OUR
     ARRAY BACK": END
```

## PROGRAM LIBRARY

### DANNY'S TEXT EDITOR

This editor is designed to work with and print operating on the Apple parallel card. It is available in both a disk and cassette tape version. When ordering, specify disk or tape, also make and model of printer and slot number used by printer I/O card. This printer has a provision to output in lower case to the printer, and displays upper case as inverse video on the screen. It has most of the usual edit-functions, including line and character insertion and selectable line length. Requires 32K Ram memory. Cost $45.00

### LIBRARY PAK 2

This Pak is now in production and comes with our lcos: Limited Cassette Operating System. It contains 7 modules with 34 programs, Color Gamepak 1 (The ill-fated program 8 from Pak 1B), Color Gamepaks II and III, Color Demopak II, Holiday Greetingpak, Battleship and Nightmare Gamepak. cost $5.00. An extra .41 for postage would be appreciated.

### PROGRAMMERS WORKSHOP (for Disk or Cassette)

Workshop is currently being produced in one version only, which includes additional commands for handling disk files. Therefore you need order one Workshop only. if you own an earlier version without disk commands, you can get an updated copy for just $2.00. Workshop is a utility module, designed to aid programmers working on their programs. it contains 16 routines with 11 commands on a menu. routines are: Renumber, Append from disk or tape, List by page, Poke Writer, Examine Basic, Bytes free and used, Kill, Save to disk or tape, Quit, Catalog, Number converter and Variable list. We recommend it also as a tool to learn more about how your Apple works. Cost $6.00.

### APPLESOFT WORKSHOP

This program is very slowly in progress. We work on it as time permits, but it is still far from completion. please do not order until you see notice of its availability.

### LIBRARY PAK 3

We expect this new Pak to become available by about the first of October. It will include Musicpak I and some new utility programs, plus more color games and color demos and Hires programs. Again, please do not order until you see it announced in Call -Apple.

### *BACK ORDERS of PROGRAMS

For the first time in more than six weeks, library pak orders are on a current basis, and all orders received prior to Sept. 1st have been shipped, and your patience is appreciated. Between running out of blank tape and a time factor, it has often difficult to maintain orders on a timely basis.

### NEW PROGRAMS

We have been gratified by the number of new programs we have recently received, particularly from some of our out of state members. We would like to take this space to thank Danny Lambert, John Cook, Ed Avelar, Dave Gordon, John Backman, Mark Cross, David Garson, Doug Trusty and many others for their contributions. Many of these programs will be turning up in future Library Paks. And that is the name of the game. A.P.P.L.E. makes it possible for these programs to be enjoyed by all members. Program submission forms are available at each meetings, or by mail for sending a S.A.S.E. Let's keep the ball rolling and share your work with others.

## MINUTES of AUG. 15th MEETING

The meeting started promptly at 7:09. We introduced ourselves and found 30 members present. The treasurer's report showed over $1400 in the treasury, of which about $150 is committed. Val has ordered more 8 minute cassettes which will be available to members at six for $5.00. They will be at the September meeting. Our Letters to the Editor feature in the August Call -Apple has met with much favorable comment. Don Williams and Bob Huelsdonk have agreed to act as technical advisors and field some of the tougher questions. Cliff Gazaway reported that Computerland in Federal Way now keeps a log of technical questions, and if they can't answer them on the spot, other Apple owners are asked to respond. They have agreed to share these questions and answers with the club. Ron Aldrich wrote a disk program to convert Integer Basic to Applesoft II.

Karl Ganders suggested we work together to exterminate the bugs from our current crop of programs. Most agreed this was a useful idea and Val volunteered to make printed program listings available to anyone interested in serving the club library in this fashion. Most area dealers will also accomodate members that need listings.

Bob Huelsdonk recently had oveheating problems with his power supply, which went intermittent on him. He solved the problem by installing a 3 inch fan from Radar Electric (Seattle). Note: before you panic and start worrying about how soon your Apple will roll over and die, you should know that Bob's Apple is neatly packaged in a wooden case with a Black Box printer on top; a Disk II on the side.

Bob also wanted to know how to detect the end of file condition of a disk data file, but no valid solutions were found. We unanimously agreed to invite Randy Wigginton of Apple Computer to our next meeting, hoping that he might find a solution (!)

The formal portion of the meeting adjourned at 7:30 PM.

## EDITORIAL by Val J. Golding

The letter which we quote below was originally scheduled for use in the "Write-Apple" letters column. However, we felt the matter important enough to be the subject of this month's editorial. Ted Oom has (in part) written as follows:

I am becoming moderately frustrated over the fact that, as fast as I run, you continue to get further ahead of me. I refer to the technical discussions of the newsletter and the APPLE group meetings which are both becoming increasingly oriented toward the computer buffs, (i.e., those with extensive computer background) or those persons who desire to analyse each and every function of the computer.

I suggest that there may be a few of us who are attempting to apply the computer to practical uses, and are not desirous, or do not have the time, to appreciate every little peculiarity of the computer. There seems to be a definite communications gap between myself and the contributors to the newsletter articles. I suspect there are others who need information on a more simplistic level.

I would like to know if all the people who own Apples are of the level of proficiency and knowledge that they understand the Aldrich/Golding/Thyng conversations. Or would it benefit the majority of the group to simplify the information; include more explanatory discussion. The solution to my particular problem of getting questions answered would probably be to get a list of Apple owners in my area with whom I can exchange information and generally coordinate.

In conclusion, I did not intend the preceeding as a criticism of you or others involved in the group. It is extremely difficult to organize and run a new and rapidly growing group such as we have. I applaud you for your efforts and accomplishments to date. But I think it may be appropriate to slow down and analyse the situation.

Ted, you have given us much food for thought. We would like to invite comment from our readers, as well as bring the subject up at a meeting. Many of your points are well taken, while on others, we feel perhaps you have not researched thoroughly.

Perhaps there is too high a percentage of technical articles in Call -Apple. Perhaps we should not have run Don Williams' Floating Point Routines in this issue. We confess to not really understanding them ourselves. Or are there readers that do understand - and appreciate - an article of that high a technical level?

Perhaps you would be willing to assist in an editorial capacity? Certainly this magazine should not be a one person operation. We have stated on numerous occasions that one of our goals is to assist the newcomers to personal computing. Are we failing you and others in this regard?

We do feel that the staff and officers of the magazine and club, respectively, must have the knowledge and must be able to keep "a jump ahead", in order to anticipate and answer questions, both at meetings, and in magazine articles and letters columns.

We believe you are mistaken when you attempt to categorize Aldrich/Golding/Thyng among those with extensive computer backgrounds. At 20, Darrell Aldrich has an "extensive computer background" of two years high school data processing. Golding had never laid hands on a computer B.A. (Before Apple). Ron Aldrich who, at 16, can write programming circles around Golding, had no Basic programming until his brother bought an Apple. Thyng is an exception. Thyng earns a living as a programmer. But in Cobol, not Basic.

But most of all, we appreciate your interest in the club, and we thank you for showing it by having written.

```
100 REM THIS ROUTINE ALLOWS EXECUTION OF M
    ONITOR COMMANDS FROM > BASIC PROGRAM W
    ITH RETURN TO BASIC
110 REM BY S H LAM, PRINCETON, N.J.
120 DIM C$(40)
130 INPUT "MONITOR COMMAND=",C$
140 C$( LEN(C$)+1)=" E88AG"
150 FOR I=1 TO LEN(C$)
160 POKE 511+I, ASC(C$(I))
170 NEXT I
180 CALL -144
190 END
```

Dear Apple Customers,

Beginning September 12, I will serve you from the B E L L E V U E   COMPUTERLAND   store   rather than the Federal Way  store.

I will be in charge of the Apple and home computer department at BELLEVUE Computerland.

I would like to thank each of you  who let me help you in the past.

If I can help you, in the future, call me at (206)746-2070 at the BELLEVUE store, or phone me at home at 935-2697. Or  visit me at the store at 14340 N.E. 20th. Street in Bellevue, Washington.

Thank you,
Cliff Gazaway

P.S. I'll  see you at the A.P.P.L.E. club meeting at BELLEVUE Computerland  on September 12  at 7pm.

**TV GAME AND QUAD BALANCING JOYSTICK!**
*Four 100K Pots
$9.95
Highest quality joystick made. Perfect for computer games, TV games, and audio balancing. Pots mounted on a 1½ x 1½ x 1" metal frame. Full rotation 1" shaft. Resistance varies with angle of shaft.

Each joystick replaces two game padales. Makes games and graphics much more fun! ! Avialable about Sept. 25.

**ComputerLand**™
**Bellevue**
14340 N.E. 20th Street
746-2070

# LINKAGE ROUTINES for the Apple II Integer Basic FLOATING POINT PACKAGE

by DON WILLIAMS

Floating point numbers are treated by the Apple II Rom Routines as four bytes represented in Figure 1, below:

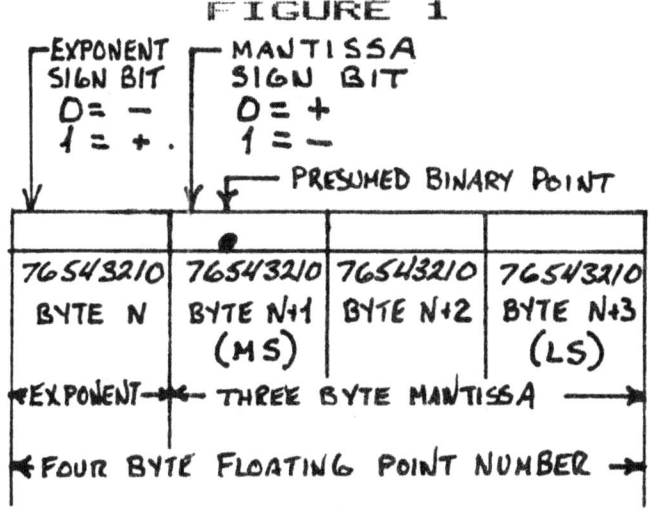

FIGURE 1

with the number being represented as in scientific notation

as: MANTISSA * 2(exponent)

The exponent byte is biased by 80 hex and represents the number of implied binary point moves to the right (80-FF) or to the left (00-7F) of the binary point. For example:

```
FIGURE 2          FIGURE 3
EXPONENTS         FLOATING POINT NUMBERS

00 IS -128        83 50 00 00        10.
01 IS -127        80 40 00 00         1.
02 IS -126        7C 66 66 66          .1
   :              00 00 00 00         0.0
7F IS  -1         7C 49 99 9A         -.1
80 IS   0         7F 80 00 00        -1.0
81 IS  +1         83 B0 00 00       -10.0
   :              80 60 00 00         1.5
FF IS  127        80 70 00 00         1.75
```

The three byte mantissa (or fractional part of the number) is standard two's complement notation with the sign bit in the most significant (MS) bit (bit 7) of the high order byte. The assumed binary point is between bits 6 and 5 of the same byte. In this representation, a properly normalized number will have a mantissa whose absolute value is between 1 and 2. A properly normalized number will have the most significant two bits unequal:

```
01.XXXXXX  positive mantissa (MS) byte
10.XXXXXX  negative mantissa (MS) byte
```

The programs documented here will build these numbers from Integer Basic numbers and call the floating point routines.

There are several parts to the floating point linkage routines you will have to understand in order to successfully use them. First I will discuss what memory locations are used, and then the several Basic subroutines that use them.

MEMORY
LOCATION

0    - This location will be incremented if an error occurs in the floating point routines (such as 2*127 * 2*127)
1    - This location will contain the floating point op code (operation).

OP
CODE        FIGURE 4

```
0 =FIX        R(B)   R(A)  →  R(C)
1 =FLOAT      R(B)   R(A)  →  R(C)
2 =ADD        R(B) + R(A)  →  R(C)
3 =SUBTRACT   R(B) - R(A)  →  R(C)
4 =MULTIPLY   R(B) * R(A)  →  R(C)
5 =DIVIDE     R(B) / R(A)  →  R(C)
6 =ABS VALUE  R(B)   R(A)  →  R(C)
7 =COMPLIMENT R(B) - R(A)  →  R(C)
8 =SWAP       R(B)   R(A)  →  R(C)
```

2,3     - These locations contain the address of the floating point array (i.e. REAL(127) or R(127))
4,5     - These locations contain the address of the first operands index (i.e., A)
6,7     - These locations contain the address of the second operands index (i.e., B)
8,9     - These locations contain the address of the results index (i.e., C)
A,1F    - These locations are used for scratch storage.
300-376 - These locations contain the machine language linkage programs.

In the description of the various program segments, I will proceed in a logical, rather than sequential, manner.

BASIC LINE   PURPOSE
400          - "Float": Store the value of "INT" into the Real array at location "A"

JMP Page 10

(from Page 9)

| | |
|---|---|
| 700-1500 | "Fix": Convert the value in the Real array at location "C" into its integer and fractional parts in "INT" and "FRAC" |
| 4500-4900 | Set up the pointer (memory 0-9) |
| 3800 | Calculate the address where the next variable defined will be stored. |
| 4300 | Poke an address into (memory 2-9) |
| 5100 | Build the floating point number 10000. (This is used in FIX and FLOAT) |
| 5300-5400 | Build the floating point number 12. (This is used in FIX) |
| 5700-5800 | Float (I) => Real (B). Note B=4 & C=4. |
| 6000-6100 | Float (J) => Real (A). Note A=0 & C=0. |
| 6400 | Real (B) (Op) Real (A) => Real (Q). |
| 6450 | SQRT (Real (Q)) => TEMP @ Real (240). |
| 450 | Print the floating value in INT and FRAC. |
| 205-260 | Calculate the square root of the number in Real (A). |

Since the program segment to calculate the square root is the least clear, I will try to delineate its operation. The derivation of the Newton iteration solution for square root is as follows:

### FIGURE 5

$$\sqrt{A} = C$$
$$A = C^2$$
$$C^2 - A = 0$$
$$IF\ C_N = ?$$
$$THEN\ C_{(N+1)} = \frac{C + (\frac{A}{C_N})}{2}$$

A flow chart outlining the square root segment is shown as figure 6 in column 2.

## WRITE —APPLE

Dear Val Golding

Below is an interesting sequence of instructions which reveals an interesting quirk in the video display. "(e)D" is used for escape D.

| OPERATION | RESULT |
|---|---|
| (e) @ | Clear screen |
| (e) C | |
| (e) C | Move cursor down |
| POKE 1024,225 | "!" appears in upper left corner. |
| POKE 1025,226 | '"' appears next to the "!" |
| POKE 1026,227 | "#" appears next |
| (e)D...(e)D (8 times) | |
| (e)B | Cursor should be over the "!" |
| | The '!"#' changes to "ABC" ! |
| GOTO Page 12 | |

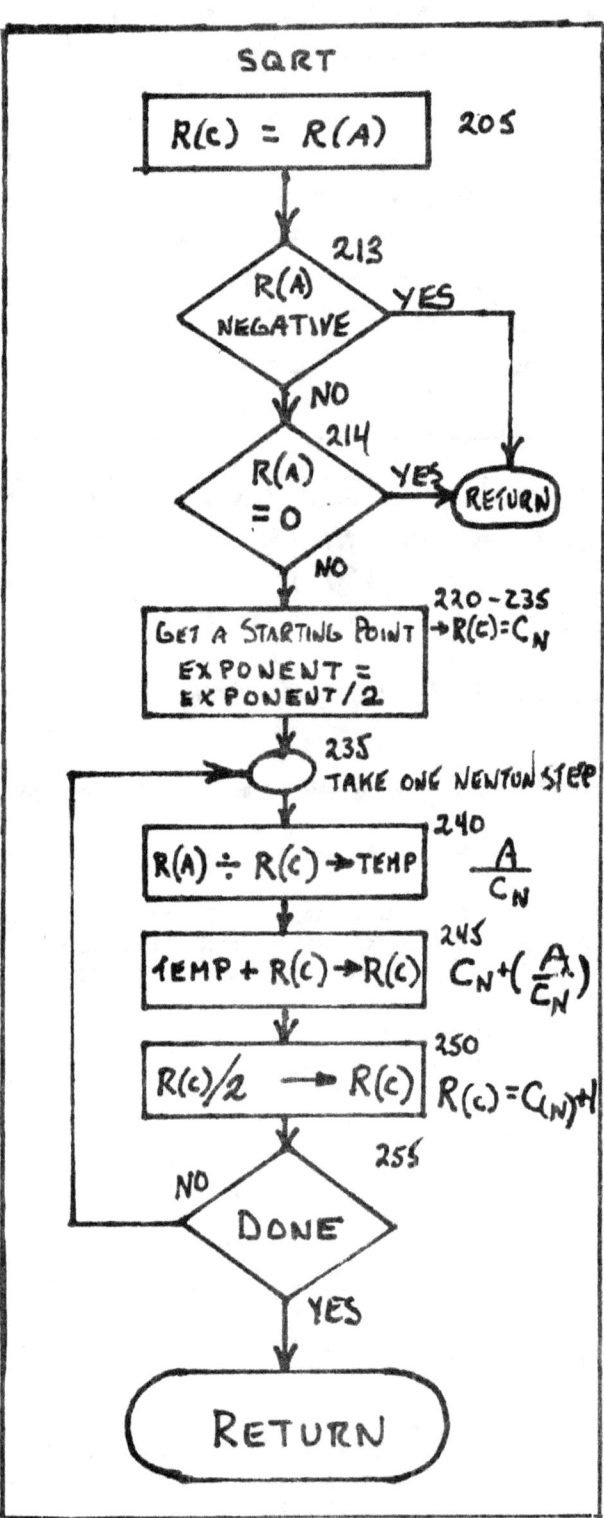

FIGURE 6

GOSUB Page 11

(from Page 10)

The "REAL" array can contain up to 64 floating point variables (The last three are used by FIX and FLOAT) indexes A,B & C represent bytes so that the first is 0, while the second is 4 and the I'th is (I-1)*4.  so the value of user indexes can range from 0-240 in steps of 4.

The machine language routines reside in Basic lines 7200 to 7500 and will be placed in memory by a small Basic routine in lines 3200-3600.  A GOSUB 7200 will place the program into memory, ready to use.

As for size and speed, the Basic program occupies 1193 bytes of memory and runs at the following rates:

## FIGURE 7

|  | TIME IN MILLISECS | | AVG #/SEC | INT. OPS/SEC |
|---|---|---|---|---|
|  | MIN | MAX |  |  |
| FIX | 5.7 | 5.8 | 174 | — |
| FLOAT | 4.7 | 4.7 | 213 | — |
| ADD | 5.1 | 17.9 | 87 | 500 |
| SUBTRACT | 5.3 | 17.9 | 86 | 500 |
| MULTIPLY | 7.1 | 7.3 | 139 | 400 |
| DIVIDE | 8.0 | 9.1 | 117 | 333 |
| ABS VALUE | 4.7 | 4.7 | 213 | — |
| COMPLIMENT | 4.7 | 4.7 | 213 | — |
| SWAP | 4.7 | 4.7 | 213 | — |

Even though these times are large in comparison with the equivalent integer operations, it should be remembered that Basic spends much more time keeping track of what it's doing than doing it.

```
 90 REM   "INTEGER BASIC FLOATING POI
         NT LINKAGE ROUTINES"

100 REM   WRITTEN BY DON WILLIAMS 2/7
         8
200 GOTO 4400
204 REM   REAL(C) = SQRT(REAL(A))
205 REAL(C/2)=REAL(A/2):REAL(C/
    2+1)=REAL(A/2+1)
210 TA=A:TB=B:TC=C
213 IF PEEK (RL+A+1)>127 THEN RETURN

214 IF REAL(A/2)=0 THEN RETURN

215 K= PEEK (RL+C)
220 IF K>128 THEN K=(K-128)/2+128

225 IF K<128 THEN K=128-(128-K)
    /2
230 POKE RL+C,K
235 FOR KK=1 TO 6
240 B=TA:A=TC:C=248: POKE 1,5: CALL
    790
245 B=248:C=TC: POKE 1,2: CALL
    790
250 POKE RL+C, PEEK (RL+C)-1
255 NEXT KK
260 A=TA:B=TB:C=TC: RETURN
300 REM   REAL(A) = FLOAT (INT)
400 REAL(A/2)=INT: POKE RL+A+2,
    PEEK (RL+A): POKE RL+A+3,0
    : RETURN
450 PRINT INT;: IF PEEK (36)>( PEEK
    (33)-6) THEN PRINT : PRINT
    FRAC+10000;:L= PEEK (36): TAB
    L-4: PRINT ".";: TAB L+3: RETURN

500 REM   INT = IFIX (REAL(C))
600 REM   FRAC = (REAL(C) - INT) * 10
    000
700 REAL(124)=REAL(C/2):REAL(125
    )=REAL(C/2+1):TA=A:TB=B:TC=
    C
800 B=C: POKE 1,0:A=C: CALL 790

900 POKE RL+C, PEEK (RL+C+2):INT=
    REAL(C/2): POKE RL+C+3,0: POKE
    1,1: CALL 790
1000 B=248: POKE 1,3: CALL 790
1100 B=252: POKE 1,4: CALL 790
1200 B=244: POKE 1,2: CALL 790
1300 POKE 1,0: CALL 790
1400 POKE RL+C, PEEK (RL+C+2):FRAC=
     REAL(C/2):A=TA:B=TB:C=TC
1500 IF FRAC>=0 THEN RETURN :FRAC=
     0:INT=-1: RETURN
1600 REM   SAVE MEMORY IN A STRING
1700 INPUT "STARTING ADDRESS ",IST
1800 INPUT "ENDING ADDRESS   ",IND
1900 INPUT "STATEMENT NUMBER ",STMT
2000 PRINT " ";STMT;" L = ";IST
2100 REM   (SL) ==> S$
2200 POKE SL,162
2300 K=1: FOR I=IST TO IND:N= PEEK
     (I):M=N/16:N=N-16*M
2400 IF M>9 THEN M=M+7:M=M+176
2500 IF N>9 THEN N=N+7:N=N+176
2600 POKE SL+K,M: POKE SL+K+1,N
2700 K=K+2: IF K<100 THEN 3000
2800 GOSUB 3100
2900 K=1
3000 NEXT I
```

JSR Page 12

(from Page 11)

```
3100 POKE SL+K,162: POKE SL+K+1,
     0:STMT=STMT+10: PRINT " ";STMT;
     " S$= ";S$;" :GOSUB 330": RETURN

3200 REM   SUBROUTINE TO STORE THE HE
     X DATA IN STRING S$ INTO MEMORY
     AT LOCATON L
3300 FOR I=1 TO LEN(S$) STEP 2
3400 J= ASC(S$(I))-176: IF J>9 THEN
     J=J-7
3500 K= ASC(S$(I+1))-176: IF K>9
     THEN K=K-7
3600 POKE L,J*16+K:L=L+1: NEXT I:
     RETURN
3800 L= PEEK (204)+ PEEK (205)*256
     +3+ LEN(V$): RETURN
4300 GOSUB 3800: POKE IA,L MOD 256
     : POKE IA+1,L/256: RETURN
4400 DIM V$(10):V$="S$": GOSUB 3800
     : DIM S$(255):SL=L: GOSUB 7200
4500 REM   DEFINE THE F.P. POINTERS
4600 V$="REAL":IA=2: GOSUB 4300:
     DIM REAL(127):RL=L: POKE 0
     ,0
4700 V$="A":IA=4: GOSUB 4300:A=0
4800 V$="B":IA=6: GOSUB 4300:B=4
4900 V$="C":IA=8: GOSUB 4300:C=8
5000 REM   REAL(126,127) = 10000.
5100 INT=10000: GOSUB 400:C=252:
     POKE 1,1: CALL 790
5200 REM   REAL(122,123) = 1./2.
5300 INT=5000: GOSUB 400:C=244: POKE
     1,1: CALL 790
5400 B=244:A=252: POKE 1,5: CALL
     790
5500 B=4:A=0
5600 FOR I=1 TO 10
5650 REM   FLOAT I==> REAL(1)
5700 INT=I: GOSUB 400
5800 C=4: POKE 1,1: CALL 790
5900 FOR J=1 TO 10
5950 REM   FLOAT J==> REAL(0)
6000 INT=J: GOSUB 400
6100 C=0: POKE 1,1: CALL 790
6200 PRINT I;"@";J;"=",
6300 FOR Q=2 TO 7
6350 REM   R(4) (+) R(0) ==> R(Q)
6400 C=(Q+1)*4: POKE 1,Q: CALL 790
6425 REM   SQRT(R(Q)) ==> TEMP
6450 A=C:C=240: GOSUB 205:C=A
6500 GOSUB 700: GOSUB 450
6550 C=240: GOSUB 700: GOSUB 450

6600 A=0: NEXT Q: PRINT
6700 NEXT J
6800 IF PEEK (-16384)<128 THEN 6800

6900 POKE -16368,0
7000 NEXT I
7100 END
7200 L=768: REM    300-376   FLOATING
     POINT LINKAGE ROUTINE
7300 S$="186502850AA5036900850B60A003
     B10A910C8810F960A0F4B90000991CFF
     C8D0F7EAEAEAA2F4860C840DB1062000
     03200C03": GOSUB 3300
7400 S$="A9F8850CA000B104200003200C03
     206003A000B108200003A003B10C910A
     8810F9A0F4B91CFF990000C8D0F760EA
     A9F6A401": GOSUB 3300
7500 S$="F002A9F448B96E0348603F506D67
     8BB131A340": GOSUB 3300: RETURN
```

(from Page 10)

So here we see that the video does not interpret lower case letters as upper case, but that the I/O routine actually converts them to upper case. The video actually misinterprets the lower case letters as special characters and numbers.

Note that ASC ("a")=225 (Base 10)
and      ASC ("b")=226
and      ASC ("c")=227.

Dan Chapman
18346 Corliss Avenue N.
Seattle, Wa. 98133

GOTO Page 14

## BACK ISSUES

July and August are the only back issues currently available. We will reprint May and June in the near future. To order, please indicate by month the back issues desired. Members who have paid 1979 dues only, please include $1.00 per copy. Others include $1.00 total for postage and handling. Address labels would be helpful if you have them.

## INTEGRAL DATA IP 125-225 DRIVER

If you own an Integral Data printer, you may be interested in these minor modifications to the Apple Red Manual teletype routine. The modifications are slight, changing only the window width and baud rate and adding a small delay loop to prevent printer buffer overflow, plus a turn off routine that restores window width to 40 columns. It loads from $0360 to $03E9 and is called from Basic with CALL 874, or from Monitor with $36BG. The Basic turn off call is 864. Window width is set at location $374, delay at $380 and baud rate at $3D4. It performs beautifully for us, running off a 20 mil current loop built on an Apple hobby board, taking data from the paddle output. Here's the disassembled listing

```
0360-   A9 F0       LDA   #$F0
0362-   85 36       STA   $36
0364-   A9 FD       LDA   #$FD
0366-   85 37       STA   $37
0368-   4C 39 FB    JMP   $FB39
036B-   A9 7D       LDA   #$7D
036D-   85 36       STA   $36
036F-   A9 03       LDA   #$03
0371-   85 37       STA   $37
0373-   A9 84       LDA   #$84
0375-   85 21       STA   $21
0377-   A5 24       LDA   $24
0379-   8D F8 07    STA   $07F8
037C-   60          RTS
037D-   48          PHA
037E-   48          PHA
037F-   A9 48       LDA   #$48
0381-   20 A8 FC    JSR   $FCA8
0384-   AD F8 07    LDA   $07F8
0387-   C5 24       CMP   $24
0389-   68          PLA
038A-   B0 03       BCS   $038F
038C-   48          PHA
038D-   A9 A0       LDA   #$A0
038F-   2C C0 03    BIT   $03C0
0392-   F0 03       BEQ   $0397
0394-   EE F8 07    INC   $07F8
0397-   20 C1 03    JSR   $03C1
039A-   68          PLA
039B-   48          PHA
039C-   90 E6       BCC   $0384
039E-   49 0D       EOR   #$0D
03A0-   0A          ASL
03A1-   D0 0D       BNE   $03B0
03A3-   8D F8 07    STA   $07F8
03A6-   A9 8A       LDA   #$8A
03A8-   20 C1 03    JSR   $03C1
03AB-   A9 58       LDA   #$58
03AD-   20 A8 FC    JSR   $FCA8
03B0-   AD F8 07    LDA   $07F8
03B3-   F0 08       BEQ   $03BD
03B5-   E5 21       SBC   $21
03B7-   E9 F7       SBC   #$F7
03B9-   90 04       BCC   $03BF
03BB-   69 1F       ADC   #$1F
03BD-   85 24       STA   $24
03BF-   68          PLA
03C0-   60          RTS
03C1-   8C 78 07    STY   $0778
03C4-   08          PHP
03C5-   A0 0B       LDY   #$0B
03C7-   18          CLC
03C8-   48          PHA
03C9-   B0 05       BCS   $03D0
03CB-   AD 59 C0    LDA   $C059
03CE-   90 03       BCC   $03D3
03D0-   AD 58 C0    LDA   $C058
03D3-   A9 14       LDA   #$14
03D5-   48          PHA
03D6-   A9 20       LDA   #$20
03D8-   4A          LSR
03D9-   90 FD       BCC   $03D8
03DB-   68          PLA
03DC-   E9 01       SBC   #$01
03DE-   D0 F5       BNE   $03D5
03E0-   68          PLA
03E1-   6A          ROR
03E2-   88          DEY
03E3-   D0 E3       BNE   $03C8
03E5-   AC 78 07    LDY   $0778
03E8-   28          PLP
03E9-   60          RTS
```

## RETURN to TEXT from GRAPHICS

by Alan G. Hill

Here is a short routine that may come in handy if working on graphics programs when you need to frequently return to text mode to correct lines. Normally, you must hit control C, return, text and call -936 or escape @. This will permit you to hit reset, control Y and return. To load this routine, go to monitor and call the mini-assembler (F666G), and enter the following:

```
03F8:  JMP  $0300   ;Go to Control Y routine
0300:  JSR  $FC58   ;Clear scrn, home cursor
       PLA           ;Pop return adr off stack
       PLA
       JMP  $E003   ;Back to Basic
```

## PRINTER DRIVER FIXES

by Bob Huelsdonk

Some protocol is a must if you use a printer with > 40 columns with your Apple. This comes about because it tries to write beyond the screen area and into the variables area in Integer Basic or into the operating system in Applesoft. The following will help prevent problems:

Start your printer driver routine with a JSR FC58. This will home the cursor and clear the screen. Do not return to the screen via FDF0. You will not get any output to the CRT but this is usually O.K. Unless you have the ROM version of Applesoft, there is also a problem using a PR#0. To solve this, use the routine given below to re-enter the CRT output with a call to 1008, if you load it at the address shown. This also resets the window width to 40 characters. For driver routines that are located in memory between $0300 and $03FF, there is also a conflict with the disk operating system, which will not permit you to directly call the printer. However, this can be overcome in most cases by addressing the printer under program control. In printing a program listing, a line must be added to the program as follows:

```
10 CALL 880 : LIST 100,900 : CALL 1008 : END
   03F0-   A9 F0      LDA     #$F0
   03F2-   85 36      STA     $36
   03F4-   A9 FD      LDA     #$FD
   03F6-   85 37      STA     $37
   03F8-   A9 28      LDA     #$28
   03FA-   85 21      STA     $21
   03FC-   60         RTS
```

DON'T CALL APPLE, CALL -APPLE !

As we have mentioned in the past, we have received only the greatest support in the world from Apple Computer, Inc. There was a time when Apple owners were a very small minority among personal computer users. Not so now, when Apple is outselling all others. We imagine that in that dim distant past, Phil or Woz or Randy probably enjoyed an occasional phone call from a user. Presently, however, we suspect that those good people may be rather plagued by calls. After all, they certainly are expected to do some programming or whatever. Anyway, what we are obtusely pointing to is before you call Apple, call -Apple, or talk to your area dealer. There are now Apple user groups in many parts of the country, and most all we know usually talk to Apple frequently. So why not first route your calls to the clubs or dealers. Many problems and questions we feel can be resolved at the local level. The Call -Apple "Hot Line" is (206) 932-6588. Try it, you'll like it!

## CLASSIFIED ADS

Members rate .05/word for non commercial ads.
Commercial rate .10/word- $3.00 Minimum

FOR SALE  The Apple Box mini-modem for your cassette I/O port. With this modem you can trade programs with your friends from the comfort of your own computer room. $18.50 with documentation; $23.50 with monitor speaker. From Apple, 6708 39th Avenue SW, Seattle, Wa. 98136. (206) 932-6588.

WANTED  Commercial advertisers. Full page $12.50; Half page $9.00. Same size camera ready copy only; no halftones. Maximum size, 7-1/2 X 10. Call -Apple, (206) 932-6588.

MICRO-PSYCH  bi-monthly newsletter for professionals interested in computers in mental health. $10./year.  Mark Schwartz, M.D., Box A, 26 Trumbull St., New Haven CT. 06511

## WRITE -APPLE (from Page 12)

Dear Mr. Goldins:

Referring to Call -Apple, Vol. I, No. 5, (June), try this subroutine which I use daily:

```
10 IF RD < .005 THEN RD$ = "0.00":RETURN
20 RD = INT(RD*100 + .5)100:RD$ = STR$(RD = .005):
   RD$ = LEFT$(RD$,LEN(RD$)-1):RETURN
```

In main program use:

XXX RD = X:GOSUB 10:X$ = RD$

This works for positive values of X to 9 digits.

If X can be + or -, then a slower routine is:

```
10 IF ABS(RD) < .005 THEN RD$ = "0.00":RETURN
20 RD = SGN(RD)*INT(ABS(RD)*100+.5)100:
   RD$=STR$(SGN(RD)*ABS(RD)+.005)):
   RD$ =LEFT$(RD$,LEN(RD$)-1):RETURN
```

I hope this may be of some value.

Wilbur C. Andrews
5212 Inglewood La.
Raleigh, NC 27609

# ComputerLand™

## **\*RAM\*RAM\*RAM\***

16 k RAM, MOTOROLA, NOW $195.00
set of eight 16kx1bit, ship 'A'

## **\*RAM\*RAM\*RAM\***

### SOFTWARE DEPT.

APPLE COMPUTER CO. SOFTWARE
1. Checkbook Cassette           $20.00
2. Startrek/Starwars            $15.00
3. Color Demo/Breakout          $ 7.50
4. Applesoft II/F.P.Demo w/mnl  $20.00
5. HiRes Graphics/HiRes Shapes  $ 7.50
6. RAM Test Cassette            $ 7.50
7. Color Math Demo/Hangman      $ 7.50
8. Blackjack/Slot Machine       $ 7.50
9. Biorhythm/Mastermind         $ 7.50
10. Apple II Capabilities Demo  $20.00
11. Finance I,(4 program set)   $25.00
12. Datamover/Telepong          $ 7.50

THE MICROMEDIA LIBRARY OF PROGRAMS,
see last months issue for some of
the discriptions of a few of them.

THE SPEAKEASY SOFTWARE LIBRARY
1. Warlords, a high level war game.
2. Bulls & Bears, the stock market.
3. Microtrivia, a party tape game.
4. Kidstuff, great for 6-12 years.

---

☐ VISA/BAC     ☐ M/C     Expiration date: _____

Card #: _____

Signature: _____

Name (Print): _____

Address: _____

City: _____ State: _____ Zip: _____

Add handling and shipping charges as per schedule. Shipped by UPS unless specified otherwise. Delivery is stock on most items. No delay in shipment for payment by cashier's check, money order or charge cards. Allow three weeks for personal checks to clear. Washington state residents ad 5.4% sales tax. Availability, prices and specs may change without notice.

---

PRINTERS, PRINTERS, AND PRINTERS!
We've done it! The Trendata is running off our Apple II. The Trendata 1000 terminal printer, is now available for only $995. The interface and software $95. This is a $3700. printer that's two years old, rebuilt, has a 30 day warrentee with it and can be used as a regular IBM Selectric typewriter too. Ship 'F', schdle
In Stock!! 2 IP125's w/printer, option, ship 'D'. Price $838.00
INTERFACE for IP125, stock $95.
Decwriter II, LA36, shp 'F' $1595.00
INTERFACE for Apple II    $180.00
AXIOM EX-820 Microplotter $795.
AXIOM EX-801-s, Printer   $495.
   Interfacing available, ship 'C'.
T.I. PRINTER, 743         $1395.00
   Interface available, ship 'D'

**\*\*\*\*\* CLOSEOUTS \*\*\*\*\***
MAKING ROOM FOR MORE APPLE II's
CHESS CHALLENGER, reg.    $199.00
   4 left, ship 'B' now   $125.00
COMPUTER BACKGAMMON, reg. $200.00
   2 left, ship 'B'   now $110.00
Video Brain, Computer,    $495.00
   2 left, ship 'B'   now $425.00
Video Brain Cartridges, 25% off
   10 assorted, ship 'A', now $15.00
   Math, $22.50, HomeMgt., $29.50
FAIRCHILD Game Cartridges, &prie
   16 asst.1,2,3,4,5,7&12  $9.98
ATARI Game Cartridges,
   Indy 500, 2 only,   now, $27.50
   Video Olympics, 1 only, $12.50
Ship both 'A', add 50¢ ea. extra
**\*\*\*\*\*\*\*\*\*\*\*\*\*\*\*\*\*\*\*\*\*\*\*\*\*\*\*\*\*\*\***

**SHIPPING SCHEDULE** — Add as per specified, handling & shipping charges.

| | |
|---|---|
| A. | $2.00 |
| B. | 4.00 |
| C. | 10.00 |
| D. | 20.00 |
| E. | 30.00 |
| F. | 40.00 |

## ComputerLand™

1500 South 336th St. • Parkway Center, Suite 12 • Federal Way, Washington 98003
Tacoma (206) 927-8585 • Seattle (206) 838-9363

CALL –APPLE
616 SOUTHWEST 152nd
SEATTLE, WASHINGTON 98166
(206) 244-5200

SEPTEMBER, 1978

PAGE 16

890 Southcenter Shopping Center
Tukwila, Washington 98188
206-246-6120

*Empire* ELECTRONICS, INC.

# COMPUTER SHOP

MEMOREX MINI DISCETTES  $ 3.80 ea.

# 16K RAM CHIPS
# $218.00 /SET

```
INTEGRAL DATA   IP-225 PRINTER ************  $ 949.00
                With GRAPHICS  ************  $1148.00
EXPANDER BLACK BOX           ****************  $ 425.00
APPLE AC CONTROLLER / REMOTE ************  $ 329.00
SOFTWARE: DATABASE, APPLEDITOR, VENDOR **  $  30.00
          SAVINGS, LOANS, LEASES ********  $   7.50
          GAMEPACK I and II    ************  $   5.00
DOW JONES PACKAGE            ****************  $  25.00
```

JOYSTIKS $8.50

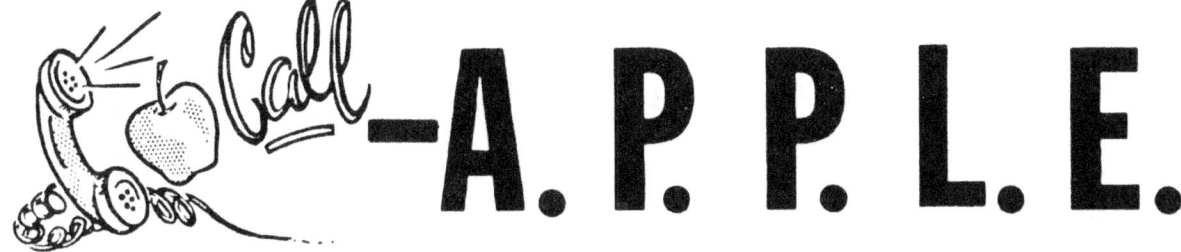

# APPLE PUGETSOUND PROGRAM LIBRARY EXCHANGE

OCTOBER, 1978  $1.00  Vol. 1, No. 9
6708 39th Avenue SW   Seattle, Washington 98136   (206) 932-6588

## BYTES from the APPLE
Software Stuff, etc., etc., etc., etc., etc., etc., et

by   Val J. Golding

Some of the news this month is no news. We had hoped at this time to be able to announce Library Pak 3, but it is still unfinished at this writing. We will go out on a limb and say that we will fill orders commencing October 20th or so. Library Pak 4 will follow close on its heels, but again we ask that you do not order until it is announced. Price will be $5.00, which we intend to hold to for all regular Library Paks. We regret at this time that we can not fully list the contents; they are still not firm. But there will be some utility programs. Library Pak 4 will contain a few business oriented programs.

You can anticipate our announcement in the November Call -Apple of a package designed especially for Integral Data printer owners. It will include a serial driver, a Hires screen dump routine, a printer oriented maze, the mini editor we use on this magazine, and other goodies, and will be priced at $7.50. The Integral Data's graphics capability is demonstrated elsewhere in this issue.

We would like to welcome Dick Hubert to the staff of both the magazine and the club. In the two short weeks that Dick has been helping us, he has already demonstrated his abilities to relieve us from some of the workload. To Dick we say thanks (though you may regret it later!) Thanks are also in order for Randy Wigginton of Apple Computer, Inc., who not only braved the unexplored great northwest to appear at our September meeting, but also brought with him a friend who turned out to be Mike Scott, the president of Apple. The meeting was extremely well attended by 76 of our approximately 70 local members, and Mike and Randy fielded many interesting questions from the audience, many of which will be published in Call -Apple. In addition, Randy presented

GOTO PAGE 4

Val J. Golding, President            (206) 932-6588
Michael Thyng, Secretary             (206) 524-2744
Dick Hubert, Administrative Asst.    (206) 255-7410
Darrell Aldrich, Program Editor
Ron Aldrich, Asst. Prgm. Editor      (206) 782-7082
Bob Huelsdonk, Technical Consultant, Basic    (206) 362-4910
Don Williams, Technical Consultant, Assembly  (206) 242-6807
Steve Paulson, Circulation           (206) 242-2700

## OCTOBER MEETING
7:00 PM     TUESDAY,    OCTOBER 17, 1978
Omega Stereo     5420 176th SW     LYNWOOD

## NOVEMBER MEETING
7:00 PM     Tuesday,    November 21, 1978
Computerland     1500 South 336th Street,     Federal Way

## IN THIS ISSUE . . .                       Page

Bytes from the Apple........................... 1
Applesoft Tone Subroutines..................... 3
6502 Program Exchange.......................... 3
A Brief History of Apple....................... 4
Sample Disk File Handler....................... 6
Write -Apple (letters).......................... 7
Minutes of the September meeting............... 8
Mystery Program Contest........................ 9
Wiz Wiz Contest................................ 9
Apple Software Bank............................ 9
Applemash(ed).................................. 11
Editing in Integer and Applesoft............... 11
& Now, the Ampersand........................... 11
Modifying Programmer's Workshop................ 12
DOS Patches.................................... 12
Apple Documentation Package (the WOZpak)....... 12
Integer Basic Token Chart...................... 13
Applesoft II Basic Token Chart................. 14

# Empire ELECTRONICS, INC.

## COMPUTER SHOP

MEMOREX MINI DISCETTES    $ 3.60 ea.

# 16K RAM CHIPS
## $210

**NOW IN STOCK: GUARANTEED CHIPS**
**NOW ONLY $174.95/SET!**

```
INTEGRAL DATA   IP-225 PRINTER  ************ $  949.00
                With GRAPHICS   ************ $ 1148.00

EXPANDER BLACK BOX              ************************ $  425.00

APPLE AC CONTROLLER / REMOTE    ************ $  329.00

SOFTWARE: DATABASE, APPLEDITOR, VENDOR **  $  30.00 EA.

          SAVINGS, LOANS, LEASES *******  $   7.50 EA.

          GAMEPACK I and II  ************ $   5.00 EA.

DOW JONES PACKAGE  ********************** $  25.00
```

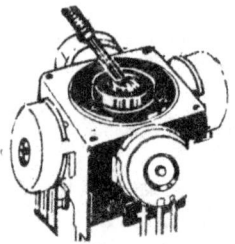

JOYSTIKS $8.50

890 Southcenter Shopping Center
Tukwila, Washington 98188
206-246-6120

616 SOUTHWEST 152nd
SEATTLE, WASHINGTON 98166
(206) 244-5200

## APPLESOFT TONE SUBROUTINES

by John D. Cook

The handy tone subroutines from the the red Apple II Reference Manual are a nice addition to many programs. Unfortunately, they won't run in Applesoft Basic. As listed in the manual, they are in the wrong place in memory. They will work, however, if relocated as listed below:

MACHINE LANGUAGE PROGRAM

```
0308-   FF                  ???
0309-   FF                  ???
030A-   AD 30 C0    LDA     $C030
030D-   88          DEY
030E-   D0 05       BNE     $0315
0310-   CE 09 03    DEC     $0309
0313-   F0 09       BEQ     $031E
0315-   CA          DEX
0316-   D0 F5       BNE     $030D
0318-   AE 08 03    LDX     $0308
031B-   4C 0A 03    JMP     $030A
031E-   60          RTS
```

```
31000 REM    BASIC "POKES"

32000 POKE 776,255: POKE 777,255:
      POKE 778,173: POKE 779,48:
      POKE 780,192: POKE 781,136
      : POKE 782,208: POKE 783,5:
      POKE 784,206: POKE 785,9: POKE
      786,3: POKE 787,240
32010 POKE 788,9: POKE 789,202: POKE
      790,208: POKE 791,245: POKE
      792,174: POKE 793,8: POKE 794
      ,3: POKE 795,76: POKE 796,10
      : POKE 797,3: POKE 798,96: RETURN

32100 REM    GOSUB

  25 POKE 776,P: POKE 777,D: CALL
     778: RETURN : REM  SET PITCH & D
     URATION

32767 REM  GOSUB 32000 ONCE AT BEGINNI
      NG OF PROGRAM THEN GOSUB 25 ANYW
      HERE IN PROGRAM
```

## 6502 PROGRAM EXCHANGE

Apple II users can now run an extended version of the high-level language FOCAL* (*DEC trademark). FCL65E is now available in Apple II cassette form for $25 from the 6502 Program Exchange, 2920 Moana, Reno, Nv, 89509. Manuals and sorce listings are also available at additional cost. Programs in FOCAL for Apple are also available.

Apple PASCAL is under development in southern California and a few copies have been released for sale. When details are available, you will read about it in Call-Apple. Rumors are also rampant about an Apple version of FORTH. If anyone can supply information about this, we would be greatful.

"ALAS, POOR BASIC, I KNEW IT WELL!"

THE PICTURE OF SHAKESPEARE, ABOVE, IS FROM THE APPLE SOFTWARE BANK, AND WAS PRINTED ON THE INTEGRAL DATA PRINTER.

Sept. Call-Apple, Page 7, add line 175 as follows, and this routine will also work with disk on:

175 POKE 72,0

## BYTES from the APPLE    from Page 1

us with a number of programs, which will be made available to the membership in various forms, and last but most definitely not least, a documentation package well over 200 pages in length, containing much valuable Apple information. See the article elsewhere in this issue that describes the package and how to obtain it. Other user groups, please make note of our special offer to make this available to you at no cost to you or your club.

Another feature implemented in this issue is contests. We are not going to guarantee there will be one every month, but we will start out with two for this month, one of which will be a contest to create a contest! If the other one appears to be too easy for you, leave it for some of the less experienced members. Prizes will be awarded winners.

Finally, we want to thank Bruce Tognazzini of the San Francisco Apple Core and Dave Gordon of the Long Beach group for furnishing us with myriads of programs, many of which you will see in the form of future Library Paks. For those of you who don't know Dave, he is no doubt the country's (or the world's) greatest Apple software collector, with his own collection of programs numbering in the hundreds. What a boon the advent of the disk must have been to him.

## TOKENS, TOKENS, my COMPUTER for a TOKEN...

By popular request (and to fill space) we are reprinting the Integer and Applesoft token charts from the May and June issues of Call -Apple. These should be saved as permanent references, and in time you will find them of considerable value to you. They may be found on pages 13 and 14.

## SOME BASIC ENTRY POINTS

```
LIST    JSR  $E04B     CALL -8117

RUN     JSR  $EFEC     CALL -4116

RUN*    JSR  $E836     CALL -6090

SAVE    JSR  $F140     CALL -3776

LOAD    JSR  $F0DF     CALL -3873

  * = VARIABLES NOT DELETED
```

## A BRIEF HISTORY of APPLE

by Michael M. Scott, President

Presented at the September 12, 1978 meeting of A.P.P.L.E

Apple was started two and a half years ago by two gentlemen, Steve Jobs and Steve Wozniak who met at the "home brew" computer club at the Stanford accelerator. There, they got together and put into manufacture the Apple 1, which was a single-board, black and white -basically a fancy monitor- that worked with a TV set. A year later, they were joined by three other gentlemen, that's myself (Mike Scott), Mike Markulla and Rod Holte, and formed Apple Computer, inc. and went about the business of making the Apple II.

To give a little background on the five of us: Jobs is from Atari and, in fact, was the inventor of the "breakout" game that you see around a lot. Wozniak was in the advanced calculator group at H-P, and tried to interest H-P in doing a home computer, but they weren't interested, so he started working in his garage. Rod Holt was previously with Hickock as head of engineering and more recently at Atari and he did Apple's switching power supply and does the analog circuits and the rest of the support engineering.

Mike Markulla was originally with Hughes aircraft and most recently had been with Intel as head of marketing and had been retired from there about a year and a half when he came to us, and I most recently was director of hybrids and transducers at National Semiconductor. So we have a mixed crew and have expanded on it.

So we had five. February, a year and a half ago, we introduced the Apple II at the first West Coast Computer Faire on April 5th, 1977. We shipped the first Apple II last June -sorry- June a year ago. This last June was out first million dollar sales month, and where we thought business was excellent and getting better, in the last three or four months it's improved even further.

The company has sought and obtained outside financing. We have a very small percentage of the company; the stock has been sold to private firms or individuals. In particular, we did this to establish more credence with banks and other people that we could obtain financing from, and also to obtain outside advice on how not to get into trouble. The principal outside contributors are: Benrock, which is part of the Rockefeller Foundation. They're the country's oldest capital venture firm. The other group is Capital Management, and they were the firm that originally financed Atari and arranged for the Warner buy-out of Atari And Capital now owns ten percent of Warner.

We have a couple of private gentlemen; one is Art Brock who is known in the San Francisco area for his financing of such companies as Intel, Intercil, Fairchild and Quantel. It's not been made public yet, but joining our board as of a week and a half ago is an Apple freak who has one of the earliest Apples, with one at his home and one at his office. His name is Henry Singleton. He does not sit on any outside boards, but has given us the honor of joining Apple's Board of Directors. For those who don't know, eighteen years ago, with fifteen hundred dollars cash, he started a little company called Teledyne, Inc., and he is still Chairman of the Board, partially retired, the head of a 2.5 billion-dollar-a-year company. He doesn't program in Basic or any of the other languages; he programs in machine language only. He's one of the five people we know who uses the internal floating point package to do financial analyses on the Apple. That's what he does at work for relaxation. And now he's working on a chess program which finds any three moves in a little less than a second right now. So we're looking forward to his participation and advice.

The company grew then, from the original five people, we currently, as of the last count, have 74 direct employees at the main Cupertino plant. We have 340 authorized stores right now and are sold internationally in almost every single country in the world, including throughout Europe, South America and the far east. International sales represent about 25% of our sales right now. We have indirectly working for Apple Computer then, about another 100 people through sub contractors. We specialize at the main plant; what we do is buy all the material. We then kit it, like Heathkit. We kit it out to sub-contractors who do the actual assembly of the PC board, and the insertion and the soldering. Then it returns to Apple where we do a board level test, a 24 hour burn in, and a final systems test.

So we try to keep down the amount of square footage that we need for expansion. One and a half years ago, we had 800 square feet. In the next six months we picked up another 3000. Last February, only six months ago, we swore it was enough space for 18 months when we moved into our new facility that was 21,000 square feet. A month ago we picked up another 5000, and we are next week picking up another 40,000 right in the same area. And that's keeping down what we do in the plant.

What we have inside now in the way of groups, is in the marketing group. We now have a fairly complex marketing group. We have an applications engineer full time in marketing; we're adding one to the engineering group to answer questions. We still encourage the local clubs or the local dealers to filter it, or that the questions that come in, come in in writing, so we can combine them and put them out in the Contact newsletter. We have hired a full time service manager who will set up a separate service department.

We have hired a full time publications group which consists of eleven people, partially made up of five text editors, and we still have not been able to keep up with the rate at which we need to document to put out a good manual. I'll give you two examples: one is the disk manual, which is atrocious, and we hope to have a revision in a couple of months, but it takes time to do it, and do it right. Applesoft II: hopefully the final revision is in print; this is a shrunk version, and it will be the same size as the Basic programming manual. It is not tutorial, but it goes exactly into the syntax of how the current released version of Applesoft II works.

Separate from the publications department, we have an inside group of ten people doing programming that's working on dedicated, user-related (DowJones types) and other types. Besides the user-contributor group, we now have under contract five different outside groups doing software packages for us. We will in the future introduce packages for small business that will be Apple supported as opposed to user-supported, where we say "you can have copies, but don't call us if there's a bug".

We're also looking at having an educational package. We have a well-known educational group doing some languages that are used for the high schools and colleges in teaching, to go on the Apple. Within the last three or four weeks we have added -he's not officially on our board till the 25th- a gentleman named Lloyd Martin from H-P who will head our applications software group. He, for your information, is the one that has headed the development software group at HP and done the applications package for the HP-45 series of programmable calculators.

We've added two additional gentlemen inside Apple, one is Bill Thomas, who is starting the 18th. Bill is one of the original founders of Four-Phase. Did their software for their systems; did their Cobol compiler. He's joining us as manager of our systems software group. The other gentleman was head of the design team at Motorola on the 6800 microprocessor; he did the 6502 design at Mostech, and is the architect of the patent. That's Chuck Pettle, and Chuck joined us yesterday from Commodore.

I'd say as a company a lot of people said "well, are you going to bring out a different product each year?". I think we've already shown that we don't have that intention. We certainly over the next couple of years will introduce other mainframe products. We think of the Apple II as being useful to the user for five to ten years and plan to continue supporting it with additional periferals and expanding the software that will run on the system. The more recent periferals out include the disk, which nobody can get enough of. This illustrates a problem we have; we have established a user base, so whenever we announce <a new product> we are immediately sold out for 8 to 12 weeks. A short example: we announced the communications card and put 500 in stock because marketing said that would be enough, and we sold out in two weeks, then we started the production cycle again.

The Applesoft ROM card: we made an initial pre-production run of 2500, and also sold those out in less than two weeks. The disk we knew we were going to be in trouble on. We are the largest supplier of mini-drives in the world now, because we do business with Shugart, who makes 90% of the drives. We're their largest customer now and have been for four months. So those who haven't got theirs yet, be patient; current lead time is about 6 to 8 weeks on new orders. Those stores who had early orders in were supplied first on the disk drive.

There are newer periferals coming; a high speed serial card is in manufacturing and should be ready in 4 to 5 weeks. As soon as the manual is ready -since the manual is most of it- we will announce what we call the "Programmer's Aid" Rom, which is in stock now except for the manual, which will be ready in about four weeks. It plugs into slot B0 on the main Apple board and gives such things as <Gary> Shannon's tone routines in firmware, hires routines in firmware, a tape verify routine and some other utility routines that are crammed on that 2K of code. We're interested in your input. You will be receiving in the mail, those of you who have your warranty cards in in the next couple of months, a questionaire to help us decide on what new periferals, or new software, or what new generation products we should look at, and we'd appreciate your inputs on it. For those of you who know people who don't have their warranty cards in, please encourage them to fill one out and send it in. That is how we key the mailing of the Contact users group and any updates that we have.

## SAMPLE FILE HANDLER

Here is a short and sweet program by Bob Huelsdonk that demonstrates (and will establish) files for data handling, using the DOS.

```
8  REM    BOB HUELSDONK
9  REM    9/12/78
10 REM * SAMPLE FILE HANDLER *
11 D$ = "": REM  CTL D IN QUOTES
12 GOTO 20
13 REM   REMOVE LINE 12 AFTER RUN
         NING ONCE
14 PRINT D$;"NOMON I,O,C"
20 GOTO 500
30 REM *** UNLOCK FILE ***
32 PRINT D$;"UNLOCK";FI$
34 RETURN
40 REM *** OPEN FILE ***
42 PRINT D$;"OPEN";FI$;",L100"
44 RETURN
50 REM *** READ FILE ***
52 PRINT D$;"READ";FI$;",R";R1
54 INPUT A,A$,B$
56 PRINT D$
58 RETURN
70 REM *** WRITE FILE ***
72 PRINT D$;"WRITE";FI$;",R";R1
74 PRINT P: PRINT C$: PRINT E$
76 PRINT D$
78 RETURN
90 REM *** CLOSE FILE ***
92 PRINT D$;"CLOSE"
94 PRINT D$;"LOCK";FI$
96 RETURN
500 REM *** INPUT DATA ***
510 HOME : PRINT : PRINT "DATA INPUT"
515 PRINT : INPUT "WHAT FILE NAME? ";FI$
520 R1 = 0
530 INPUT "A NUMBER (-99 TO READ BACK)";P
535 IF P = - 99 THEN 585
540 INPUT "A PHRASE";C$
550 INPUT "ANOTHER PHRASE";E$
560 GOSUB 40: REM   OPEN
570 GOSUB 70: REM   WRITE
580 R1 = R1 + 1: GOTO 530
585 GOSUB 70
590 GOSUB 90
600 REM *** READ BACK ***
610 HOME
620 PRINT : INPUT "DO YOU WISH TO READ THE FILE NOW? ";Q$
630 IF  LEFT$ (Q$,1) < > "Y" THEN 1000
640 GOSUB 40
645 R1 = 0
650 GOSUB 50
655 IF A = - 99 THEN 1000
660 PRINT A: PRINT A$: PRINT B$
670 R1 = R1 + 1: GOTO 650
1000 REM *** QUIT ***
1010 GOSUB 90
1015 PRINT D$;"MON I,O,C"
1020      END
```

### Write -Apple

September's editorial stirred up some interesting responses to Ted Oom's letter concerning the technical level of articles in Call -Apple, some of which are reprinted here. It is our opinion, after reading them, that we should not reduce the level of our article. However, it is also plain that in order to serve our readers best interests, we must also include more articles designed to explain some of the inner workings of the Apple's various routines for beginners, and this we shall do.
Read on...

Dear Val:

I have two responses to the letter from Ted Oom which you printed in your editorial. The first is personal; I have also felt the feelings of frustration with technical articles I could not understand. (That includes much of what is in the red Apple II Reference Manual.) However, I have found that after several weeks or months, I have come back to these articles (or the Red Manual), and it suddenly makes sense. Usually it's when I need the information to solve a specific problem. So, my advice to Ted is to save your back issues of Call -Apple. It's a valuable reference.

My second response is a not-too-technical article (especially if you ignore the machine language program) which you might want to print in Call -Apple.

John B. Cook
1905 Bailey Drive
Marshalltown, Iowa 50158

WE APPRECIATE both your letter and the program, which appears elsewhere in this issue

Dear Val and fellow Club Members:

I just got the September issue of Call -Apple. You guys are doing a fantastic job. What a stab in the back for anyone to suggest a lower dues for out of state members. May termites invade their Apples.

I am somewhat up the same tree as Ted (Oom) when it comes to machine language listings and some of the Basic routines found in our newsletter. However, I have every intention of "catching up". I urge you to maintain the course you have set. The only criticism I have is that the magazine doesn't come more often. (I know.) Broaden the scope, yes, but lower it? NO!

THANK YOU RON ALDRICH FOR "CONVERT". I had wondered if such conversion was possible but didn't know where to begin. The program will get a workout when my disk and Applesoft ROM comes in.

Thomas W. DeWinter
Route 2, Box 55
Colona, Il. 61241

WE'RE PRETTY PROUD of Ron and Convert, too!

Mr. Val J. Golding:

I do agree with Ted (Oom) on the direction the club is I do believe you are way, way ahead of me on the technical level. But I've only read the past two issues. In short, I would like to see more simple basic information along with the more technical articles. Perhaps in that way we can all be satisfied. Just don't go too far ahead too soon, remember, as more Apple II's become available to the public, the more beginners you'll have to deal with. After all, Apple II is a personal computer, isn't it?

Library Pak 2 will not auto-run because line 70 (on the Cassette Operating System) reads "CLR: GOTO 0". It should be changed to simply "GOTO 10", since all programs contained on the Library Pak 2 begin with line 10.

Steve Toth
(no address)

AS ALWAYS, your comments are appreciated. earliest copies of Library Pak 2, one line was omitted from each module, which enables the LCOS to function properly. It reads: "0 REM". This is what line 70 on the LCOS menu is actually looking for.

Call -Apple:

With regard to your editorial: I don't agree there is too high a percentage of technical articles in Call -Apple. A smaller number might make it easier to keep track of them for later reference, but I see no other advantage.

Sincerely yours,

Stanley Sawyer
Beau Jardin, Apt. 10-12
2550 Yeager Road
West Lafayette, Ind. 47906

PROF. SAWYER just recently moved from the Seattle area. We're happy to see his continuing interest in the group.

Dear A.P.P.L.E.-

I noticed you have some 8 minute cassettes available to members at six for $5.00. Is this just for Seattle members or can us poor out-of-state-ers buy them also?

I disagree with Ted Oom's suggestion that there might be too many "technical" articles in Call-Apple. You may want to ADD a few more articles which are less oriented toward the computer buff, but don't DROP any of those excellent "technical" articles. I don't understand many of them myself, but I don't think it will be too long before both Ted and I DO start understanding them.

I read in your August issue that I should have "a set of three 14 pin sockets on hand for memory select jumpers" (p5) when I but memory expansion chips. Where can I obtain them?

Gene Boggess
Star Route, Box 220-6
Columbus, Miss. 39701

WE'RE GLAD you asked about the short length cassettes, since we had intended to mention them, and this provides the opportunity. They are manufactured by DAK in Hollywood, and we have used them in audio work for a number of years without any real problems. You can call (800) 423-2636 and get a catalogue and sample tape. To obtain the jumper sockets, contact any of our advertisers.

Call Apple:

I'd like to comment on the September editorial.

First, Mr Oom is correct, but he is short-sighted. Let us consider why the condition exists. The main reason is the market itself and the new things Apple is selling, i.e., interfaces, Disk II, Rom, etc.

If I had to wait for Apple to provide the excellent service that Golding & Co. provide, it may be long coming. They provide a service not available ANYwhere else, and I say good job done.

I know it's hard to keep up, but let these things accumulate in your buffer, and lo and behold in a few months you may be glad for their efforts. It is hard in any club to provide for all, but the answer may lie within the club itself. Let the advanced ones help the novice. After all, isn't that what your club is for?

Finally, have you got a sample program to demonstrate how to open a file, write to it, close it and recall same later? If so, would appreciate it.

Ken Hossatt, President
Apple Portland Program Library Exchange

9195 SW Elrose Court
Tigard, Or. 77223

ASK and YE SHALL RECEIVE. Your sample file handler appears elsewhere in this issue.

Call Apple:

Ted Oom is mostly right, but we're all victims of Apple Computer, Inc., not the club. If REAL documentation existed for the computer, instead of that disaster-series "reference manual", the clubs newsletter would be quite appropriate.

Instead, we are forced to either wade through back issues of Byte, DDJ, etc., to find out how to use standard tools. I've never heard of a company including source code in their "reference manual", but no instructions! What do people without the appropriate magazines do?

So it is natural for Ted and some of the rest of us to look to the club for help, not because it's the clubs responsibility, but because we're desparate.

Alan Winston
1771 NW 59th Street - #2
Seattle, Wa. 98107

THE FOREGOING responses seem to be pretty typical of those we have received, both by mail and on the phone. It would appear that our editorial position was supported by something like 65% of those responding. Ted Oom has also helped point out that this is YOUR club, and as always, we welcome the comments of our members.

## MINUTES of the MEETING - Sept. 12

The meeting was called to order at 7:12 PM by Val Golding with 76 members present. The minutes of the previous meetings were approved and Val then turned the meeting over to Randy Wigginton and Mike Scott of Apple Computer, Inc. Mike delivered a most interesting history of Apple Computer which is printed elsewhere in this issue, and the two of them then fielded questions for the balance of the meeting. A number of interesting questions, both technical and non-technical were asked and answered, and these may be expected to appear in the next Call-Apple. The meeting was adjourned at approximately 9:20 PM.

## APPLE SOFTWARE BANK

Apple Computer has now gotten their software bank under way. All Seattle area dealers have now received copies of Volumes 1 and 2 of User Contributed Programs in diskette form, and it works like this: buy a diskette or tape (or bring your own) to your dealer, and ask to see his catalog of User Contributed Programs, then select those you want and copy them to disk or tape. Depending on dealer policy, these programs will be available at little or no cost. Apple Computer expects a new release about every two months.

## MYSTERY PROGRAM CONTEST

The object of this contest is to write an Integer Basic program that does nothing whatsoever, and will be used as a contest in the December Call-Apple. First prize will be a Wozpak and $10 cash, or $25 cash if you have ordered the Woz Pak. Second prize will be a Wozpak or $15 cash, and third prize will be a copy of the newest version of Programmer's Workshop. Ties will be decided on the basis of earliest postmark. Seattle entrants will have a three day postmark handicap and Washington and Oregon state entrants will have two day handicap. All entries must be received no later than November 21, 1978. Just follow these simple rules:

1. The program must be written in Integer Basic.
2. It must run on a machine with only 16K of RAM.
3. It must not require use of disk or printer. They may be optional, however.
4. The program must serve no useful purpose whatsoever.
5. End results must be identifiable (i.e., something must occur during the run of the program).
6. Algorhythms must be as devious as possible.
7. One or more Basic lines must change during run.
8. Author's name, address and phone must be in REM lines.
9. Bruce Tognazinni is disqualified!

## WIG-WIZ CONTEST

Here is a simple contest to test your understanding of the Apple. Five prizes of Programmer's Workshop will be awarded for the five best answers. The same postmark handicaps will be observed as in the other contest. All entries must be received no later than October 20th. To qualify, each of the following questions must be answered:

1. What is the function of Line 0?
2. What is the function of the Pokes in lines 20-30-40?
3. What happens to the display while the program is running?
4. Describe how this program could be utilized as a subroutine in another program.

All you need to do is enter the program as shown in the listing below, and run it.

```
0   POKE (( PEEK (202)+ PEEK (203
    )*256)+37),17
1   PRINT 3072
10  REM  "WIG WIZ" BY RANDY WIGGINGT
    ON
12  DIM C$(40)
20  POKE 768,173: POKE 769,0: POKE
    770,192: POKE 771,41: POKE
    772,127: POKE 773,32: POKE
    774,168: POKE 775,252
30  POKE 776,173: POKE 777,85: POKE
    778,192: POKE 779,173: POKE
    780,0: POKE 781,192: POKE 782
    ,41: POKE 783,127: POKE 784
    ,32: POKE 785,168
40  POKE 786,252: POKE 787,173:
    POKE 788,84: POKE 789,192:
    POKE 790,76: POKE 791,0: POKE
    792,3
100 GOSUB 490
105 GOSUB 2000
110 C$="800<400.7FFM E88AG"
120 FOR I=1 TO LEN(C$)
130 POKE 511+I, ASC(C$(I))
140 NEXT I
145 POKE 72,0
150 CALL -144
200 GOSUB 490
210 GOSUB 2000
300 CALL 768
470 REM  GR LINES
475 GR
500 FOR I=0 TO 39: COLOR= RND (
    16): HLIN 0,39 AT I: COLOR=
    RND (16): VLIN 0,39 AT I
510 COLOR= RND (16): VLIN 0,39 AT
    39-I: COLOR= RND (16): HLIN
    0,39 AT 39-I: NEXT I: RETURN
2000 CALL -936: PRINT "HIT ANY KEY TO
     CHANGE FLIP FREQUENCY"
2010 PRINT "TRY CONTROL AND EDIT KEYS
     , BUT NOT RESET": RETURN
```

# AUTOMATED TRAINING SYSTEMS     PHONE (206) 935-2697

Automated Training Systems has been a Washington State Licensed Proprietory School since 1968. These classes are taught by Cliff Gazaway who has had 20 years of electronics hardware experience and ten years of teaching.

In addition to the classes listed below, informal "fun get-togethers" will be held once each week at 7906 34th S.W. in West Seattle. The schedule will be :

First week------6502 interests.Pet.Apple.Ohio Sci.
Second week----Radio Shack interests.
Third week-----S-100,8080,Z80
Fourth week----RCA 1802,Little Elf,VIP

---

**These classes will meet in west Seattle or Bellevue. They will be scheduled as soon as suffiecient interest is shown in them.**

### BEGINNING APPLE BASIC.

This class is for beginners who have never programmed in BASIC or for those who already know BASIC but have never had their hands on an APPLE computer. The graduates of this class will be able to use ALL of the Integer BASIC & Applesoft I &II commands. $55.00 plus materials.

### POKING & PEEKING AT YOUR APPLE.

This class shows you how to use the powerful POKE,PEEK,& CALL commands to do exciting things with you APPLE.
$55.00.

### APPLE CIRCUIT THEORY.

You will know the purpose of every IC chip in your APPLE upon completion of this course. You will get more out of your APPLE if you know how it works. $55.00 plus materials

### CONNECTING TO THE REAL WORLD.

We will study a collection of magazine articles on interfacing and adapt the articles to the APPLE. We will help you custom build the hardware. Subjects of special intrest include clock and calendar, burglar alarms, AC appliance controls, temperature and photo input. $55.00 plus materials.

### CHRISTMAS PRESENTS FOR APPLELOVERS.

Every APPLE owner wants something for his APPLE for Christmas. 1978 will be the first"home computer Christmas". This class helps you build or buy something for your APPLE computer owner.
$55.00 plus materials.

# AUTOMATED TRAINING SYSTEMS    PHONE (206) 935-2697,

7906 34th.S.W.,Seattle,Wa.98126

## APPLEMASH

by Mike Thyng

## EDITING in INTEGER or APPLESOFT

Reprinted from the April, 1978 Call -Apple, used by permission!

Here are two tools that will help speed up your program editing: First, to avoid those long end of line gaps in PRINT or REM statements, first clear your screen with a CALL -936. Then, POKE 33,33. Finally list the program lines you want to work on and, presto, they are all scrunched up. You have just reset the right window of your display, and those gaps have disappeared like magic! To return to normal, just type TEXT and hit return.

Have you ever found you needed to insert a word in your program statement, but there was no room? The easiest way to do that is with the escape keys, A, B, C and D. To insert a word, use escape D to go above the line, escape C to return to the line, and escape B to back up to where you left off. Unlike the forward and reverse arrow keys, the escape keys do not copy when you trace over characters.

## & NOW, the AMPERSAND

Inside the elaborate labyrinths of Applesoft II there lurks a mysterious and shady character. This character can perform marvelous and incredible feats however, when beckoned forth to perform his many functions. This character goes by the name of Mr. Ampersand. We'll call him & for short. By cleverly using Mr. &, the user can extend Applesoft II indefinitely. HOW ? ? ?

When Applesoft is executing a program, if it encounters a & at the beginning of a statement, a JSR to location $3F5 is executed. At this time, the user is free to do anything from assembly language. To fully utilize the capabilities of the ampersand, a list of some useful subroutines contained in the ROM version of Applesoft will be published in the October issue of Call -Apple.

APPLE BOX deliveries are running very slow at present; kindly hold thy tongues.

DISK PROBLEMS? If you are as confused by the DOS documentation as we are, drop us a note quickly and we'll try to get some answers in the next issue.

## MODIFYING WORKSHOP

For those of you who may be so inclined and are interested in adding your own routines to, or otherwise modifying Programmer's Workshop, it is necessary to bring those high numbered lines down to where they are accessable. The Workshops own renumber routine will help on this, but it is a operation. First run Workshop to set the poke statements into memory. Then reload Workshop and save lines 0 to 420 separately. Call them the "head", if you like. Then enter the following pokes, to set up the renumbering process:

```
POKE 2,32500 MOD 256
POKE 3,32500/ 256
POKE 4,2
POKE 5,0
POKE 6,32765 MOD 256
POKE 7,32765/ 256
POKE 8,255
POKE 9,255
```

Next call 776, which will accomplish the actual renumbering. When work is completed, Workshop can be renumbered back up using its own routine. Just use a starting number of 32765 and an increment of 1. Remember that the value of B in line 32765 is set to equal the exact number of bytes in the program. This can be verified by testing with the bYTE routine. The value of P in the same line may also need to be changed as it determines the GOTO used in the POKE routine. After restoring the original high line numbers, then use the Workshop's own APPEND routine to put the head back.

---

A limited number of the May Call -Apple have been reprinted

## DOS PATCHES

Here are patches that will correct two of the bugs that occured in earlier versions of DOS. Just follow the directions exactly as given below.

CORRECTION NO. 1
The MASTER.CREATE program does not always function correctly. Boot the Master Diskette and type the following:

```
UNLOCK MASTER.CREATE
LOAD MASTER.CREATE
 97 X=PEEK(1528)
100 PRINT "DcBLOAD RAWDOS"
105 POKE 14313,X:POKE 14327,X
110 CALL 6912:END
SAVE MASTER.CREATE
LOCK MASTER.CREATE
```

CORRECTION NO. 2
In Applesoft II, reading or writing data to a file will not work on a line number over 255. Boot the Master Diskette and type the following (do not type "hit reset"):

```
UNLOCK RAWDOS
BLOAD RAWDOS
(hit reset)
25D6:4C D5 3F
25DC:2E
3FD5:E8 F0 01 60 4C DD 25
3D0G
BSAVE RAWDOS,A$1B00,L$2500
LOCK RAWDOS
```

Next, initialize a diskette through the MASTER.CREATE program. Whenever this newly initialized diskette is booted, Applesoft II will work properly with READ and WRITE statements. Also note that any slave diskettes initialized from the corrected master diskette will also have the problem corrected.

## DOCUMENTATION PACKAGE

We have been able to obtain, through the kindness and courtesy of Randy Wigginton and Apple Computer, Inc., a superb package of Apple documentation, consisting of well over 200 pages. It is our intention to make this available to our membership for only slightly more than the cost of printing and shipping, for $12.50, postpaid. Because our print run will be limited to orders received, it will be essential for your orders to reach us no later than October 27th. This package will be distributed to local members at the meeting of November 21st, and they may deduct $2.50 from their remittance. Envelopes containing orders MUST be marked on the outside "WOZPAK" in order for us to handle them in the most expeditious manner.

The following is a partial list of contents:
Disassembler (12 pgs)
Cassette file handling (18 pgs)
Using Apple II color graphics (7 pgs)
Integer floating point package (23 pgs)
Sweet Sixteen (30 pgs)
Renumber-Append (27 pgs)
Use of read-write track sector (13 pgs)
Apple II Trek (14 pgs)
Lower case Apple (6 pgs)
Apple II system monitor (29 pgs)

USER GROUPS: you may obtain a copy for your group at no cost by submitting two original programs from your own group that may be distributed to our membership.

**APPLE II INTEGER BASIC INTERPRETATION OF MEMORY**

Val Golding + Don Williams  3-27-78

|   | 0 | 1 | 2 | 3 | 4 | 5 | 6 | 7 | 8 | 9 | A | B | C | D | E | F |
|---|---|---|---|---|---|---|---|---|---|---|---|---|---|---|---|---|
| 0 | HIMEM: | HIMEM: | — | : | LOAD | SAVE | CON | RUN | RUN | DEL | ? | NEW | CLR | AUTO | ? | MAN |
| 1 | END OF STMT | LOMEM: | + | — | * | / | = | # | >= | > | <= | <> | < | AND | OR | MOD |
| 2 | < | + | ( | ? | ( | THEN | ? | ? | " | " | ( | ! | . | ( | PEEK | RND |
| 3 | SGN | ABS | PDL | RNDX | ( | + | — | NOT | ( | = | # | ! | ASC( | SCRN( | ? | ( |
| 4 | ?/÷ | ?/÷ | ( | ? | ? | ? | ? | ? | ? | ? | # | LEN( | GR | CALL | DIM | DIM |
| 5 | TAB | END | INPUT | INPUT | INPUT | FOR | = | TO | STEP | NEXT | ? | RETURN | GOSUB | REM | LET | GOTO |
| 6 | IF | PRINT | PRINT | PRINT | POKE | ? | COLOR= | PLOT | ? | HLIN | ? | AT | VLIN | ? | AT | VTAB |
| 7 | = | = | ) | ) | LIST | ? | LIST | POP | NODSP | NODSP | NOTRACE | DSP | DSP | TRACE | PR# | IN# |
| 8 | NUL | SOH | STX | ETX | EOT | ENQ | ACK | BEL | BS | HT | LF | VT | FF | CR | SO | SI |
| 9 | DLE | DC1 | DC2 | DC3 | DC4 | NAK | SYN | ETB | CAN | EM | SUB | ESC | FS | GS | RS | US |
| A | SP | ! | " | # | $ | % | & | ' | ( | ) | * | + | , | - | . | / |
| B | 0 | 1 | 2 | 3 | 4 | 5 | 6 | 7 | 8 | 9 | : | ; | < | = | > | ? |
| C | @ | A | B | C | D | E | F | G | H | I | J | K | L | M | N | O |
| D | P | Q | R | S | T | U | V | W | X | Y | Z | [ | \ | ] | ^ | _ |
| E | ` | a | b | c | d | e | f | g | h | i | j | k | l | m | n | o |
| F | p | q | r | s | t | u | v | w | x | y | z | { | \| | } | ~ | del |

**LEAST SIGNIFICANT DIGIT** (columns)
**MOST SIGNIFICANT DIGIT** (rows)

Rows 0–7: TOKENS
Rows 8–F: ASCII CHAR. & CONTROLS (ASCII EQUIV 0–7)

## Pointers & Tokens — Figure 2

### Applesoft II Tokens — Var Golding 05.28.78

|     | 0 | 1 | 2 | 3 | 4 | 5 | 6 | 7 | 8 | 9 | A | B | C | D | E | F | | Decimal |
|-----|---|---|---|---|---|---|---|---|---|---|---|---|---|---|---|---|---|---------|
| 8   | END | FOR | NEXT | DATA | INPUT | DEL | DIM | READ | GR | TEXT | PR# | IN# | CALL | PLOT | HLIN | VLIN | B | 128-143 |
| 9   | HGR2 | HGR | HCOLOR= | HPLOT | DRAW | XDRAW | HTAB | HOME | ROT= | SCALE= | SHLOAD | TRACE | NOTRACE | NORMAL | INVERSE | FLASH | 9 | 144-159 |
| A   | COLOR= | POP | VTAB | HIMEM: | LOMEM: | ONERR | RESUME | RECALL | STORE | SPEED= | LET | GOTO | RUN | IF | RESTORE | & | A | 160-175 |
| B   | GOSUB | RETURN | REM | STOP | ON | WAIT | LOAD | SAVE | DEF | POKE | PRINT | CONT | LIST | CLEAR | GET | NEW | B | 176-191 |
| C   | TAB( | TO | FN | SPC( | THEN | AT | NOT | STEP | + | - | * | / | ^ | AND | OR | > | C | 192-207 |
| D   | = | < | SGN | INT | ABS | USR | FRE | SCRN( | PDL | SQR | RND | LOG | EXP | COS | SIN | | D | 208-223 |
| E   | TAN | ATN | PEEK | LEN | STR$ | VAL | ASC | CHR$ | LEFT$ | RIGHT$ | MID$ | | RETURN WITHOUT GOSUB | SYNTAX | OUT OF DATA | ILLEGAL QUANTITY | E | 224-239 |
| F   | OVERFLOW | OUT OF MEMORY | UNDEF'D STATEMENT | BAD SUBSCRIPT | REDIM'D ARRAY | DIVISION BY ZERO | ILLEGAL DIRECT | TYPE MISMATCH | STRING TOO LONG | FORMULA TOO COMPLEX | CAN'T CONTINUE | UNDEF'D FUNCTION | ERROR | ( | ( | ( | F | 240-255 |
|     | 0 | 1 | 2 | 3 | 4 | 5 | 6 | 7 | 8 | 9 | A | B | C | D | E | F | | |

— LEAST SIGNIFICANT DIGIT —

MOST SIGNIFICANT DIGIT

NOTE: Values 00 to 7F (0 to 127 decimal) are used by the standard Ascii character set.

# Bellevue ComputerLand

14340 N.E. 20th Street
746-2070
Bellevue, WA 98007

*Prices good only if this ad mentioned.

## APPLE II SERIAL I/O INTERFACE *

Part no. 2
Baud rate is continuously adjustable from 0 to 30,000 • Plugs into any peripheral connector • Low current drain. RS-232 input and output • On board switch selectable 5 to 8 data bits, 1 or 2 stop bits, and parity or no parity either odd or even • Jumper selectable address • SOFTWARE • Input and Output routine from monitor or BASIC to teletype or other serial printer. • Program for using an Apple II for a video or an intelligent terminal. Also can output in correspondence code to interface with some selectrics. Board only —
With parts —      Assembled and tested — $68

COME IN AND SEE CLIFF AND TELL HIM WHAT YOU WANT TO SEE AT YOUR APPLE STORE.

CARRYING CASE. Makes the apple a nice piece of luggage. Lots in stock. $30.

* 16K MEMORY $169.
32K $319

## MODEM *

Part no. 109
• Type 103 • Full or half duplex • Works up to 300 baud • Originate or Answer • No coils, only low cost components • TTL input and output-serial • Connect 8 ohm speaker and crystal mic. directly to board • Uses XR FSK demodulator • Requires +5 volts • Board
With parts  $32

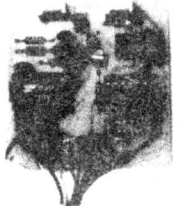

STOP WAITING FOR A PRINTER!
$995 plus $85 interface, cable, & software.
We have IBM Selectrics up and running on the Apples. Worth over $800 as regular typewriter. Add a telephone modem for a stand alone timeshare terminal (Apple not needed) to talk to big computer for only 50 cents per hour. Once you use a printer for developing and debugging programs you will never write another program without it. You have to wait months for other printers to be delivered---take delivery on this IBM today!

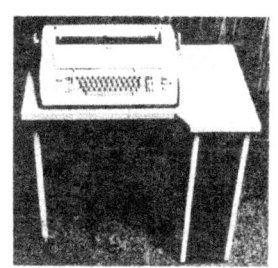

## RS 232/TTY * INTERFACE

Part no. 600
• Converts RS-232 to 20mA current loop, and 20mA current loop to RS-232 • Two separate circuits • Requires +12 and -12 volts • Board only     With parts $9

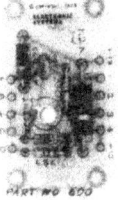

FREE PROGRAMS.
Hammurabi. Pinball. Sink The Ship. Catch. Curves. Towers Of Hanoi. Nightmare #6. Color Math. Magic Lantern Slide Show. Math. Magi. Mastermind. Othello. Blackjack. Bone Tumor Differential Diagnosis. Yahtzee. Hex Converter. Morse Code. Integer Basic CHR$ Function.

**THE APPLE MAGIC LANTERN**     F R E E !

1. Musical notation, with drawings of instruments obbligato.
2. A map of the world. Careful observers will find a new continent.
3. A handsome woman's face.
4. An isomorphic view of a double Bessel function with hidden line suppression. Or, if you'd rather, a fantasy landscape.
5. A woodcut of William Shakespeare.
6. Uncle Sam, who can tapdance.
7. "Joe sent me . . ."
8. Spirallellogram. Whatever that is.
9. Rocky Raccoon
10. A neat set of characters that can be generated on the APPLE II. You *can* get upper and lower case—at least in a drawing.
11. One United States Dollar. Well, Most of One Dollar.

## RS 232/TTL * INTERFACE

Part no. 232
• Converts TTL to RS-232, and converts RS-232 to TTL • Two separate circuits • Requires -12 and +12 volts • All connections go to a 10 pin gold plated edge connector • Board only     with parts $9
with connector add

master charge   PLEASE ADD FOR POSTAGE & HANDLING   BankAmericard

# Bellevue ComputerLand

14340 N.E. 20th Street
(206) 746-2070
Bellevue, WA 98007

# ComputerLand™

# 16K APPLE II RAM $175.00
NEW SHIPMENT AT LOWEST PRICES EVER, NEC UPD 416D CHIPS.

```
*******************************
      S O F T W A R E   D E P T .
*******************************
```

### APPLE COMPUTER INC. SOFTWARE

```
 1. CHECKBOOK CASSETTE              $20.00
 2. STARTREK/STARWARS               $15.00
 3. COLOR DEMO/BREAKOUT             $ 7.50
 4. APPLESOFT II/F.P. DEMO W/MNL.   $20.00
 5. RAM TEST CASSETTE               $ 7.50
 6. COLOR MATH DEMO/HANGMAN         $ 7.50
 7. BLACKJACK/SLOT MACHINE          $ 7.50
 8. BIORYTHM/MASTERMIND             $ 7.50
 9. APPLE II CAPABILITIES DEMO      $20.00
10. FINANCE I(4 PROGRAM SET)        $25.00
11. DATAMOVER/TELEPONG              $ 7.50
12. APPLE DEMO DISK'S (SET OF 2)    $25.00
    NEW VOL 1&2 W/DOCUMENTATION
13. VOL. 1&2 ON CASSETTES (2)       $20.00
```

### MICROMEDIA SOFTWARE FOR APPLE II

```
 1. SUPERMATH            $12.00
 2. TRUE/FALSE QUIZ      $12.00
 3. VARIABLE MESSAGES    $12.00
 4. MATCHING QUIZ        $12.00
 5. DON'T FALL           $12.00
 6. MEMORY AIDE          $12.00
 7. STUDY AIDE           $12.00
 8. KEYBOARD ORGAN       $12.00
 9. GRADING ROUTINE      $12.00
10. DRAWING              $12.00
```

### SPEAKEASY SOFTWARE FOR APPLE II

```
1. KIDSTUFF                       $12.00
2. MICROTRIVIA                    $12.00
3. BULLS AND BEARS (8 PLAYERS)    $12.00
4. WARLORDS (4 PLAYERS)           $12.00
```

### CALL A.P.P.L.E. SOFTWARE

```
1. PROGRAMMERS WORKSHOP   $ 7.00
2. LAB PAK IB             $ 6.00
3. LAB PAK II             $ 6.00
4. BASIC TUTORIAL         $20.00
```

----------------------------------------
ALL SOFTWARE SHIPPED SCHEDULE A.
----------------------------------------

```
*******************************************
    PRINTERS    PRINTERS    PRINTERS
*******************************************
```

| PRINTER | PRICE | SHIP. |
|---|---|---|
| AXIOM EX-801-s | $ 495.00 | C |
| AXIOM EX-820 | $ 795.00 | C |
| INTEGRAL DATA IP-125 | $ 838.00 | D |
| INTEGRAL DATA IP-225 | $ 988.00 | D |
| TRENDATA 1000 | $ 995.00 | F |
| TEXAS INSTRUMENTS 743 | $1395.00 | D |
| DECWRITER II, LA36 | $1595.00 | F |

Add handling and shipping charges as per schedule. Shipped by UPS unless specified otherwise. Delivery is stock on most items. No delay in shipment for payment by cashier's check, money order or charge cards. Allow three weeks for personal checks to clear. Washington state residents ad 5.4% sales tax. Availability, prices and specs may change without notice.

**SHIPPING SCHEDULE**  A. $2.00   C. 10.00   E. 30.00
                      B.  4.00   D. 20.00   F. 40.00

☐ VISA/BAC    ☐ M/C    Expiration date: _____
Card #: _____
Signature: _____
Name (Print): _____
Address: _____
City: _____ State: _____ Zip: _____

## ComputerLand™

1500 South 336th St. • Parkway Center, Suite 12 • Federal Way, Washington 98003
Tacoma (206) 927-8585 • Seattle (206) 838-9363

# -A.P.P.L.E.

## APPLE PUGETSOUND PROGRAM LIBRARY EXCHANGE

NOVEMBER-DECEMBER 1978     $1.00     Vol. 1, No. 10
6708 39th Avenue S.W.     Seattle, Washington 98136     (206) 932-6588

## BYTES from the APPLE
Software Stuff, etc., etc., etc., etc., etc., etc., etc., etc., etc., etc.,

by Val J. Golding

The BIG NEWS for this issue is APPLESOFT WORKSHOP is here! The cost is $6.41 postpaid, and orders will be accepted, subject to the following conditions: This preliminary version will be updated several times over the next few months. Updates will be available at $2.00 postpaid. This version is disk-dependent in that it requires disk for certain routines, including Append. Every attempt has been made to debus it, but some may still remain. Please allow 30 days for delivery on this and the other new Library Paks.

Library Paks 3 and 4 are expected to be available by the time you read this. Pak 3 will contain Home Ecpak 1, Musicpak 1 and more games. Pak 4 will contain a complete financial program, amortzation, etc., along with the usual compliment of games and demos. Price is $5.41 each, postpaid.

Elsewhere in the software world, Jim Hoyt of Apple Computer has asked us for permission to reprint Ron Aldrich's CONVERT in Contact! We need your programs and articles for Call-APPLE and the library. Don't be shy!

We've limited ourselves to this one page this month. Even with 20 pages, we ran out of space. Don't miss Gene Jackson's Checkbook modifications for disk in this issue, or the feature of Lo-res color assembly language routines.

| | |
|---|---|
| Val J. Golding, President | (206) 932-6588 |
| Michael Thyng, Secretary | (206) 524-2744 |
| Dick Hubert, Administrative Asst. | (206) 255-7410 |
| Darrell Aldrich, Program Editor | (503) 581-8600 |
| Ron Aldrich, Asst. Prgm. Editor | (206) 782-7082 |
| Bob Huelsdonk, Technical Consultant, Basic | (206) 362-4910 |
| Don Williams, Technical Consultant, Assembly | (206) 242-6807 |
| Steve Paulson, Circulation | (206) 242-2700 |

## IN THIS ISSUE.................. Page

Bytes from the Apple ................................ 1
LO-RES Color Assembly Routines ..................... 2
Checkbook Patches for Disk ......................... 5
Use of the Game Paddles ............................ 5
Write-Apple ........................................ 7
Applemash .......................................... 7
& Now, the Further Adventurs of Mr. Ampersand ...... 8
Transient Voltage Protection ....................... 8
Minutes of the October Meeting ..................... 8
Apple-Sharing ..................................... 10
The Apple Widow ................................... 12
PEEKS, POKE and CALLS ............................. 14
Apple Source ...................................... 15
Binary Disk Program Identifying ................... 17
Resurecting the Dead (Programs) ................... 18
LO-RES Graphics Screen Map ........................ 18

## NOVEMBER MEETING
7:00 P.M.     TUESDAY     NOVEMBER 21, 1978
Computerland     1500 South 336th Street     Federal Way

## DECEMBER MEETING
7:00 P.M.     TUESDAY     DECEMBER 19, 1978
Empire Electronics     616 S.W. 152nd St.     Seattle

# ComputerLand™

***********************************************

## WE'RE TIRED OF THE RAM RACE !!!

***********************************************

<u>16K RAM CHIPS</u>  
<u>N.E.C. UPD416D</u>  
CERAMIC CHIPS

| | | |
|---|---|---|
| 1-5 | SETS | $120.00 |
| 6-11 | SETS | $112.00 |
| 12-24 | SETS | $104.00 |
| 25-UP | SETS | $ 96.00 |

<u>4K RAM CHIPS</u>  
<u>N.E.C. UPD414D</u>  
PLASTIC CHIPS

| | | |
|---|---|---|
| 1-5 | SETS | $48.00 |
| 6-11 | SETS | $40.00 |
| 12-24 | SETS | $32.00 |
| 25-UP | SETS | $24.00 |

THESE CHIPS ARE IN STOCK AND READY FOR **IMMEDIATE DELIVERY!** COME AN' GET 'EM !

FOR THOSE WHO CANNOT COME INTO OUR STORE SHIP. SCHEDULE "A" + $.50 CENTS FOR EACH SET THEREAFTER FOR SHIPPING & INSURANCE.

***********************************************

COME TO OUR STORE AND MEET OUR **NEW STAFF!**

COME SEE THE NEW APPLE SOFTWARE, MORE NOW THAN EVER BEFORE. **IN STOCK!**

ASK ABOUT OUR NEW EXTENDED MAINTENANCE WARRANTEE FOR **YOUR** APPLE II COMPUTER.

---

Add handling and shipping charges as per schedule. Shipped by UPS unless specified otherwise. Delivery is stock on most items. No delay in shipment for payment by cashier's check, money order or charge cards. Allow three weeks for personal checks to clear. Washington state residents ad 5.4% sales tax. Availability, prices and specs may change without notice.

**SHIPPING SCHEDULE**  
A. $2.00  C. 10.00  
B. 4.00  D. 20.00

☐ VISA/BAC   ☐ M/C   Expiration date: _____  
Card #: _____  
Signature: _____  
Name (Print): _____  
Address: _____  
City: _____ State: _____ Zip: _____

---

**ComputerLand™**  
1500 South 336th St. • Parkway Center, Suite 12 • Federal Way, Washington 98003  
Tacoma (206) 927-8585 • Seattle (206) 838-9363

# USE OF APPLE-II COLOR GRAPHICS IN ASSEMBLY LANGUAGE

The APPLE-II color graphics hardware will display a 40H by 48V grid, each position of which may be any one of 16 colors. The actual screen data is stored in 1K bytes of system memory, normally locations $400 to $7FF. (A dual page mode allows the user to alternatively display locations $800 to $BFF). Color displays are generated by executing programs which modify the "screen memory." For example, storing zeroes throughout locations $400 to $7FF will yield an all-black display while storing $33 bytes throughout will yield an all-violet display. A number of subroutines are provided in ROM to facilitate useful operations.

The x-coordinates range from 0 (leftmost) to 39 (rightmost) and the y-coordinates from 0 (topmost) to 47 (bottommost). If the user is in the mixed graphics/text mode with 4 lines of text at the bottom of the screen, then the greatest allowable y-coordinate is 39.

The screen memory is arranged such that each displayed horizontal line occupies 40 consecutive locations. Additionally, even/odd line pairs share the same byte groups. For example, both lines 0 and 1 will have their leftmost point stored in the same byte, at location $400; and their rightmost point stored in the byte at location $427. The least significant 4 bits correspond to the even line and the most significant 4 bits to the odd line. The relationship between y-coordinates and memory addresses is illustrated on the following page.

The APPLE-II color graphics subroutines provided in ROM use a few page zero locations for variables and workspace. You should avoid using these locations for your own program variables. It is a good rule not to use page zero locations $20 to $4F for any programs since they are used by the monitor and you may wish to use the monitor (for example, to debug a program) without clobbering your own variables. If you write a program in assembly language that you wish to call from BASIC with a CALL command, then avoid using page zero locations $20 to $FF for your variables.

Color Graphics
Page Zero Variable Allocation

| Name  | Address |
|-------|---------|
| GBASL | $26     |
| GBASH | $27     |
| H2    | $2C     |
| V2    | $2D     |
| MASK  | $2E     |
| COLOR | $30     |

GBASL and GBASH are used by the color graphics subroutines as a pointer to the first (leftmost) byte of the current plot line. The (GBASL),Y addressing mode of the 6502 is used to access any byte of that line. COLOR is a mask byte specifying the color for even lines in the 4 least significant bits (0 to 15) and for odd lines in the 4 most significant bits.

These will generally be the same, and always so if the user sets the COLOR byte via the SETCOLOR subroutine provided. Of the above variables only H2, V2, and MASK can be clobbered by the monitor.

Writing a color graphics program in 6502 assembly language generally involves the following procedures. You should be familiar with subroutine usage on the 6502.

1. Set the video mode and scrolling window (refer to the section on APPLE-II text features)
2. Clear the screen with a call to the CLRSCR (48-line clear) subroutines. If you are using the mixed text/graphics feature then call CLRTOP.
3. Set the color using the SETCOLR subroutine.
4. Call the PLOT, HLINE, and VLINE subroutines to plot points and draw lines. The color setting is not affected by these subroutines.
5. Advanced programmers may wish to study the provided subroutines and addressing schemes. When you supply x- and y-coordinate data to these subroutines they generate BASE address, horizontal index, and even/odd mask information. You can write more efficient programs if you supply this information directly.

PLOT1 subroutine (address $F80E)

Purpose: To plot squares in standard resolution mode with no Y-coordinate change from last call to PLOT. Faster than PLOT. Uses most recently specified COLOR (see SETCOL)

Entry: X-coordinate in Y-Reg (0 to 39)

Exit: A-Reg clobbered. Y-Reg and carry unchanged.

Example: (Plotting two squares - one at (3, 7) and one at (9, 7))

| | |
|---|---|
| LDY #$3 | X-coordinate |
| LDA #$7 | Y-coordinate |
| JSR PLOT | Plot (3, 7) |
| LDY #$9 | New X-coordinate |
| JSR PLOT1 | Call PLOT1 for fast plot. |

(continued on page 4)

## SPECIAL NOTICE

This issue of Call -Apple, as you may have noted, is dated November-December, the reason for this being our switch last issue to a bulk mailing rate. While we had anticipated some delay, it turned out being considerably more, and forced us to drop back on our publishing schedule, since it was not possible to pick it up. This has resulted in a number of changes, notably the next issue will be dated January. The monthly frequency will not be changed.

Deadline for the Wiz-Wiz contest has been extended to January 15, 1979 and the mystery program contest to February 15th.

## COLOR GRAPHICS (from page 3)

### HLINE subroutine (address $F819)

Purpose: To draw horizontal lines in standard resolution mode. Most recently specified COLOR (see SETCOL) is used.

Entry: The Y-coordinate (0 to 47) is in the A-Reg. The leftmost X-coordinate (0 to 39) is in the Y-Reg and the rightmost X-coordinate (0 to 39) is in the variable H2 (location $2C). The rightmost x-coordinate may never be smaller than the leftmost

Calls: PLOT, PLOT1

Exit: The Y-Reg will contain the rightmost X-coordinate (same as H2 which is unchanged). The A-Reg is clobbered. The carry is set.

Example: Drawing a horizontal line from 3 (left X-coord) to $1A (right X-coord) at 9 (Y-coord)

```
LDY #$3          Left
LDA #0$1A        Right
STA H2           Save it
LDA #$9          Y-coordinate
JSR HLINE        Plot line
```

### SETCOL subroutine (address $FS64)

Purpose: To specify one of 16 colors for standard resolution plotting.

Entry: **The least significant 4 A-REG bits contained a color code** (0 to $F). The 4 most significant bits are ignored.

Exit: The variable COLOR (location $30) and the A-Reg will both contain the selected color in both half bytes, for example color 3 will result in $33. The carry is cleared.

Example: (Select color 6)
```
LDA #$6
JSR SETCOL ($F864)
```

Note: When sitting the color to a constant the following sequence is preferable.
```
LDA #$66
STA COLOR ($30)
```

### PLOT subroutine (address $F800)

Purpose: To plot a square in standard resolution mode using the most recently specified color (see SETCOL). Plotting always occurs in the primary standard resolution page (memory locations $400 to $7FF).

Entry: The x-coordinate (0 to 39) is in the Y-Reg and the y-coordinate (0 to 47) is in the A-Reg.

Exit: The A-Reg is clobbered but the Y-Reg is not. The carry is cleared. A halfbyte mask ($F or $F0) is generated and saved in the variable location MASK (location $2E).

Calls: GBASCALC

Example: (Plot a square at coordinate ($A, $2C))
```
LDA #$2C         Y-coordinate
LDY #$A          X-coordinate
JSR PLOT (F800)
```

### SCRN subroutine (address $F871)

Purpose: To sense the color (0 to $F) at a specified screen position

Entry: The Y-coordinate is in the A-Reg and the X-coordinate is in the Y-Reg.

Exit: The A-Reg contains contents of screen memory at specified position. This will be a value from 0 to 15). The Y-Reg is unchanged and the "N" flag is cleared (for unconditional branches upon return).

Calls: GBASCALC

Example: To sense the color at position (5, 7)
```
LDY #$5          X-coordinate
LDA #$7          Y-coordinate
JSR SCRN         Color to A-Reg.
```

### GBASCALC subroutine (address $F847)

Purpose: To calculate a base address within the primary standard resolution screen memory page corresponding to a specified Y-coordinate. Once this base address is formed in GBASL and GBASH (locations $26 and $27) the PLOT routines can access the memory location corresponding to any screen position by means of (GBASL), Y addressing.

Entry: (Y-coordinate) / 2 (0 to $17) is in the A-Reg. Note that even/odd Y-coordinate pairs share the same base address)

Exit: The A-Reg is clobbered and the carry is cleared. GBASL and GBASH contain the address of the byte corresponding to the leftmost screen position of the specified Y-coord.

Example: To access the byte whose Y-coordinate is $1A and whose X-coordinate is 7.
```
LDA #$1A         Y-coordinate
LSR              Divide by 2
JSR GBASCALC     Form base address
LDY #$7          X-coordinate
LDA (GBASL), Y   Access byte
```

Note: For an even/odd Y-coord pair, the even-coord data is contained in the least significant 4 bits of the accessed byte and the odd-coord data in the most significant 4.

**(see Color Graphics Screen Map on page 18)**

## CHECKBOOK CHANGES FOR DISK

### BY GENE JACKSON

```
1110 PRINT " 8.   SAVE DATA ": PRINT
     " 9.   CHECK FILE LENGTH": PRINT
     "10.   QUIT"
1112 DZ$="": REM   CTL D
1114 PRINT DZ$;"NOMON C"
1200 CALL -936: PRINT "ARE YOU GOING
     TO ENTER DATA FROM": INPUT
     "THE KEYBOARD 'K', DISK 'D' OR T
     APE 'T' ?",C$
1210 IF C$="T" THEN 1300: IF C$=
     "D" THEN 2100: IF C$#"K" THEN
     RETURN
2100 INPUT "REPLACE CURRENT DATA OR A
     PPEND TO IT (R/A) ?",L$: REM   DI
     SK LOAD ROUTINE
2105 INPUT "FILE NAME TO LOAD ?"
     ,N$: IF L$="R" THEN 2130: IF
     L$#"A" THEN RETURN
2110 BCM=LM:LM=CM+0: GOSUB 2130:
     LM=BCM: RETURN
2130 PRINT DZ$;"BLOAD CB.HDR ";N$
     :B=LM+A: IF B>HM OR A<Z THEN
     GOSUB 20000:CM=B
2140 PRINT DZ$;"BLOAD CB.FILE ";
     N$;",A";LM: RETURN
2150 P=LM: GOSUB 2
2155 D(5)=R(0):P=CM-S-S+0: GOSUB
     2:D(6)=R(0)
2160 A=CM-LM: IF A<Z THEN RETURN
     : PRINT DZ$;"BSAVE CB.HDR "
     ;N$;",A2048,L102"
2165 PRINT DZ$;"BSAVE CB.FILE ";
     N$;",A";LM;",L";A
2170 PRINT DZ$;"LOCK CB.HDR ";N$
     : PRINT DZ$;"LOCK CB.FILE "
     ;N$: RETURN
2610 INPUT "OK, TYPE IT IN- (NO COMMA
     S PLEASE) -",N$
2620 INPUT "DO YOU WISH TO SAVE TO DI
     SK 'D' OR TAPE 'T' ?",C$: IF
     C$="D" THEN 2150: IF C$#"T"
     THEN RETURN
3205 PRINT DZ$;"MON C"
```

A number of master diskettes were inadvertantly sent out blank by Apple. If your brand new disk wont boot, this possibly could be the cause.

## USING GAME-PADDLE BUTTONS
by Steve Paulson

In looking over a few of the programs currently in our game-paks I happened upon two programs which could be improved through the use of paddles. They are: "Klingon Capture" and "Pin Ball" (marbles).

During the operation of these programs, one must control part of the game by operating the game paddle and part by "hitting" a key on the keyboard. This seems a waste of human maneuvers. By a few simple changes and yes, additions, these programs can be made more interesting and easier to operate.

In the game of "Klingon Capture" we can change one line and add another changing the game from a strictly one-man game to the possibility of two players. Here are the changes:

Line #4340: change to: KEY = PEEK (-16287): IF KEY > 127 THEN 4400
Add line #4342: KEY = PEEK (-16286): IF KEY > 127 THEN 4400
Change #4400 to: REM

These changes and additions will cause the paddle-buttons to be used in place of the keyboard. In this program two people can now play together. Paddle 0 will control vertical and paddle 1 will control horizontal movement of the ship. Both paddles will now fire the torpedos.

In the instance of "Pin Ball," we have a nice relaxing game that both children and adults can play. I have two young children interested in the computer and sometimes I like to have them experience it with me. "Marbles" is just the thing.

By changing two lines and deleting one, the kids can play the game without touching the computer. Here are the changes:
Line #2740: change to: F = PEEK (-16287)
Line #2750: change to: IF F < 128 THEN 2680
Line #2760: delete this line.

These changes will cause the paddle-button to drop the marble instead of the keyboard.

In the case of "Klingon Capture" an extra line is added permitting two to play, and the program is easier to use.

In the case of the "Pin Ball", one may now sit back in the chair and watch the marbles fall. This is quite a change from having to constantly reach over and hit a key.

These changes add a little more ease to the games and a lot more character. They alter the technique, making the programs more "professional" in style and lend a higher quality to one's programming ability.

---

Wozpak orders will be filled. If you have not heard of this superb documentation package, available postpaid at $12.50, the remaining copies will be supplied on a first come, first served basis.

# Bellevue ComputerLand

14340 N.E. 20th Street
746-2070
Bellevue, WA 98007

PRICE CHANGES: E.S. interface boards that require after-sale-support have had price increases. "FREE" programs are now up to $2 each.

* 16K MEMORY $169.
32K $319

SELL YOUR SOFTWARE.
Let us sell your programs. No matter how simple or how elaborate, whether complete or not, we want it.

SOFTWARE OR INTERFACE CONSULTING?
Are you available, as a paid consultant, to help our customers develop software for business, education, engineering, and other applications. Call Cliff at (206)746-2070 and get on our list of paid consultants.

QUESTION & ANSWER LOGBOOK.
Cliff is nearly overwhelmed by the volume of questions he is being asked. He does not want to discourage your calls or in-person questions, since AFTER-THE-SALE service is the most important reason for buying from the BELLEVUE COMPUTERLAND store. However, it would help if you would present some of your questions in writing. Come in to the Bellevue store and log your question in Cliff's Question & Answer book. Or mail your question to him. Cliff will write his answer in the log and other readers will proofread it and perhaps add a more accurate answer. Do not let this request discourage you from calling, when you need to. Calls are always welcome.

OVER-THE-COUNTER DISK DRIVE SALES ????
Believe it or not, we got caught up on our Apple Disk waiting list. We even sold a couple of drives over the counter. ORDER YOUR DISK NOW WHILE WE ARE STILL ALMOST CAUGHT UP. A 100 % deposit <u>might</u> bring your disk next week (no promises).

APPLE II OVER-THE-COUNTER TOO.
We have plenty of Apple computers in stock, so send your friends, relatives, and neighbors over---while they last.

**MICRO** "MICRO" The 6502 Journal is an excellent magazine for Apple owners. Bellevue Computerland has a good stock of volume 6. We also have ample back issues of the last three issues of CALL-APPLE.

We can ship almost any Apple product advertised in this magazine, or its back issues, (no matter who's ad) to anywhere in the U.S. Telephone orders, welcome.

"THE BEST OF MICRO VOLUME 1" The book will be organized by subject. Aside from these minor changes, the content will be identical to that of MICRO numbers 1 through 6. If you already have them, you will not profit by getting the new edition. If you do not have them, then this will be the only way to get the information.

"The BEST of MICRO Volume 1" will be available about the first of November. It will be about 160 page long in an 8 by 11 format, soft cover.

# Bellevue ComputerLand

14340 N.E. 20th Street
(206) 746-2070
Bellevue, WA 98007

## WRITE - APPLE

Dear Val,

I noticed that you have a note about the "&". I just got my Applesoft II ROM a month ago and find your notes about undocumented features and tokens helpful.

Another undocumented (in my manual, at least) token is the WAIT. From the listing, it appears to work like this:

WAIT adr, mask, change

will remain in a tight loop reading the location at "adr." When any of the bits at "adr" that are set in mask are not zero, the loop is broken and control goes to the next command. The argument, "change" is optional - any bits set in "change" are changed (from 0 to 1 or 1 to 0) in the word read from "adr" before testing, allowing a test for a change from 1 to 0. In brief, it is

Loop until ((adr). EOR. change) .AND.mask <> 0

It would be normally used to look at an I/O address. For example, WAIT - 16287, 128 delays until the button # 0 is pressed. ('change' is 0 in this example and hence is not needed. WAIT - 16287, 128, 128 loops until button 0 is released!)

Another feature not documented is the DRAW S AT X, Y. The "S" seems to refer to an index of shapes. The routine seems to expect the number of shapes to be in the first two bytes of the table. The next two bytes seem to have an offset from the beginning of the table to the start of the first shape, etc. I haven't tried that yet - perhaps some of your associates have and can confirm or correct.

Richard F. Suitor
166 Tremont Street
Newton, MA 02158

HOW ABOUT IT, Readers? Can you come up with anything?

Dear Mr. Golding:

I'm wondering if you can help me with something.

I'm paralyzed from an accident and wonder if you could ask members if there was any money making ways I could use my Apple computer at home. Can you please find out if anybody could make an automatic phone dialer for the Apple, because I have an idea for a business where I would have to call about 200 persons a day. It would be easier if there was a way of using the computer.

Any help you would give me would be greatly appreciated.

Gerald Schwader
R. 6 Riverside Pk.
Janesville, Wisc. 53545
Phone (608) 756-4006

AGAIN we will ask the readers help.

Dear Val:

This is in answer to your editorial in CALL -APPLE of September '78 Vol. 1 No. 8, pg. 7 in which you ask for feedback on the technical level of the articles in CALL-APPLE.

First let me say that the newsletter is terrific! I read and re-read them and try out the programs. I agree that it is good to stretch one's capabilities by learning new techniques.

However, like "Ted" in your editorial, I have been frustrated (even more than mildly) when I read about some new technique or program that looks so useful and interesting and then find that the writer has only hinted at what it was all about and assumes my technical level to be much higher than it actually is. This means I don't understand what the program is supposed to do, why you would want to do it, or how to actually use it. In many cases, a specific example would help. Also a little more hand-holding for us newcomers to the Apple II. In my own case, I have a fair knowledge of 6502 machine language, but on the KIM-I (2 years), not as applied to the Apple.

An example of what I mean is found in Aldrich's tempting hintsin Vol. I, No. 6, July '78, pg. 9 on Color Mask Byte. What was this all about? Example?

In general the style and explanations given in System Monitor (July '78, pgs. 12 - 14) is very good. Note that they give examples of how to use the techniques suggested!

Huelsdonk's Free Byte suggestion doesn't work with my 48K Apple II. Some of the calculations are over 32767!

Another case where more information on significance and utility is needed is Dan Chapman's routine on the Video Display, September '78, pg. 4.

Please note that the above comments are meant to be constructive. I really do like the newsletter. But since I am a neophyte, I get frustrated by temptations I can't deal with.

Dr. William R. Dial
438 Roslyn Avenue
Akron, OH 44320

**YOUR COMMENTS** are appreciated and we will try and follow through.

## 1979 DUES PAYABLE NOW!

For those members who have not yet renewed, now is the time. Don't miss out on our new library paks and the next year of Call -Apple! Please show your membership number when renewing. It costs only $7.50.

## & NOW, THE FURTHER ADVENTURES OF THE MYSTERIOUS AMPERSAND

(Continued from last month)

When last we saw this shady character named Ampersand, he was hiding in a memory location known only as 3F5. Now, as our story resumes, we find some of the Applesoft subroutines that Mr. & can use in the ROM version.

CHRGET ($00B1) - This routine gets the next sequential character or token from the program. At all times, TXTPTR ($00B8, $B9) points at the next character. After executing the & and jumping to location $3F5, Applesoft will leave TXTPTR pointing at the character immediately following the &, and leave that character in the accumulator register. Upon a JSR to CHRGET, the character next in the program is returned in the A-register, and the status flags are set as follows:

Zero flag - set if the character is a terminator (end-of-line or a colon ":").

Carry - Set if the character is non-numeric, i.e. not a digit. Cleared if the character is a digit.

CHRGOT ($00B7) - This subroutine gets the current character from the program. Whereas CHRGET increments TXTPTR to get the next character, CHRGOT does not change TXTPTR.

FRMNUM ($DD67) - This subroutine evaluates a formula expression into the floating point accumulator.

GETADR ($E752) - Subroutine converts the floating point accumulator into a two-byte integer, in locations $50 and $51.

GETBYT ($E6F8) - Evaluates a formula and converts it to a one-byte value in the X-register.

SNERR ($DEC9) - Prints "SYNTAX ERROR" and halts the program.

Note that after the user subroutine RTS's to Applesoft, the TXTPTR must point at a terminator, indicating the end of this statement. See example program on other page.

## MINUTES OF OCT. 17, 1978

Our meeting started promptly at 7:15. Val led us in introductions and we unanimously chose to pass reading the minutes.

Val suggested that we go to a commercial typesetter to make the Call-A.P.P.L.E. more readable. Unanimous approval.

It was suggested that Val use a larger type size than that which he's currently using.

He said the size he's using saves us about 25 to 30% over the next larger size. He will look into it.

Jim Hoyt liked Ron Aldrich's Convert program so well he's asked for permission to print it in APPLE'S CONTACT.

Integral Data System Printer Driver routines are being prepared in a printer pak and should be available by (?) next meeting.

Comments solicited on the mystery programs tell us to make the contests no closer together than every 3 to 4 months.

Val suggested that wise APPLE owners should not miss out on the Woz Pak documentation. This is the bunch of stuff that Randy Wiggington dropped off with Val that contains what is reported to be loads of hints. A bargain at $10.00 ($12.50 for those that have to be mailed).

Secretary's comment — Buy this documentation.

Mike Thyng and Bob Huelsdonk conducted a disk seminar. They commented on the proper way to use the disk and which statements cause what to happen. Next meeting the seminar portion will discuss strings and arrays. Meeting dissolved at 8:40.

## TRANSIENT VOLTAGE PROTECTORS

By Steve Paulson

The transient voltages that we are concerned about are those which occur when any electric or electronic device is energized or de-energized. These interruptions in current flow cause "spikes" or peaks of voltage which are then transmitted to the computer. Since the computer uses very defined voltages and currents for it's memory, logic and timing functions, these sudden changes in voltage and current can do great harm.

The Transient Voltage Protector is a device that utilizes several varistors to detect any transient voltages and then disperse them to ground. Sometimes (as in the turning on of an electric range, refrigerator, light switch, or any number of electric devices), these transient voltages can be as high as 1200 volts and more. One might imagine the damage that could occur if these voltages were to enter the small silicon chips of the Apple.

The Transient Voltage Protector is a simple device that plugs into the wall outlet and then the computer (or any device) is then plugged into the protector. One should make sure the protector is rated at a sufficient level to provide protection. A rule-of-thumb is that it should be able to handle voltages of at least four times the source. That is, for the Apple, one would need protection of at least 500 volts.

A Transient Voltage Protector can be purchased from Computerland of Federal Way for about 12 dollars and at many electronic stores. This is a small price to pay for the protection afforded.

```
***************************
*                         *
*      SIMPLE TONES       *
*   A DEMONSTRATION FOR   *
*      EXTENSIONS TO      *
*       APPLESOFT-II      *
*                         *
*      SEPTEMBER, 1978    *
*                         *
*       R. WIGGINTON      *
***************************
*
* SIMPLE TONE PROGRAM FOR APPLESOFT-II
* INSIDE THE APPLESOFT PROGRAM:
*    &T <NOTE>,<DURATION>
* THIS MUSIC ROUTINE IS NOT CALIBRATED TO ANY SCALE
* WHATSOEVER.
*
                CHRGET  EQU     $00B1
                CHRGOT  EQU     $00B7
                SPKR    EQU     $C030
                GETBYT  EQU     $E6F8
                SNERR   EQU     $DEC9
                WAIT    EQU     $FCA8
                        ORG     $0300
0300 C9 54      SIMTON  CMP     #$54 ;'T' FOR TONE?
0302 D0 0F              BNE     GIVERR ;IF NOT, GIVE A SYNTAX ERROR
0304 20 B1 00           JSR     CHRGET ;GO OVER THE 'T'
0307 20 F8 E6           JSR     GETBYT ;AND GET A VALUE FROM 0-255 FOR THE NOTE
030A 8A                 TXA     ;PRESERVE
030B 48                 PHA
030C 20 B7 00           JSR     CHRGOT ;IS IT A COMMA NEXT?
030F C9 2C              CMP     #$2C
0311 F0 03              BEQ     OK
0313 4C C9 DE   GIVERR  JMP     SNERR ;NO IT WASN'T A COMMA, BLOW HIM AWAY.
0316 20 B1 00   OK      JSR     CHRGET ;EAT THE COMMA.
0319 20 F8 E6           JSR     GETBYT ;NOW GET THE LENGTH OF THE NOTE.
*
* NOW PLAY THE NOTE.
*
031C 68         PLAY    PLA     ;GET NOTE FROM STACK.
031D 48                 PHA     ;COPY BACK ONTO THE STACK
031E 20 A8 FC           JSR     WAIT ;DELAY BEFORE CLICKING SPEAKER AGAIN
0321 AD 30 C0           LDA     SPKR ;CLICK THE SPEAKER.
0324 CA                 DEX
0325 D0 F5              BNE     PLAY ;KEEP PLAYING.
0327 68                 PLA     ;CLEAR UP STACK.
0328 60                 RTS     ;GO BACK INTO APPLESOFT.
*
* APPLESOFT EXTENSION LINK:
*
                        ORG     $3F5
03F5 4C 00 03   EXTLOC  JMP     SIMTON
```

## APPLE-SHARING
by Jeffrey K. Finn © 1978
Part I of II

(Part I is intended primarily for those with only a limited knowledge of computer time-sharing. It's the stuff I didn't know but would have found helpful when I was getting started. Part II, next month, will contain technical information gathered by myself through the school of "tough luck.")

Time-sharing is the way many large-memory, high-speed computers are utilized to maximize their production and return on investment. I'm sure you've already realized while using your Apple, that you're usually the reason it doesn't work faster. When you're sitting at the keyboard, you're not typing at the 120 characters per second that the Apple reads your cassette tapes. Nobody is blaming you. After all, you're only human. In the meantime, the disk is merrily reading in information at a rate in the average range of three or four thousand characters per second. But even the disk is not taking advantage of Apple's Central Processor Unit, the 6502, and its memory chips. They are screaming for characters which they are able to manipulate at a rate some fifty times faster than the disk. That is in the range of 200,000 characters per second. We're talking about memory chips with read access time in the hundreds of nanoseconds. (One nanosecond equals a billionth of a second.) This is approaching the speed of light which travels one foot in one nanosecond. Please remember that it physically takes a certain amount of time for an electrical impulse to travel through the length of the wiring itself.

You are probably as confused as I was when I first tried to comprehend the speed of Apple's Central Processor Unit, (CPU), and its memory. To put these figures in a more understandable ratio, let's slow the whole thing down like a slow motion movie. Suppose the CPU were to operate at a speed where it could manipulate a character somewhere in the range of 3/4 of a second. Relative to that speed, the disk provides one character every 1/2 minute. The tape cassettes are providing a character every 3/4 of an hour, and a good typist at a keyboard terminal can put in a character every three to five hours. Next, consider all the times you've stopped to think a second, just one second, about the next key to type. In the relative time frame we're using, a real second is like a whole day to your Apple's CPU. That CPU is in there asking itself, "Hasn't that fool at the keyboard sent me a character yet?"

As you can see, a CPU which uses a keyboard, or most any other mechanical input/output device for moving information, has a lot of free time in which it could be doing something else. A large central memory core is needed to keep the CPU working at its full capacity as well as handle the few large jobs which require large memory areas for data bases and/or intermediate results. In these large computer installations when large jobs weren't being run, it was found several small jobs could be run simultaneously by having the CPU processing a small job in one section of its memory while loading and unloading the other jobs in other parts of its core memory. The information is transferred to and from the core memory in complete blocks, usually via a hard disk system. Except in times of high demand, the fact that several jobs are being run is not perceptible to the individual user.

To keep the core memory filled with information for the CPU to process, a master program which does several things is run continually. (You might think of this master program as something similar to your Apple's monitor program.) This master program 1) Tells the CPU which of the programs in memory to work on next; 2) Keeps track of what the CPU is doing; 3) Keeps track of what sections of core memory are being used for what; 4) Keeps track of which input/output devices, (printers, keyboard terminals, card readers, tape decks, disk files), are ready to send or receive information; 5) Organizes input/output into logical and complete blocks of information; and, 6) Directs the movement of those blocks of information among the various input/output devices and the computer's memory.

Through this master management program, the CPU is kept continually operating at a speed close to its potential, and its associated core memory is kept as full as possible, thus maximizing the central computer's use. To further assist your understanding of this subject, the following is a description of a typical, but much simplified, operating sequence of one of these master, (time-sharing), programs. First the program checks all input devices to see if there are any that want to send information to the main computer. If it sees that a punch card needs to be read at a card reader, a signal is sent to the reader to "read." While the card reader is starting to feed the card through its reading mechanism, the program recognizes that someone has depressed a key at a keyboard terminal. It issues a command to store the code for the key depressed in a particular area of the hard disk. It then goes back to the card reader in time to get the code from the card being read and stores that in a different area on the hard disk. All this takes place in less than the blink of an eye.

The program continues this process until it gets a code from one of the input devices that says this is the end of the information (job) from this particular device. The program then checks the area(s) on the hard disk where it had been storing the particular input to see how much there is, and estimates how much CPU time the requested processing will take. If there is sufficient CPU time and available core memory locations, it will transfer the block of information from the hard disk to the core memory and tell the CPU in what order it should start work on the information beginning at that location in core memory.

At the same time, the time-sharing program is also checking to see what information the CPU has finished processing. When it spots some, it moves the block of completed work back out to the hard disk. It then searches for the specified output device to see if it is ready to receive the information. These output devices include printers, card punches, tape punches, monitors, etc. When the device is ready to receive the information, the time-sharing program sends the information to the device.

One of the input/output devices that can be used is a telephone port. It enables information coded in that computer's format and an agreed-upon code, commonly ASCII, to be transmitted and received by ordinary telephone lines. In order to transmit on telephone lines which carry only tones, a device called a Modulator/Demodulator (MODEM) is placed between the computer's telephone port and the telephone handset. (The sophisticated operations combine all this with automatic answering and dialing and connect to lines without a phone.) The MODEM changes the ASII coded information into tones and tones into ASCII code.

Obviously, for this system to work, there needs to be a MODEM at both ends of the telephone line — one at the end where the central computer is located, and one at the other end which must be connected to some kind of terminal. The terminal decodes the central computer's format, (seven or eight bits, parity, etc.), for transmitting characters and uses the decoded characters in the manner it has been built to present information. It could punch cards, print on paper, or be a TV monitor.

This is essentially the way time-sharing works, and through the use of the Apple Communication Card you can participate yourself using the card as the encoder and decoder for your Apple. It enables your Apple to act as though it were a "dumb" terminal which can only send or receive characters from the central computer. It also allows your Apple to be a "smart" terminal and process information received from the central computer utilizing some of the powerful graphic capabilities of Apple's software. The potential is boundless.

One thing that you should remember if you are getting a MODEM for your Apple, is that with the Communication Card, your Apple can act as either the central time-sharing computer or the terminal. This means that your MODEM should be able to operate in both "originate" and "answer" modes. These terms refer to an adopted convention where the terminal's MODEM, the one doing the calling, is known as the "originate" MODEM and the time-sharing system's MODEM is the "answer" unit. This is done so the two MODEMs can go through a "handshaking" procedure to align their timing and tone generators.

In this handshaking procedure, the MODEM you call sends out a tone which your MODEM hears. That tone is saying, "Hello! Hello! Anybody there?" Your MODEM sends back a different tone which says, "It's me! I think we're in tune!?" If everything is in order, the answering MODEM sends back tones which mean, "Yes, we're in tune and I'm ready to receive information." If you've followed the procedures for that particular time-sharing computer you should be able to read a message on your monitor that requests you to properly "log in" on that time-sharing system.

A more complete article on MODEMs, their operation, and how to build them, is contained in the May, 1978 (3-4) issue of the Northwest Computer Society's Northwest Computer News.

My article next month will be about methods to avoid the pitfalls I experienced while attempting to get the "log in"message to appear on my monitor. If you avoid these pitfalls, most any computer in the world that has a telephone port can be connected to your Apple. In this way your Apple can be enhanced to equal the capabilities of those computers.

There may be errors in my statements or calculations due to my own misunderstandings. Though some of the information I have presented would not pass the rigorous scrutiny of professional engineers or computer experts, I felt required to write an article for our Call -Apple from a layman's point of view. I did it as an encouragement to other A.P.P.L.E. members who have gained valuable information which should be shared. I would appreciate hearing from those who discover errors in my writing so I can correct my misunderstandings. Val can put you in contact with me.

The following program is a simple illustration of the time-sharing principles I have discussed. It is intended to demonstrate the speed with which the Apple can simultaneously accommodate incoming information from four sources and display it. Imagine the Apple's game paddles and swiches as four terminals and that they are connected to four Apple telephone ports. See what happens when you twist the dials or push the buttons. To illustrate the speed of the CPU, see what happens if you push both buttons simultaneously. How perceptible is the delay in the screen's display? If the display for both buttons' condition didn't change at the same time, you didn't push at the same time. Can you perceive the time difference needed to push the buttons so that the status of button 0 changes on one line of output and the status of button 1 changes on the next output line?

```
100 REM TIME-SHARING DEMONSTRATION
110 REM BY JEFFREY K. FINN 9/17/78
120 REM THIS PROGRAM DEMONSTRATES
    THE SPEED WITH WHICH THE CPU
    REACTS TO EXTERNAL, MECHANICAL
    INPUT. <INTEGER BASIC>
200 CALL -936
210 PRINT "PRESS ANY KEY TO STOP PRO
    GRAM": PRINT "PADDLE0 PADDLE1 SW
    ITCH0 SWITCH1"
220 POKE 34,2
230 A= PEEK (-16287):B= PEEK (-
    16286): IF PEEK (-16384)>127
    THEN 300
240 IF A>127 THEN 280
250 IF B>127 THEN 310
260 PRINT PDL (0), PDL (1),"OFF"
    ,"OFF"
270 GOTO 230
280 IF B>127 THEN 330
290 PRINT PDL (0), PDL (1),"ON "
    ,"OFF"
300 GOTO 230
310 PRINT PDL (0), PDL (1),"OFF"
    ,"ON"
320 GOTO 230
330 PRINT PDL (0), PDL (1),"ON "
    ,"ON"
340 GOTO 230
```

Dear Sirs:

Being the wife of an Apple computer nut, I felt other women in my predicament would appreciate this little tribute. I would appreciate it if you would publish it in your next monthly newsletter.

"For the Apple Widows"

Attention ladies ...
I'm in distress!!
My eyelids are twitching
My head's all a mess.

I married into
A strange family
Where life is comprised
Of monitors and keys.

With PEEK and POKE
and LOAD and RUN
Any sabotage
Is a job well done!

From Qubic, Artillery,
Pong and Star Wars,
My brain has just about
Run it's course!!

I know computers
Are entertaining and neat,
But when your husband
Forgets to breathe and eat???

I suppose, I suppose I could
Refuse to fight
Just wash the dishes
And accept my plight.

Would someone, somehow,
Somewhere please
Help me control this
New disease?

If you have an idea
That's unusually great
I'll be in EMMANUEL
Psych. Ward, Rm. 208.

Cindy Rogers
934 N.E. 73rd
Portland, OR 97213

WE'RE SURE you are not alone!

## APPLEMASH

By Mike Thyng

Last time, we talked about single dimensioned numerical arrays. We also considered how and why the DIMension statement works. This time, we'll look at Alpha String arrays, INTEGER and Floating Point arrays and Multi-Dimensioning.

First some basics. We must tell the computer what type of data we're working with. Let's consider a variable called A. If we want A to store numeric values with results from "hard core" mathematics, we're talking about floating point variables, conveniently thought of as numbers with decimal points 5.6, - 8.13, .00477, etc. If we need counters or simple arithmetic variables without decimals, then we'd use integers. Now, when we want alphabetic data, like names or alphanumeric data like addresses or secret formulas (formulae) then we need string variables. For our example of A, A would be floating point, A% would be integer and A$ would be string or alphanumeric.

Now back to arrays. Last time we talked about keeping track of Quarterback Jim Zorn's passing yardage with a numerical array. This time let's find a way to keep track of the whole team's 100 yard dash times. First we set up space for each team member. They're allowed 45 players, so we set up our players names by DIM PNAMES (45). PNAME is our variable (players name), $ denotes string, and 45 sets up space for 46 players. Remember: PNAMES (0) through PNAMES (45). We'll use 1 through 45. Next, DIMension for their times. PTIME (a floating point variable should be DIMensioned.) DIM PTIME (45). Now let's take a look at one approach to recording the necessary data.

```
10 REM ALPHA-NUMERIC ARRAY TEST
20 DIM PNAMES (45)
30 DIM PTIME (45)
40 SB = 1
50 INPUT "PLAYER    "; SB;"  "; PNAMES (SB)
60 INPUT "PLAYER    "; SB; "'S   TIME   "; PTIME (SB)
70 SB = SB + 1
80 GO TO 50
```

This won't let you do much with the data you'd record, but after you've recorded players and times, you can refer to a player and his time with one subscript. That is PNAMES (18) and PTIME (18) refer to the player. This gives you an idea of how alpha and numeric arrays can work together.

Multi-Dimensional Arrays are set up like this:

DIM A (6, 5, 4). They're great for games and solving linear algebra through matrices. But that's outside the scope of this article. In example A (6, 5, 4) a down to earth use might be that you want to keep track of how many sales your salesmen are making in 4 attempts in each of 5 areas. Let's say you have 6 salespeople. Each one has a salesperson number. Each one must try to sell some gizmos in each of 5 areas. In each area the salesperson gets 4 chances. So, with multi-dimensioning you can record the number of sales per area per salesperson.

(continued on page 16)

# AUTOMATED TRAINING SYSTEMS   PHONE (206) 935-2697

Automated Training Systems has been a Washington State Licensed Proprietory School since 1968. It is a fun school, now operated from Cliff Gazaway's home at 7906 34th. S.W. in West Seattle. Many of the classes have been taught by Cliff, who has had 20 years of electronics hardware experience, ten years of teaching, and formal education in biology, teacher training, and business administration.

In addition to classes, tours, and social activities the following fun computer oriented get-togethers are offered at 7906 34th.S.W., Seattle at 7:00 to 9:00 PM Monday evenings. These are not formal meetings but a place for people to meet and talk and enjoy soft drinks and snacks.

```
First Monday each month--------6502 interests.Pet.Apple.Ohio Sci.
Second Monday each month-------Radio Shack interests.
Third Monday each month--------S100, 8080,Z80 interests.
Fourth Monday each month-------RCA 1802, Little Elf,VIP.
```

Brink food and soft drinks to share. Also bring your computer, books, and ideas. We plan to provide a computer library and book store.

THE FOLLOWING CLASSES HAVE BEEN OFFERED IN THE PAST WITH GREAT SUCCESS. If enough interest is shown, they will be repeated in the future.

### 320 Put Microswitches Under Its Toes and It Is Your Equal

The adult white male thinks he is intellectually superior to anyone and anything. Any adult, male or female, black or white, feels more intelligent than any child, animal, or machine. This course is a writing and research workshop that will challenge the superiority of man. We will write a magazine article or book to show that man's conceit has altered his perception of intelligence. We will show that a two year old can understand as much as the adult will let him (He can learn to repair radios at age 3 if his parents think he can.) We will show that a chimpanzee can learn, speak, and understand a thousand-word vocabulary (probably more if I could conceive of it). We will show that computers can do anything that the human brain can do. We will study an electric turtle, that has a brain simpler than a pocket radio, but that can act as intelligently as a 5-year-old human. We will show electromechanical ways of compensating for the real physical (not mental) deficiencies in children and "lower" animals—so that they can match our (!) intellect.

### 519 Biofeedback and Electrical Control of the Mind
Clifford M. Gazaway

Biofeedback, a technique which allows you to control the state of your health, happiness and well being solely through the power of your mind, without the use of drugs. Sounds like science fiction. But in hospitals and laboratories across the country it is becoming science fact. This course is a comprehensive report on a spectacular scientific breakthrough. By listening to your body or brain waves on a special electronic machine, you can learn to control them to achieve inner peace and joy, and even a drugless alpha-wave high. This course is not a clinic but we will discuss how to select a clinic without getting ripped off. We will also discuss where to buy or build your own equipment for less than $60.00.

### 380 The Mating of the Celestial Spheres

A pair of 3-D radiant spheres pursue each other, embrace erotically, dance exotically, twisting and turning to the beat of the music from your radio or hi-fi. Connect a microphone to the lovers and they obey your every command. Clap your hands and they fly apart. Hum and they snuggle together, purring contentedly. Makes a beautiful hanging lamp! This is a workshop for unusual lighting.

### 117 Psychedelic Electronics and Lighting
Clifford M. Gazaway

Floating, exploding, multi-colored patterns, created inside your body with your eyes shut. Same effect produced by LSD but this electronic method is still legal. Electronics can do almost anything drugs can do. This course in psychedelic electronics shows the fun and euphoria as well as it warns of the dangers of sensuous electronics. Subjects include amateur shock therapy, electrical sex devices, black lights, sound lights, heart beat lights, bio-feedback, etc. Class includes theory and construction. No technical ability needed for some sections.

### 116 Million Dollar Light-Show for $999.99
Clifford M. Gazaway

I will show you how to make the best light show ever built. This fantastic light show would cost you well over $1,000,000.00 if you were to purchase it or to hire it built. I am not exaggerating one bit. Your $7.00 course fee will be refunded if you are the first student to show me documentation proving that there is a more fantastic light show, anywhere, that can be bought for less than a million dollars. If you can wire up a light bulb and use ordinary hand tools you can tackle this project. If you do not have a $999.99 budget you can build a mini-light show for 29 cents.

See back issues of CALL-APPLE for course descriptions of:
BEGINNING APPLE BASIC; POKING & PEEKING AT YOUR APPLE; APPLE CIRCUIT THEORY; CONNECTING THE APPLE TO THE REAL WORLD; and CHRISTMAS PRESENTS FOR APPLELOVERS.

SOFTWARE WANTED: Apple computer programs are wanted. These program will be sold nationwide. You can make some money from programs that you did not even realize were worth selling. Cliff is marketing two series of programs. One is called Quick and Dirty Software. It will be ten to twenty short programs for ten to twenty dollars. The other series will be called "Bigger and Better" programs and will sell for ten dollars to $200 per program. Cliff has had considerable experience selling by mailorder. He would like to sell your Apple software.

## AUTOMATED TRAINING SYSTEMS   PHONE (206) 935-2697,

7906 34th.S.W.,Seattle,Wa.98126

## PEEKS, POKES and CALLS

Peeks, Pokes and Calls are among the powerful commands at your disposal. They permit you to wander through the passageways and corridors of your Apple's memory. RAM memory may be looked upon as a huge old-fashioned post office file cabinet, with 65,536 pigeon holes, which are actually memory "locations", numbered from 0 to 65535 (decimal) or from 0 to FFFF (hex). Each location is capable of holding one one byte (or unit) of data (information). A "byte" is a hexidecimal number with a value between 0 and FF (0 to 255, decimal).

Hexidecimal is a number base in which the unit column may have a value between 0 and 15. The numbers 10 to 15 are expressed as the letters A through F, thus F equals 15, while hex 10 equals 16. The dollar sign ($) is commonly used to indicate a hex number. In number systems, hex is known as base 16. Other number systems used in microcomputers are octal (base 8) and binary (base 2). Your Apple actually works in binary, but this is essentially an internal process that most users are unaware of.

Any hex number greater than FF must be stored in memory as two consecutive bytes, with the low order byte stored first. To convert a two byte hex number to decimal, we must do more than simply convert the hex values to decimal. For an example, let us take the hex number 7FFF (remembering that this will appear as FF7F (in reverse order) as you look at it in memory) and convert it to decimal. The procedure is always the same: the high order (second) byte is multiplied by 256 and the value of the low order (first) byte is added to the result. Therefore, 7F=127, 127*256=32512, and FF=255, so 32512+255=32767. We have just converted 7FFF stored as two consecutive hex bytes of FF and 7F to their decimal equivalent of 32767!. A working knowledge of hex is needed to put all the power of Apple at your beck and CALL.

We're sorry Applemash did not make the last issue in time. Mike apologizes and we apologize and... oh, the hell with it!

The CALL command is to assembly (or machine) language what GOSUB is to Basic. Instead of saying GOSUB and specifying a Basic line number, you write a Call to a memory location. The effect is the same: you are asking Apple to execute a subroute, only in machine language instead of Basic.

POKE and PEEK are opposites, and aptly named. POKE is the command that allows you to store data in memory, perhaps for use at a later time. For example, a tone subroutine in Integer Basic may be located in hex locations 2 to 18. Locations $0 and $1 are to be used to store the values of the variables PITCH and DURATION, (commonly P & D. So a line in your program might read:
100 P=25: D=150: POKE 0,P: POKE 1,D: CALL 2

A PEEK command allows you to look inside the very core (pun intended) of your Apple and see what is stored there. Example: you want to know what your high mem is set at. The values of "HIMEM" are stored in decimal locations 76 and 77 (remember, this is a two byte figure), so you can use this simple algorhythm to find out:

PRINT PEEK (76) + PEEK (77) * 256

Incidently, these are called "pointers" because they "point" to where high memory actually is. Another example of useing the PEEK command is when you want the computer to "peek" at the keyboard to see if the user has typed a character or not. A common way to do this is as follows: Assume you are asking the user to type a Y or N to indicate yes or no. You could write it like this:

```
100 KEY = PEEK(-16384)
110 IF KEY < 128 THEN 110
120 IF KEY = 217 THEN 200
130 END
```

In Integer Basic, the "Ascii" character set has values between 128 and 255. If the variable "Key" in our example is less than 128, it means no key has been typed, and the program has been sent back to read the keyboard again, until such time as the user actually types a character. 217 is the Ascii value for the character "Y".

## APPLE SOURCE
Transcribed by Mike Thyng

The following transcription is an approximation of the question and answer session held at the September meeting at Computerland of Bellevue where Apple President Mike Scott and Randy Wigginton addressed members. Many people were too far away to be clearly recorded. Other times, someone would cough or shuffle when a key word was spoken by a distant or soft speaker. So I have tried to relate as accurately as possible the intent of the questions and remarks by both sides.

In this portion Q. = club members. A. = Mike Scott
A. The Apple disk drives are not intended to be used with other computers. The APPLE hardware was designed to be integral and interactive within the APPLE. The APPLE disks are soft sectored. The drive is not a standard Shugart 400 drive. The Shugart Standard Analog Board has 23 IC's; APPLE had 4. The S-100 controller card has 30 IC's - the APPLE has 8. APPLE accomplished substantial savings by tying the design together of the software firmware, and hardware. You can cut a notch in the other side and use both sides of the diskettes.

2A is the identifier of the most current version of APPLESOFT II. Disk was released with only the right version of APPLESOFT. The ROM card is gospel.

Q. You changed the definition of LOMEM in APPLESOFT. Is there any way to get the equivalent Integer Basic LOMEM from APPLESOFT?

A. You mean so it doesn't use memory belowa certain point? Yes, there is. Do a POKE of 103, 104. This is the base address of your APPLESOFT program. If you have a ROM card and disk and your programs are saved onto the disk, with the RAM version you have to do a call. What's happening is that we have to relocate all the pointers down for the ROM Card and back up for the RAM version. So if you adjust 103, 104 then you're going to have to do those calls. From RAM to ROM call 54514. From ROM to RAM (in memory) call 3314. Loading from tape you never have those problems. It does it all automatically. See Val's write up about the ampersand.

Q. I've had problems initializing disks from my master create program. A. Easiest solution is to move the disk card from slot 6 to slot 7. When the new version of the DOS comes out, we'll have that corrected. We wanted to standardize the slots and leave slot 7 open for a possible video interface card if and when we ever do an 80 character or some other video interface. When APPLE wrote the DOS for the European Market the boards were in slot 7. Then shortly before USA release they were switched from slot 7 to slot 6. Not all the software routines were changed back. There's a new manual being printed that will explain much more about your APPLE. Expected distribution is in OCTOBER. 180 pages long; detail about how exactly APPLESOFT works.

Q. Is PASCAL software being developed for the APPLE? A. Not by APPLE but by a company in San Diego. Q. What languages are you planning to introduce? A. I'm not at liberty to say which, but APPLE has contracted with outside software suppliers to provide a second and a third generation language. Q. When will we get a real time clock? A. We've worked on it some. The problem now is the high cost. It's on our list of things to do. Q. How many APPLEs are there? A. Everybody wants to know. It's a well kept secret. Many, many thousands. A. We allocate product on a first order in - first order out. If we don't have enough to fill all the orders fully then we allocated a percentage to each order so everybody gets some.

THE NEXT PORTION IS BEING FIELDED BY RANDY WIGGINTON. RANDY WRITES SYSTEMS SOFTWARE DID APPLESOFT II AND WROTE PART OF THE DOS.

Memory allocation starts at hex location 800 for the ROM cards. The variables are located immediately after the program. First it's simple variables, then array variables. String arrays have pointers. A$ = "HELLO" has pointers that point inside the program. A$ = B$ then B$ points to A$. Strings are allocated memory from high memory down. If you set A$ = something and B$ = Something, and C$ = something, and then change it, you are leaving blanks. These blanks stay there until you run the program; then the program shifts things around. This explains why a large program may take many minutes to run. It has a lot of number crunching to do. I gave Val Golding about 2 inches of documentation and miscellaneous things.

You could have 6 colors in HIRES: HCOLOR = 0, 4 black 3, 7 white then 1, 2, 5, 6 could be four other colors but unnamed because the way you adjust the TV set would alter the colors. Future versions of DOS call for it to be about 3K rather than the present 11K. Val has the RWTS routines that let you use the disk directly. All the new stuff will be on DOS. The Interface to disk requires that when you write to disk you input the command number, specify whether you want to format the disk, read or write the track and sector data.

Q. You can't write a "to disk" can you? A. Anytime you want to get a "to the disk, write CHRS(n), where n is the numerical decimal equivalent of the character." A. The new manual will have stuff about how to create your own save tape. A Macro assembler will be coming out ... Q. I've got a file on my disk that was written with an illegal character and now I want to delete it. A. Initialize the disk. Only way presently. Q. What about a copy? A. That would only transfer the bogus data to the new disk. Q. I did an open, a write and a CATALOG and the CATALOG cancelled out the write. I wanted to get a copy of the CATALOG out on a text file so I could bring it in later and .... A. Whenever you go into write mode, anytime you print a control D or try to do an input you'll move out of write mode. Basically there is no way presently that you can get your catalog written out. The Catalog is located on disk at tracks 17 & 18. APPLE has spent many hours trying to find ways to neatly read the Catalog but so far no success. Checkbook II has a way to do this, but it's not elegant.

Many questions about the disk format. Data written out is in ASCII Mode. When or if you Print A, B the data would go out as it would look on the display screen. But, and this is a big one, you could not read back that A, B as A, B. The disk sees that as all one variable. Don't panic. The solution is to PRINT A: PRINT B. What's required is to get the variables seperated by a carriage return symbol. Individual Prints do that. Q. I have trouble converting programs from magazines (written for other computer's BASIC's) to programs for my APPLE. A. We're working on it.

Q. How often will CONTACT come out? A. We're working on every two months, but not yet. In the future, perhaps every month. Q. Does the APPLE see A and shift A as the same character? A. Unmodified, yes. I have given Val information on lower case. If you add a wire to the keyboard then lower case characters will display as reverse video. Q. I can't get the other square bracket to print. A. Try PRINT CHR$ (154). Or something close to 154. Q. Does the disk store PR # someplace? A. You mean it's own character out switches? Q. Where are they? A. Up in High Memory somewhere.

My printer is hooked up to the Communications interface card and when I use a comma, it doesn't seem to recognize it. A. When we hit a comma, we change the cursor horizontal directly in memory. On the printer card we check to see if the cursor horizontal jumps by more than 1. If it does, it puts in the extra spaces. The Communications Card does not do that. I suggest you TAB or use the Space command. Q. When I try to print out 3 strings A$, B$, C$ and use commas, depending on the length of the second string, I may print on line 1 or line 2 ... what gives? A. Plain and simple, I made an error. I meant to check 33 instead of 23. Q. How do you determine how much space you have left on your disk? A. You know those Numbers just ahead of the program names in the CATALOG? Well those are completely random. Actually there isn't a way.

Q. My APPLE's DOS won't let me read or write above 256. What gives? A. You have an earlier version. Your club has the patch. Q. HTAB doesn't work above 40 characters on my printer. A. POKE 36, value will do it for you. Q. Do we have indirect addressing in BASIC? A. No. A. DOS documentation and a revised version of the DOS will be coming out.

A. When you have problems, suggestions, or comments ... write them in - don't call. We can't be effective by phone. Q. I have a mix of 16K and 4K chips ...A. DOS can handle it. Q. Does the Communication Interface card handle the IBM BAUD rate of 134? A. I think that is one on the standard selections ... if not, the manual that came with it can tell you how to set it to that rate. A. There is a new high speed serial interface card coming out - up to 19K baud. Switch and software selectable. Q. I have an idea for a change to the case of the APPLE II. A. We're not likely to make any changes to the APPLE II case design because it costs $80,000.00 for tooling to make the case. A. 80% of the failures that occur in the field, are caused by plugging the ribbon in improperly. Plugging the ribbon one pin off will cause the LS125 chip to fry and put your disk out of commission.

Q. Can I handle files without a disk? On the cassette tape? A. You need a disk. Q. We have a program that uses illegal line numbers and sets HIMEM. It works fine when loaded from cassette tape but doesn't work loaded from disk. A. I don't know. Q. When you use random access to write on record 97 of a 250 record file, do you mess up records above 97?

A. No, not at all. Q. How do we determine end of file? A. Either put in a special code in the last record and test for it when reading, or reserve the first record of the file for telling your program where the end is. See the ANIMALS program. When you read or write, be sure you start and end with a control D. Q. Any plans to put some kind of joysticks into production? A. No. Q. Are the new HIRES routines done any differently than the old routines? A. While we've had many versions of HIRES they are still being done the same.

Q. Explain the EXEC file. A. It is a sequential text file which contains execute statements. Someone wrote "well, Randy" on the front of the Call-APPLE magazine, referring to the statement I made that you can't convert from Integer to APPLESOFT. The conversion shown doesn't convert TAB to HTAB. I got out of that one. On the APPLESOFT CARDS I gave you HPLOT X, Y to X, Y to X, Y (applause) Q. Do you have a fix for the PIA? A. APPLE has a schematic for a PIA on an interface card.

A. We're working on a General Purpose Serial and a General Purpose Parallel cards. APPLE would like to solicit your comments. Write to APPLE, tell us what you want these cards to be able to do. Q. What about lightpens. A. We've hooked one up and had it working. Q. How many peripheral devices can one APPLE II handle? A. 8 APPLE peripheral cards and 48K. Q. Do you have any X-Y Plotter plans? A. We're working with AXIOM trying to develop an inexpensive plotting device. We're looking into a bit pad too. Approximate cost six to eight hundred dollars. Our product line will be expanding. Q. Will you be expanding to an eight inch floppy? A. Not for the APPLE II. However, we may be getting into hard disk for the APPLE II in 1½ to 2 years. Earlier maybe double density, double sided disks with half a megabyte per drive. Q. COLOR Monitor plans? A. We're talking to 3 manufacturers. Haven't chosen yet.

APPLEMASH (from page 12)

Again, as with single dimension arrays, you're setting aside space for your variables. For our 6 x 5 x 4 array above, we set aside places for 120 variables. I've had some arrays in testing that were 8 dimensional. I suppose core size is the only limitation on how many dimensions you can have, though it's really not practical to go much beyond 3 dimensions.

Next issue, we'll discuss how to use the APPLE Disk "T" files, random access — great stuff.

There is one bit of philosophy I want to end with. If it was more practical to have million byte core computers, then arrays of 8 or even more dimensions could be used instead of disk files. Remember, accessing data from an array is MUCH faster than accessing it from disk. In an array there is only solid state electronics between you and the data. On a disk file there's that mechanical arm and rotating diskette which must coordinate before you can get your data. Arrays are faster. Disks are more practical. I'll try to teach you how to use both. It is up to you to decide which is best for your application.

## IDENTIFYING BINARY DISK PROGRAMS

Here are two ways to help you save and identify binary (machine language) programs on disk. First, follow this procedure, (which conflicts with the method suggested by Apple Computer), for BSAVEing your machine language programs: 1. If DOS is not up, boot it up. 2. CALL -151 (This puts you in Monitor without resetting. 3. load your machine language program from tape. 4. Control C back to Basic (or Applesoft). 5. Type "BSAVE PROGRAM,A$a,L$l" (where a= starting address and l= length). 6. Enter a NEW command (to insure nothing is in memory) and type "SAVE PROGRAM A$a L$l". What this accomplishes is to save a "dummy" basic program (composed of nothing) which identifies where the binary program stores.

Another problem may occur where you have an existing binary program on disk and would like to copy it. This is a wee bit difficult if you have forgotten the address or length. To this end, we have written a program called "BINADR", which will load a binary program and tell you its address and length. It appears on this page.

Finally, a housekeeping hint, not directly related to the foregoing. We use this little trick to show when a disk is full. Again, this involves SAVEing a "dummy" program, and we do the title in inverse, to make it stand out.

POKE 50,63. PRINT "THIS DISK FULL". POKE 50,255. Now the words "THIS DISK FULL" will have appeared on the screen in inverse form and you should next type "SAVE". Then, using the escape (edit) keys, trace over the inverse characters and hit return. You now have a program named "THIS DISK FULL", and the title is displayed in inverse video!

```
50 REM   BINADR BY VAL J GOLDING
51 REM   APPLE PUGETSOUND PROGRAM
              LIBRARY EXCHANGE
52 REM   WRITTEN IN INTEGER BASIC
53 REM   THIS PROGRAM OUTPUTS A$ &
              L$ INFO FOR BINARY PROGRAMS
100 GOTO 500
110 IF PEEK (77)<64 THEN 150
120 PRINT 16384: REM SET LOMEM:16384

130 DIM FILE$(40): GOTO 160
140 PRINT 2048: END : REM RESET LOMEM

150 PRINT (( PEEK (77)-5)*256): GOTO
    130: REM LOMEM FOR 16K MACHINE

160 D$="": REM  CONTROL D
170 PRINT D$;"NOMON C,I,O"
180 TEXT : CALL -936: VTAB 14: INPUT
    "INPUT FILE NAME ",FILE$
190 IF FILE$="" THEN 180
200 PRINT D$;"BLOAD ";FILE$;",V0"

210 IF PEEK (77)>127 THEN 400: REM GO
    TO ROUTINE FOR 48K MACHINE

220 REM FIND POINTERS

230 HM= PEEK (76)+ PEEK (77)*256
    :LS=HM+5045:HS=HM+5046:START=
    PEEK (LS)+ PEEK (HS)*256
240 LL=HM+5027:HL=HM+5028:LENGTH=
    PEEK (LL)+ PEEK (HL)*256
250 CALL -936: VTAB 10: TAB 6: PRINT
    "DECIMAL STARTING ADDRESS IS: "
    ;START: PRINT : TAB 6: PRINT
    "DECIMAL LENGTH IS: ";LENGTH
260 PRINT : TAB 6: INPUT "MORE ?"
    ,Z$
270 IF Z$="Y" THEN 160: GOTO 140

400 START= PEEK (-22091)+ PEEK (
    -22090)*256:LENGTH= PEEK (-22109
    )+ PEEK (-22108)*256: GOTO 100

500 IF PEEK (203)>127 THEN 550
505 PP= PEEK (202)+ PEEK (203)*256
    : REM REPLACE PRINT WITH LOMEM:

510 IF PEEK (PP)=98 THEN POKE PP,
    17: IF PEEK (PP)=75 THEN 110
    :PP=PP+1: GOTO 510
550 PP=( PEEK (202)-256)+256*( PEEK
    (203)-255)
560 IF PEEK (PP)=98 THEN POKE PP,
    17: IF PEEK (PP)=75 THEN 110
    :PP=PP+1: GOTO 560
```

## RESURRECTING a DEAD FP PROGRAM

Have you ever had an Applesoft II program "blow up" while you were working on it, only to find that you had not SAVEd it and could not remember the algorithms you used? (They were probably based on the trial and error method, anyway), and it cost you a couple hours to recreate them?

Here is a short routine for Applesoft ROM that may help you recover your program. It requires that you be able to look into your memory and be able to identify the first two line numbers of the lost program. In addition, you must know the make-up of Applesoft Basic. It is as follows: The first two bytes are the address of the next line, and the next two bytes are the actual line number, stored low byte first. The last byte of a line is a "00" token, indicating the end of a line.

ROM Applesoft stores starting at decimal location 2049. On a disk reboot, the two locations that normally contain the address of the next line will have zeroes in them. The zeroes must be replaced with the correct next line address. Then you must estimate the length of the original program, and reset pointers as follows:

Say your program was about two K long. That is, approximately 2048 bytes. Add the program length to 2048 (start of memory), and divide by 256. (4096/256=16). Then poke your pointers (from the keyboard) as follows:

POKE 105,0:POKE 106,16:POKE 107,7:POKE 108,16: POKE 109,7:POKE 110,16: POKE 175,0:POKE 176,16:CALL 54514.

The pairs (107-8) and (109-10) must always be seven bytes more than the pairs (105-6) and (175-6). The CALL 54514 is a routine that helps you reassign the next line address pointers.

## COLOR GRAPHICS SCREEN MEMORY MAP

Y-Coordinate

```
0 0 A B C D E F
```

BASE (leftmost) address

```
0 0 0 0 0 1 C D        E A B A B 0 0 0
```
GBASH                  GBASL

Data Byte

```
X X X X Y Y Y Y
```

odd    even
line   line
data   data

| LINE | | BASE ADDR | | PG2 BASE ADR | |
|---|---|---|---|---|---|
| HEX | DEC | HEX | DEC | HEX | DEC |
| $0, 1 | 0, 1 | $400 | 1024 | $800 | 2048 |
| $2, 3 | 2, 3 | $480 | 1152 | $880 | 2176 |
| $4, 5 | 4, 5 | $500 | 1280 | $900 | 2304 |
| $6, 7 | 6, 7 | $580 | 1408 | $980 | 2432 |
| $8, 9 | 8, 9 | $600 | 1536 | $A00 | 2560 |
| $A, B | 10,11 | $680 | 1664 | $A80 | 2688 |
| $C, D | 12,13 | $700 | 1792 | $B00 | 2816 |
| $E, F | 14,15 | $780 | 1920 | $B80 | 2944 |
| $10,11 | 16,17 | $428 | 1064 | $828 | 2088 |
| $12,13 | 18,19 | $4A8 | 1192 | $8A8 | 2216 |
| $14,15 | 20,21 | $528 | 1320 | $928 | 2344 |
| $16,17 | 22,23 | $5A8 | 1448 | $9A8 | 2472 |
| $18,19 | 24,25 | $628 | 1576 | $A28 | 2600 |
| $1A,1B | 26,27 | $6A8 | 1704 | $AA8 | 2728 |
| $1C,1D | 28,29 | $728 | 1832 | $B28 | 2856 |
| $1E,1F | 30,31 | $7A8 | 1960 | $BA8 | 2984 |
| $20,21 | 32,33 | $450 | 1104 | $850 | 2128 |
| $22,23 | 34,35 | $4D0 | 1232 | $8D0 | 2256 |
| $24,25 | 36,37 | $550 | 1360 | $950 | 2384 |
| $26,27 | 38,39 | $5D0 | 1488 | $9D0 | 2512 |
| $28,29 | 40,41 | $650 | 1616 | $A50 | 2640 |
| $2A,2B | 42,43 | $6D0 | 1744 | $AD0 | 2768 |
| $2C,2D | 44,45 | $750 | 1872 | $B50 | 2896 |
| $2E,2F | 46,47 | $7D0 | 2000 | $BD0 | 3024 |

# EMPIRE ELECTRONICS

## COMPUTER SHOP

YOUR FRIENDLY APPLE DEALER

## MEMOREX DISKETTES
### $3.60 EA.

## 16K RAM CHIPS
### $174.95 INSTALLED

*****SOFTWARE**SOFTWARE*****

```
CHECKBOOK  ---$20.00 (TAPE)
DATABASE   ---$50.00 (TAPE)
VENDOR     ---$30.00 (TAPE)
PRB.SEC.   ---$94.95 (DISC)
LEDGER     ---$54.95 (TAPE)
INVOICE    ---$49.95 (TAPE)
LIB. PAKS  ---$ 5.00 ea.
```

******PRINTERS******

EXPANDER- INTERFACE AND
POWERSUPPLY
$549.95

INTEGRAL DATA IP 225
with GRAPHICS
$1148.00

JoyStiks  $8.50 EA.

890 Southcenter Shopping Center
Tukwila, Washington 98188
206-246-6120

PLEASE ADD FOR POSTAGE & HANDLING

616 SOUTHWEST 152nd
SEATTLE, WASHINGTON 98166
(206) 244-5200

# 6502 SYSTEM SPECIALS

## SYSTEMS*
**Apple II** 16K RAM $1195⁰⁰ • **Commodore PET** 8K RAM $795⁰⁰ • **Commodore KIM I** $175⁰⁰
Synertek **VIM** $269⁰⁰ • Microproducts **Super KIM** $395⁰⁰

*Delivery on most systems is usually stock to 2 weeks. Call or write for specific information.

## CLASSES AND WORKSHOPS

All classes and workshops listed here are free of charge but have limited enrollment. Preference will be given to regular CCI customers in the event of an overflow crowd.

### WORKSHOPS: Call for details.
KIM—2nd Saturday of the Month • PET—3rd Saturday of the Month
APPLE—4th Saturday of the Month

### CLASSES: Apple Topics
We offer a series of free classes on Apple II to aquaint owners with some of the unique features and capabilities of their system. Topics covered are Apple Sounds, Low Res. Graphics, Hi Res. Graphics, Disk Basics, and How to Use Your Reference Material. Sessions are held every Thursday Night at 7:00 p.m.

## SOFTWARE

**We now have a complete software catalog.**

**APPLE:**
| | |
|---|---|
| Appletalker* | $15.95 |
| Bomber* | 9.95 |
| Space Maze* | 10.00 |
| Applevision* | 5.00 |
| Color Organ* | 9.95 |
| Las Vegas Black Jack | 10.00 |
| Name and Address | 10.00 |
| Othello | 10.00 |
| Microproducts Assembler—Tape | 19.95 |
| Microproducts Assembler—Disk | 24.95 |
| RAM Test | 7.50 |
| ROM Test | 7.50 |
| Apple Music | 15.00 |
| Softape Instant Library | 39.95 |
| (8 tapes plus softape membership!) | |

**ON DISK:**
| | |
|---|---|
| Inventory System | 125.00 |
| Text Editor | 50.00 |
| Mailing List | 30.00 |
| Backorder Report | 50.00 |
| Electronic Index Card File* | 19.95 |
| Best of Bishop* | 49.95 |
| (6 programs on one disk) | |

*Programs by Bob Bishop

**PET:**
| | |
|---|---|
| Finance | $9.95 |
| Draw | 5.00 |
| Othello | 5.00 |
| Black Jack | 5.00 |
| Life | 5.00 |
| Star Wars | 5.00 |
| Star Trek | 5.00 |
| Mugwumps | 5.00 |
| Read/Write Memory | 10.00 |
| Galaxy Games | 9.95 |
| Off The Wall/Target Pong | 9.95 |
| Mortgage | 14.95 |
| Diet Planner/Biorythm | 14.95 |
| Basic BASIC | 14.95 |
| Pet System Monitor | 19.95 |
| Point & Figure Stock Market Plot | 7.50 |
| TNT Game Pack –1 | 10.00 |
| TNT Game Pack –2 | 10.00 |

## HARDWARE

**APPLE II HARDWARE:**

- **Programmable Printer Interface** (Parallel)
  on board eprom printer driver, full handshake logic, driver program for Centronics, Axiom, T.I. SWTPC PR-40, and others assembled & tested . $80.00

- **Power Control Interface** (From T.W.C. Products)
  Up to 16 channels of A.C. control per card. Controlled from BASIC. Each channel capable of 12 amps at 110V. Optically isolated from A.C. line. A.C. loads are switched via a low D.C. voltage on a ribbon cable (cable included). Complete system equipped for 4 A.C. circuits.
  Kit .................................................. $95.00
  Assembled ....................................... $135.00
  Additional 4 circuit A.C. Power Modules
  Kit .................................................. $35.00
  Assembled ....................................... $55.00

- **Joystick** With 3 Switches
  Great for Apple Games like Star Wars. Includes trimmers to calibrate for full deflection ....................................... $35.00

- **Upper & Lower Case Board**
  Now you can display both upper and lower case characters on your video with the Apple II. Includes assembled circuit board and sample software ........................................ $49.95

- **Apple Disk II*** ....................................... $595.00
- **Applesoft ROM Card*** ......................... $200.00
- **Heuristics Speechlab** ......................... $189.00
- **Apple High Speed Serial Interface*** ... $180.00
- **Apple Communications Card*** ........... $180.00
- **Apple Prototyping Board** ................... $24.95

* We are assuming that these items will be available from stock by the time this is published.

**PET HARDWARE**

- **Beeper** ............................................... $24.95
- **Petunia**—for computer generated sounds ... $29.95
- **Video Buffer**—to put your pet's pictures on a television set or monitor ............................................. $29.95
- **Joystick**—with four switches, speaker, and volume control ... $49.95
- **PR-40 Printer**—with cable for pet and printer driver software.
  Software Kit ..................................... $300.00
  Assembled ....................................... $425.00
- **Centronics P-1 Microprinter**—with cable and software for pet ... $520.00
- **Commodore Hardcopy Printer**—(available November ?) ... $695.00

## WHY SHOULD YOU BUY FROM US?

Because we can help you solve your problems and answer your questions. We don't claim to know everything, but we try to help our customers to the full extent of our resources.

# COMPUTER COMPONENTS OF ORANGE COUNTY

6791 Westminster Ave., Westminster, CA 92683      714-898-8330

Hours: Tues-Fri 11:00 AM to 8:00 PM—Sat 10:00 AM to 6:00 PM (Closed Sun, Mon)
Master Charge, Visa, B of A are accepted. No COD. Allow 2 weeks for personal check to clear.
Add $1.50 for handling and postage. For computer systems please add $10.00 for shipping, handling and insurance. California residents add 6% Sales Tax.

www.ingramcontent.com/pod-product-compliance
Lightning Source LLC
Chambersburg PA
CBHW080923170526
45158CB00008B/2210